M

W

J

THE
Generous
MAN

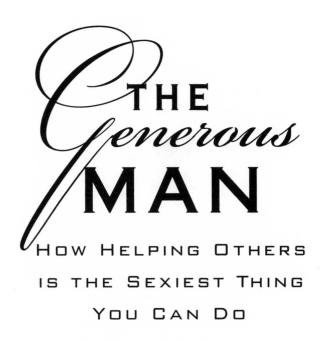

THE
Generous
MAN

How Helping Others
is the Sexiest Thing
You Can Do

TOR NØRRETRANDERS

Translated by JONATHAN SYDENHAM

THUNDER'S MOUTH PRESS
NEW YORK

THE GENEROUS MAN:
How Helping Others Is the Sexiest Thing You Can Do

Published by
Thunder's Mouth Press
An Imprint of Avalon Publishing Group Inc.
245 West 17th Street, 11th Floor
New York, NY 10011

AVALON
publishing group incorporated

Copyright © 2002 and 2005 by Tor Nørretranders
Translation copyright © 2005 by Jonathan Sydenham

First published in 2002 by the People's Press
First Thunder's Mouth Press edition October 2005

Library of Congress Cataloging-in-Publication Data is available

ISBN: 1-56025-728-8
ISBN 13: 978-1-56025-728-8

9 8 7 6 5 4 3 2 1

Book design by India Amos
Printed in the United States of America
Distributed by Publishers Group West

Contents

Acknowledgments ~ ix

Prologue ~ xi

1 *Experiments*
HOMO ECONOMICUS IS A FICTION ~ I

2 *Game Theory*
COOPERATION BETWEEN EGOCENTRICS
IS POSSIBLE ~ I5

3 *Darwin I*
FOLLOW THE LINE OF LEAST
RESISTANCE ~ 29

4 *Reciprocity*
HELPING ONE ANOTHER IS NATURAL ~ 37

5 *Darwin II*
TAKING THE EASY WAY OUT ~ 7I

6 *Handicap*
THE PEACOCK AND HIS STRIKING
PLUMAGE ~ 9I

7 *Generosity*
WHERE GOOD DEEDS COME FROM ~ I2I

CONTENTS

8 *Double Darwin*
TWO HUMANS IN ONE ❧ 131

9 *The Theory of Culture*
THE FREEDOM MESSAGE:
MAKE AN EFFORT AND YOU'LL
MAKE OUT ❧ 147

10 *Commodities and Gifts*
THE MARKET MECHANISM AND THE
HUMAN FACE ❧ 191

11 *Creativity*
BEING GIVEN AN EXPERIENCE ❧ 219

12 *Openness*
THE MANY ADVANTAGES OF SHARING
EVERYTHING ❧ 233

13 *Public Spirit*
WELFARE PAYS; GLOBALLY, TOO ❧ 259

14 *The Future*
KEEP SEXUAL SELECTION ❧ 287

Epilogue ❧ 309
Notes ❧ 315
Index ❧ 341

I paint to get pussy.

—JENS JØRGEN THORSEN

Acknowledgments

I SHOULD LIKE TO thank all the people who have contributed down the years to the process that led to this book. They include among many others Peter Bastian, Claus Bindslev, Gert Birnbacher, Nikolaj Cederholm, Chris Calude, Greg Chaitin, Claus Clausen, Wilfred Dolfsma, Thomas Hylland Eriksen, Lars Friberg, Don Foresta, Steve Gangestad, Marty Golubitsky, Karl Grammer, Martin von Haller Grønbæk, George Hersey, Peter Hesseldahl, Lars H.U.G., Timmi Jacob Jensen, Kevin Kelly, Ole Fogh Kirkeby, Morten Lund, Benoit Mandelbrot, George Markowsky, Pia Maria Marquard, George Miller, Poul Nesgaard, Nikolaj Nyholm, Anders Pape Møller, Ulla Puggaard, Howard Rheingold, Cecilie Rubow, Thomas Ryan Jensen, Christer Sturmark, Randy Thornhill, and Steven Weber.

None of the above bear any responsibility whatsoever for the flaws and deficiencies in this book, let alone its shameful propensity to try and explain far too much of life.

WELCOME TO THIS book about sex, or, more precisely perhaps, a book about how to get it.

The instructions are simple: go for the opposite. You don't get sex by thinking about it. You get it by thinking about all kinds of other things, by doing your best at something you're good at, such as playing the violin, being friendly, saving the world, or painting pictures.

You show what you're worth by doing something that's difficult. This is a central—though hitherto completely overlooked—factor in the development of life on earth; indeed, it's a central fact in anyone's life.

The last few decades of research into biology indicate a simple connection: in order to win a partner to mate with, animals and humans display their best sides. They strive for perfection, prove that they're willing to help others, do that bit extra, show consideration, and go out of their way. In other words, they are *generous.*

This book investigates how characteristics such as generosity, creativity, cooperativeness, and cleverness derive from the instinctive pull of sex and love toward *the other,* the object of desire. As we shall see, to a great extent it is our attraction to a sexual partner that brings out the best in us—wisdom, beauty, and philanthropy.

It may be expressed in one short phrase of quite unashamedly universal validity: make an effort and you'll make out.

EVOLUTION IS NOT only about survival. It's also about convincing the opposite sex that you have something to offer.

Charles Darwin's theory of the origin of man by biological evolution has two sides, one of which has been forgotten for more than a hundred years. *Natural selection,* which is about survival and efficiency, is familiar to us. But there is also *sexual selection,* which is about seducing a member of the opposite sex in order to have offspring (the "mating choice," as J. P. Jacobsen termed it, in his translation of Darwin's major works).

Sexual selection is the creative motor not just in natural history, but in the development of culture and society. Our intellects, creative powers, and ability to work together are developed through mating rituals and courtship.

A DRAMATIC SHIFT IN our image of man is taking place at present—from a perception that involves a cold, selfish, rational struggle for survival in nature and the marketplace to a perception based on generosity, mutual benefit, and being there for one another.

This shift has been started by decisive breakthroughs in several scientific fields: experimental economics, game theory, the theory of evolution, anthropology, knowledge sociology, technology theory, and welfare theory.

Together they draw a breathtakingly simple picture showing

not only the origins of care, assistance, and community, but also creativity, curiosity, and the desire to explore the world. It is all about sex, but the road to sex is *not* obtained through the perverse preoccupation with copulation prevalent in the media today but, ironically, through the preoccupation with anything other than sex: creative power, big game hunting, and human reserves in everyday life. Magnanimity. Generosity.

There are two persons in man: *Homo economicus,* who is created from the survival instincts of natural selection, and *Homo generosus,* as I call him, who is created by the courtship instincts of sexual selection.

WE ARE HEADING for a global community of man in which gifts are as important as goods, cooperation as important as competition, where attracting attention is on its way to becoming the most important form of wealth, and where welfare and freedom from hunger will be a matter of course for every member of the species.

This development is not due to charity or sentimentality but merely to the fact that the pursuit of selfish interests has assumed new and more creative forms. Biologically, there is no fundamental opposition between selfishness and cooperation, or between egoism and altruism, and, today, people display their worth in a different way from Stone Age man. The challenge is the same: to find a sexual partner. But the effort you have to make in order to do so is different now, and its fruits are of quite another order of interest.

So, yes, this book is about sex. But only because sex actually involves other things entirely—intellect, wisdom, and aesthetics. By observing something very limited (sex), we discover something much greater.

Let's begin with something that really and truly arouses our selfish interests: money. Let's play a game.

The stakes? Our philosophy of life.

THE
Generous
MAN

1
Experiments

HOMO ECONOMICUS
IS A FICTION

WANT TO PLAY? Here are the rules. You can have $100, on one condition: that you will split it with me in a way that I find acceptable. You have to make a one-time offer. If I refuse it, neither of us gets a cent. The Ultimatum Game.

How much will you offer me? Half? Well, you could, but you're privileged. You're the first mover, whereas I can only accept or reject your offer. So maybe you should weigh things in your favor a bit, and offer me $40 and keep $60? Or keep $70 to my $30? Or $80 to my $20? How far do you dare go? How far down do you think I'll go?

Let's swap roles. Now I've been given $100. You'll have to accept or reject my offer.

I could choose to offer you half. But no: I want a larger piece of the booty.

So I'll be brazen and offer you $5 out of the $100. Take it or leave it. That's $95 for me.

What do you say? "Shove it!"? Are you disgusted by my greed? Do you think I'm an S.O.B for suggesting such an unfair split? Do you feel like hitting me with a brickbat and leaving me to kick myself for being so greedy? Will you leave me to stew in my own wretched juices? Will punishing me give you a kick?

But you'd be cutting off your nose to spite your face. You could've made $5 for nothing. All you had to do was to accept: you would've had five bucks for free.

Do you really want to hurt yourself just to get back at me?

As it turns out, you do. The ultimatum game has been played by thousands of people since it was thought up twenty years ago by Werner Goth and his colleagues from Humboldt University, Berlin. The results have been amazing every time: people refuse the money if they think the other player is behaving too greedily. When the offer made is less than 20 percent of the total amount, it is usually rejected.[1]

In other words, humans are not particularly selfish. Because it is not selfish to reject $5 of $100. This does not at all accord with the assumption behind the most fashionable economic theory: that man is a *Homo economicus*, selfish and based on reason.[2] It is neither particularly selfish nor rational to reject money just because you're angered by the other person's greed.

The selfish thing would be to accept—even if you were only offered five cents. Yet most guinea pigs refuse low offers. There's got to be a limit. But why?

All kinds of sophisticated versions have been tried. Anonymous players. Making sure no two players play each other twice. Raising the stake to several months' wages. Checking the gender, educational qualifications, and mathematical abilities of the participants. Yet the results are always the same.

For one major study published in 2001 a number of prominent experimental economists teamed up with eleven anthropologists to examine the results of the ultimatum game in cultures other than those with business colleges.[3] Could they find more selfish behavior in the hunter-gatherer cultures still scattered about our planet?

But no matter whether the game was played by the Hadza of Tanzania, the Kazak of Mongolia, the Aché of Paraguay, or the Au or Gnau from New Guinea, the answer was the same: *Homo economicus* did not exist. Low offers were rejected.

There were variations between cultures, but the history of human behavior goes back further everywhere than the history of selfish, rational individuals who are in it for themselves and indifferent to anybody else.

Homo economicus is not the whole history of mankind.

T HE MOST THOUGHT-PROVOKING experience from the ultimatum game is perhaps this: somebody playing against a computer that suggests a split is more willing to accept a lower share than somebody playing another human.

What?! Surely a buck is a buck! If I get $10 it's worth the same to me whether I get it from a computer or from a business college student, right?

Why would you or I refuse an offer from a human but accept the same offer from a computer?

Because we humans apparently have other interests and priorities in life than money. When a human counterpart acts greedily we feel an urge to punish him. When computers are greedy we don't care. They can never learn any better.

But when members of our own species are involved we're willing to pay in order to show our loathing and contempt for pettiness. We show our pride, our resentment, our thirst for revenge—"oh, be like that then!"—even when it costs us.

Similarly, the experiments reveal that if the roles the players play—i.e., the question of who presents the ultimatum and who decides whether to accept or reject it—are determined by a quiz or another test rather than just by tossing a coin, the responder is more willing to accept a tiny crumb. It matters to us that we're playing with another human whom we respect.

ARE ECONOMISTS GREEDY because being an economist makes you greedy, or because greedy people become economists?

A good question, because there's no doubt that students of economics are more likely to be uncooperative in games like these than other groups of students. This was discovered back in 1981.[4] But why?

To examine this phenomenon, an ultimatum game was played by two groups of students.[5] One group consisted of students of economics, the other of students of other subjects. Astronomy, for example.

When the results were analyzed, the two groups were subdivided once more: into first-year students and more senior students. The idea behind this subdivision was to see whether beginning economists and their more experienced classmates exhibited differing levels of greed. If greed was something you could acquire by studying economics, it would of course increase as time passed.

But, conversely, if students of economics always came from the group of humans who happen to be born greedy, no change would be observable as the course progressed.

The scientists behind this study wanted to determine whether greed in economists was the result of learning or selection.

The first stage of the study was a word game. Players had to make as many words as they could out of a bunch of letters—an exercise that had nothing to do with economics. The players who did best were chosen to present the ultimata to the others.

Then, these "first movers" wrote on slips of paper the amount of the stake they were willing to share with another student. The stake was $10, and offers had to be divisible by $0.50. Thus, the largest amount anyone could say he wanted to keep was $9.50. At the same time, the second group of students had to note the lowest amount they would accept from the first movers. The lowest possible amount was $0.50.

Finally, the slips of paper were randomly paired. An ultimatum might be $2.50, for example, which would be fine if the responder had set $2 as the lower limit. If the ultimatum was $1.50, neither player got any money at all.

The results? Firstly, the economists were greedier than the students of other subjects. But the difference diminished by the year: economists are greedy because greedy people become economists. They lighten up as their studies progress. Good news for economics professors.

Young students of economics started by demanding to keep an average of $6.30 when they issued their ultimata, while more senior students of economics only demanded $6 of the $10. Young non-economists wanted an average of $5.70, while older ones would be happy with $5.20.

If we look at how small a share of the pie they could live with as responders, we observe a remarkable development as the students progressed through college. Young economists refuse splits of less than $1.40, while more senior students want at least $2. Young non-economists want $2.90 to play along, but as time passes they learn that you can make do with $2; just like the experienced students of economics.[6]

The two groups converge. You do learn something at university. Or perhaps it is from life.

B UT ANOTHER RESULT was just as remarkable: not one of the students of economics, freshman or senior, indeed not one single player in the study, and there were almost a hundred of them, behaved the way economic theory of human behavior predicts: the way *Homo economicus* would behave.[7]

A rational, selfish analysis tells you very clearly what you ought to do: as the responder you must ask for at least $0.50. This way you will not reject any offers, and you may hope that the offer you actually receive is bigger. There is no rational sense in asking for $1, $2, $3, or $4 because you will not get more than the ultimatum, regardless. But by asking for more than the lowest amount possible, you merely add to the likelihood that you're asking for more than you'll be offered and thus risk not receiving anything at all.

As the first mover you surely realize that any rational, selfish responder will have asked for the $0.50 minimum (because asking for anything more would be dumb). So that is what you offer. And you get to keep $9.50.

Yet not one person in the study behaved the way economic theory says people should behave: rationally and selfishly. Not one!

Economists are greedy because greedy people choose economics, but they are not nearly as greedy as economics says they should be. Economists are more cynical than the rest of us but not nearly as cynical as their theories assume we all are.

But this behavior was not completely irrational. Common sense tells a rational person charged with presenting an ultimatum that an offer of $0.50 is liable to be rejected, so he offers what will profit him the most: i.e., the smallest amount there is a good chance of getting away with. This is more like $7 than $9.50.

But how do we explain the refusal by the recipient to accept anything less than $2? After all, it's not particularly rational or selfish. And it is this that is the riddle, the divining rod that will lead us to man's secret source of sociality: there are limits to how little another human can offer us.

This experience has been repeated in other games.

PUBLIC GOOD GAMES are another kind of game being explored in a new discipline that is providing astonishing insights into human behavior: experimental economics.[8] The results here are perhaps even more astounding.

Four players are each given $10. They will be able to take it home after the game. But they can also make more money if they play the game.

The experimenter makes an offer: if a player puts some of his money into the bank, the experimenter will double it and share it among the other players equally.

If each player puts all $10 into the bank he or she will get twice as much in return (the $40 is doubled to $80 and then shared among the four players; i.e., they each receive $20).

So it is in the obvious interests of the group to contribute as much as possible to the bank. But is it also in the interests of the individual player?

If three players put their money into the bank to be doubled and shared out again, while the fourth keeps his money up his sleeve, the latter will gain an advantage.

The $30 in the bank is doubled to $60 and shared in equal portions. The result? Each player receives $15 from the bank. The three contributors now have one-and-a-half times their original stake, which is just fine. But the fourth, who did not stake his money, receives $15 on top of the original $10 he failed to contribute. So, there's an obvious advantage to the individual player in sitting it out and biding his time. But it's an obvious disadvantage to the group as a whole.

If two contribute while the other two wait and see, things look really galling for the former. They each get their $10 back, while the other two also get $10 on top of the $10 they kept.

If only one player contributes his stake, and the other three hold back, the player does terribly: he gets $5 total while the others each receive $5 dollars on top of their original $10. The sole contributor actually loses money on this deal while the others, who made no contribution, profit from his naiveté.

So the logic is clear: a selfish, rational player will always decide not to contribute anything to the bank, because he will never receive more than a quarter for himself. But he can hope that the others will put something into the bank because he will receive a quarter of it no matter what he chooses to do.

Do we kind of recognize this situation from real life?

B UT WHAT DO the subjects actually do? Do they all sit it out? No! On average they actually contribute half of their stake to the bank. Again, evidence that people are not as selfish as you might think.

But you can also play the public good game for several rounds. Most players start out with the same behavior as when only one round is played: they contribute a goodly chunk of their money to the pool.

But after a few rounds, people stop putting anything into the pool. They stop working together. Unless everyone contributes, it just does not pay. Goodbye community.

A sad tale. But it does not stop there.

IN JANUARY 2002, two Swiss professors of economics, Ernst Fehr from the University of Zurich and Simon Gächter from the University of St. Gallen, astonished the readers of the world's leading scientific periodical, *Nature,* with their account of the impact of punishment on public goods experiments.[9]

If the players are allowed to punish participants who fail to contribute to the pool, behavior changes as the rounds progress.

The punishment is financial: if a player imposes a punishment on another player for free riding, the offender must give the experimenter a certain amount of his original $10, like $1.50. The amount goes to the experimenter, not to the pool where the other players would get a share of it.

The player who decides to impose a punishment must pay for doing so: $0.50, for example, which also disappears from the amount available to the players and into the experimenter's pocket.

The possibility of punishment makes the game proceed in a very different way. The desire for cooperation is maintained by the players for round after round. Ultimately, more than 80 percent of them invest all their money in the pool. They cooperate, and everybody benefits.

The interesting thing is not that sanctions discourage free riding. The really astonishing thing was that 85 percent of the players punished another player at least once.

This is surprising because punishing costs money. Of course, it is also an advantage for the group to punish—since it tends to lead to more money for everyone—but the experiment was set up so that the players, 240 students, never played twice against the same player. Players were rematched with others each time.

Every round, each player simultaneously announced how much he or she wished to put into the bank. Then the endowments were published and there was an opportunity to punish free riders. Once punishment had been allocated, the group was changed.

Individual players did not benefit from the effects of the punishment meted out. The punishment affected players they would not meet again. But the price of imposing punishment, $0.50, had to be paid anyway.

So there was no immediate self-interest in imposing punishments; it's more profitable to let other players do so. Yet the players almost all imposed punishments. Why? Surely *Homo economicus,* the rational, selfish man, would not waste his savings on punishing somebody he'd never see again?

The punishment does not benefit the player who pays for it, but it very much benefits the other players, who will meet the free rider in the next round: it's a real deterrent and increases the likelihood that the punished player will contribute his funds in the future.

Ernst Fehr and Simon Gächter call this behavior *altruistic punishment.* The individual player is willing to sacrifice something in order to mete out punishment. As what he sacrifices benefits others but not him, it is labeled altruistic.

Altruism is a term invented by the Frenchman Auguste Comte in the nineteenth century.[10] Comte is best known as the founder of the philosophy of positivism, but he intended the term altruism to describe human actions performed for the sake of others (*altre* is Old French for *other*, related to the Latin word *alter*). An altruistic action is one not in the doer's own interests but exacts a price from him and benefits others. Classic examples of altruism include rescue operations in which rescuers save people from rivers and run the risk of drowning themselves.

Homo economicus is not madly enthusiastic about acting altruistically. But the players in the public good experiment were eager to. Why?

Emotions. The players had clearly negative emotional reactions to the free riders and obtained corresponding emotional satisfaction by punishing them. "They seem to be more interested in obtaining personal revenge than in increasing their overall economic performance," Ernest Fehr and two other researchers wrote of this behavior.[11]

We humans feel great pleasure in punishing those who display behavior we regard as underhand, greedy, or offensive. It feels just and good. It makes us feel warm all over.

We seem to have a built-in urge to do good deeds and to take revenge on those who do not.

We ask again: why? Why do we feel this glow? Where does it come from? Why is it there? And why are all our economic theories based on the assumption that we do not feel the remotest inclination to help the community or make any sacrifices?

T HE ECONOMIST ROBERT Frank points out that we are happy to devote plenty of time, energy, and money on pursuing a thief who steals our bag, even though the value of the bag is lower than the loss of earnings resulting from expending energy on having the man punished.[12] Something other than self-interest plays a part: anger, indignation, and our sense of fair play. "The ruthless pursuit of self-interest is often self-defeating," Frank writes, pointing out that the emotions we display in such situations, which emotions are so irrational from the economics point of view, are profoundly meaningful, because they develop cooperativeness and punish deceit.[13] We therefore obey emotional impulses that lie completely beyond the horizon of *Homo economicus*.

So far, three strange things have emerged from these experiences of experimental economics: firstly, we would rather do without a bit of cash than passively witness unfair sharing. Secondly, we are actually prepared to pay to punish greed even if we do not directly benefit from doing so. Thirdly, we do not feel the same way when a computer is involved.

In other words we're willing to pay in order to educate other people. We want to invest in good behavior in those around us; we're willing to pay to be part of a good community. We're willing to pay to ensure that people act decently. We want to invest in social behavior. We're far from being purely selfish, rational *Homo economicus*.

We are social creatures. We commit to one another.

The strange thing is that science discovered this by starting at the opposite end altogether: with game theory, a cold, rational realm of mathematics.

The parts of the brain where the reward centers reside are activated when we decide to cooperate constructively. A study of the brain metabolism during one of the little games played by experimental economists yields a pronounced result.

A group of researchers at Emory University got a number of women to play the prisoner's dilemma game. This game gives each player the following dilemma: she can decide to cooperate with the other player, but by doing so she exposes herself to the risk that the other player will not cooperate with her; in that scenario, the cooperative player loses more than she would have had she, too, decided not to cooperate. The problem, then, is that of trust.

Brain scans undertaken while the game was underway showed that when the players decided to cooperate, the brain displayed clear signs of satisfaction; in fact, it was the same neurological response we display when taking drugs. We just love working together. "We are wired to cooperate," as one of the researchers said of this result.[14]

But just as remarkable is the fact that when the women played against computers they were less likely to cooperate. And even more sensationally: when they played the computer and cooperated, their reward centers did not light up.[15] There is no satisfaction in cooperating with a computer. The pleasure and the glow only appear when we cooperate with another human (or think we are; none of the players could see each other).

The glow of cooperation and the warm feeling of doing a good deed are real and genuine. Of course we did not need science to tell us such, but it nevertheless warms the cockles of one's heart to know these things are scientifically measurable. Happiness and altruism go hand in hand. Even for economists.

2
Game Theory

COOPERATION
BETWEEN EGOCENTRICS
IS POSSIBLE

To me game theory has always seemed to be a shrill, sophomoric mathematical discipline aimed at accounting for all the tactical and strategic considerations you can exercise in a game if you'd rather not enjoy it in the meantime: a nerdish, dry-brained notion that you can work it all out.

But it is not like that at all.

Game theory[1] really started to make headway via a book that appeared in 1944: *The Theory of Games and Economic Behavior* by the mathematician John von Neumann and the economist Oskar Morgenstern. The two scientists attempted to apply game theory as the basis for the development of an economic theory.

During World War II the Hungarian-born John von Neumann, already a legend among mathematicians, worked with the mathematician Jacob Bronowski, who became widely known many years later for his brilliant television series *The Ascent of Man*. Bronowski describes a cab ride in London during which Neumann talked about his and Morgenstern's book on game theory:

> "You mean, the theory of games like chess?" Bronowski asked.
>
> "No, no," von Neumann replied. "Chess is not a game. Chess is a well defined form of computation. You may not be able to work out the answers, but in theory there must be a solution, a right procedure in any position. Now real games," von Neumann explained, "are not like that at all. Real life is not like that. Real life consists of bluffing, of little tactics of deception, of asking yourself what is the other man going to think I mean to do. And that is what games are about in my theory."[2]

GAME THEORY, THEN, isn't about determining the rules governing chess moves but those governing the chess players' behavior. It's about trying to identify patterns in the way people try to trick one another, deceive one another, tempt one another into traps, and to checkmate one another. Game theory is the theory of the way we relate to our opponents' intentions and plans; and of an endless stalemate: if

I think that he thinks that I think that he is thinking, well, he will know that I'll act *this* way. So I do something quite different.

The question is: are there patterns in the behavior of such players that make them act differently from the way they think they should act? Patterns that lead them to get stuck in situations where they do not do what they really want to?

As I say, it sounds very dry and peculiar . . . but it makes a lot of sense. In the fifties and sixties game theory assumed great influence on the analysis of war, rearmament, and political measures. In the seventies it assumed great influence on economics. Since the nineties it has embraced many sciences, such as psychology and sociology, but perhaps most surprisingly, the theory of biological evolution: the development of a species.

In 2000 the influential economist Herbert Gintis wrote in a game-theory textbook that "game theory is a universal language for the unification of the behavioral sciences."[3] In other words, game theory presents itself as the theory that will unify all the sciences dealing with human behavior, from psychology to sociology to economics. "This may seem an extraordinary thing to say," the *Stanford Encyclopedia of Philosophy* notes, but adds, "but it is entirely plausible"[4]; i.e., it does make good sense. There are sound reasons for examining game theory more closely—but first, let's look at a few games.

One good game is the stag hunt.[5]

It involves hunting stags: large, speedy animals that a huntsman would have trouble bringing down on his own. But if you hunt as a group, you can beat the brush and drive the beast into the sights of a marksman—on condition that all the beaters remain at their posts, keeping the stag from slipping away. But do they?

The seventeenth-century French mathematical philosopher Jean-Jacques Rousseau wrote in a discourse on inequality: "If it was a matter of hunting deer, everyone well realized that he must remain faithfully at his post; but if a hare happened to pass within the reach of one of them, we cannot doubt that he would have gone off in pursuit of it without scruple and, having caught his own prey, he would have cared very little about having caused his companions to lose theirs."[6]

And then the trouble begins: a large group of hunters cooperates in order to surround a stag, but the ring is broken by an impatient hunter chasing a hare. A hare is a fine catch for the hunter who catches it, of course, but of no benefit to the others; whereas the stag would feed the whole group.

The game examines whether the cooperation between the hunters can remain stable in the face of the disruption caused by somebody going for a rapid but diminutive payoff.

Two strategies clash: an individual strategy by which each hunter goes after a small animal that a single man can bring down; and a collective strategy by which the hunters hunt together to bring down a much larger beast with a much larger yield.

The point of game theory analysis is to show that there are two different strategies (or equilibria, as they are termed by game theorists) that are stable: either everybody chases his own hare or everybody cooperates in bringing down the stag.

The calculation for each player is simple: there is more meat on a stag, even after it has been shared out—but you can only catch it if everyone pulls together; if anybody sets off after a hare, the hunt will fail.

So, the vital question facing each player is: can he trust the others? If they all stick to their posts his best bet is to do likewise. But if just a few go off on their own he's best served by going, too.

It's a matter of trust. The problem is how to establish it.

It's not difficult to achieve the equilibrium involving hares. Everybody goes off on his own and keeps whatever food he catches. It's harder to move from the hare equilibrium to the stag equilibrium. It entails agreement between the hunters, and that, in turn, entails trust.

In reality, then, the stag hunt becomes a game about whether cooperation is possible at all.

ANOTHER EXAMPLE OF the way the individual gains a brief advantage by breaking ranks—but is rapidly overtaken by the group and has his advantage neutralized—is the open-air concert. Members of the audience stand in order to enjoy a better view; one by one they do so, until everybody is standing and nobody is getting anything out of it but backache. At a rather more serious end of the scale is the huge, massively expensive advertising campaigns of competing products—or, more gravely, the arms race.[7]

The classic of game theory is the prisoner's dilemma, which we touched upon briefly before. The prisoner's dilemma is a peculiar game that was developed by the RAND Corporation think tank in California just after World War II. RAND played a vital role in the development of game theory through studying its application to the nuclear arms race.

The name and the classic edition of the game are due to a popular version developed by the mathematician Al Tucker: Two robbers commit a major robbery and get caught in a stolen getaway car by the police. The police don't have enough evidence to prove they actually committed the robbery, but they are convinced the pair did so. The police give each prisoner a choice: you can implicate your partner and go free. Or you can keep your mouth shut and refuse to confess to anything—but if your partner implicates you, you'll get a hefty ten years. If you both refuse to confess you'll both get one year for stealing the getaway car. If you both implicate each other you'll both get five years.

What do the prisoners do? They may think this way: the best option for both of us, by far, is to remain silent. Then we get a year behind bars, which isn't so bad. But if I keep my mouth shut and he implicates me, I'll get a much heftier sentence (and he gets off entirely). So if he implicates me, it's better for me to implicate him, too; at least then I get off with five years instead of ten. So I'll implicate him and hope he doesn't implicate me; and if he does, the damage won't be as great as it would've had I not cooperated.

The result? Both prisoners implicate the other, and both go to prison for five years.

The interesting thing, of course, is that it would've been better for them to cooperate with each other and not the police: then they would've been out in a year to commit new robberies.

But cooperation entails trust, something they clearly did not have.

The game is important, because it shows that a rational, selfish analysis will lead to a result that is not in the best interests of all involved. Not trusting each other is bad. But trusting each other isn't easy.

THE MOST CELEBRATED achievement of game theory is the discovery of equilibria, thanks to the legendary mathematician John Nash (familiar from the book and movie *A Beautiful Mind*) who won the Nobel Prize for economics in 1994 for his discovery of . . . the Nash equilibria.

The idea of a Nash equilibrium is that it describes a state of a game players end up in—even though they are not interested in doing so—because they find themselves in deadlock.

In the prisoner's dilemma mutual implication is one such state. It is an equilibrium because neither party can gain by deviating from it unilaterally. The players are stuck in this equilibrium. They can only obtain an advantage if they both depart from the equilibrium.

From the point of view of each of the players this would seem to be the best solution for them individually, even if another solution would be better for them both. They just can't find it.[8]

The Nash equilibrium is most apparent in coordination games, where you have to pull together.

On the roads, for example: it is not very neat to have everybody driving around however he or she likes. It's better to choose a recipe for driving: that everybody will drive on the left, for example. This avoids head-on collisions. So driving on the left is a Nash equilibrium. Once everybody has chosen this strategy it's not a good idea for an individual player to choose another one, such as driving on the right or meandering along in the middle of the road.

Driving on the right is also a Nash equilibrium; in fact the two equilibria are as good as each other, because they possess the same property: as soon as everybody chooses one or the other nobody gains by deviating from it. This means it's stable, even in the face of deviants who get a kick out of driving on the opposite side (because they pretty soon disappear from the game).

So there are two equilibria in the traffic game. In many other games there are loads of equilibria, not all of equal value.

What matters is that the discovery of a Nash equilibrium tells us where the players may end up in a game, even if they have no intention of doing so; but once they get there they cannot get out of this state again, because no player can benefit from leaving the equilibrium by himself.

In other words, game theory is a mathematical theory for defining how the selfish interests of a series of individuals lead to an equilibrium that is not always equally optimal for the players.

The reason why economists like Herbert Gintis think that game theory may be the theoretical language to unify the images of mankind presented by the behavioral sciences is that much social intercourse between humans involves the interpretation of each other's strategies and intentions and adapting our behavior accordingly. This is true of seduction, auctions, chess, dealing in real estate, poker, selling, marriage, electronic games, moving along the sidewalk, warfare, tall stories, political conniving, peace-keeping missions, children's games, and playing dice. A considerable proportion of human intercourse is about reading each other's intentions and working out what the other person thinks you think he is thinking.

Such games provide game theory with analytical tools. Game theory tells us precisely and clearly how we may be expected to behave in a whole range of situations. Game theory is able to hone its statements so clearly that we can apply them to real life and see whether its predictions, based on a set of assumptions, prove correct.

They don't.

Nowhere near. Game theory tells us how we will behave if we're selfish and rational. By using controlled experiments in the laboratory you can see if it's so; will we really act like that? And the answer is no.

"Ironically, game theory is often hoisted on its own petard," Herbert Gintis wrote: "Many of its most fundamental predictions—predictions that would have been too vague to test with any confidence in the pre-game-theoretic era—are decisively and repeatedly disconfirmed in laboratory settings."[9]

DOES THIS MEAN there is something wrong with game theory? No; it means there is something wrong with the assumptions used in the analyses: that humans are rational and selfish in any situation. Game theory is a tool for working out the consequences of a set of assumptions about the way people will act. You can then test whether the consequences prove correct. If they do not, there is something wrong with the assumptions you have made.

The methods of experimental economics are based on game theory and investigate whether the assumptions of game theory are valid.[10] And they are not. Humans are not so selfish and rational as we should be if the assumptions of game theory were correct and the economists' notion of *Homo economicus* were valid.

Humans are apparently less selfish than we usually think. Now, surely that is good news?

THE WHOLE WORLD watched in horror and disbelief as two skyscrapers in southern Manhattan were leveled in a despicably virtuoso act of terror on September 11, 2001. A couple of box cutters and a piece of devilishly intelligent planning enabled a small group of people to transform airliners into firebombs capable of demolishing the Twin Towers. The towers collapsed, illusions shattered, and an entire world was forced to take a long, hard look at itself.

Why do we build cities where we concentrate so much power and so many people in such a small space?[11] What makes people commit such acts of insanity? Just what drives them?

Perhaps most important of all, the attack on the World Trade Center posed a profoundly philosophical conundrum: is it in the interests of the community if people do not care about their own lives?

September 11 involved a group of fanatics sacrificing their own lives with great joy and determination in order to kill thousands of other people and give the rest something to think about. The suicide hijackers were not interested in saving their own skins. On the contrary. They probably flew happily to their deaths.

The same phenomenon is familiar from the Japanese Kamikaze pilots in World War II and the Palestinian suicide bombers in Israel.

They remind us of a silent precondition for social life in modern society: that we all value our own lives.

It's extremely disturbing to think about just how many everyday occurrences imply a tacit expectation that the other person will protect himself. The roads are not nice places to be if we can't take such an expectation for granted. After all, the Nash equilibrium of everyone driving on the right is based on the assumption that no one wants to get killed in an auto accident.

Our shuddering at the thought of people voluntarily breaking the Nash equilibrium was superbly exploited—at least for us in Denmark—by Lars von Trier in his television series *The Kingdom,* in which doctors from the Kingdom Hospital, in Denmark, place bets on whether an ambulance driver will survive his mad drive up the wrong side of the freeway, siren blaring and blue lights flashing. Since then, I haven't been able to take that particular freeway without those scenes reappearing on my inner movie screen.

On planes, in elevators, at football stadiums, in restaurants: there are loads of places in life where we blithely assume everyone else will act in his own interest. If he doesn't, it becomes very difficult for us to feel safe.

It's a splendid arrangement, too. An equilibrium in which everybody promotes his own interests by obeying the highway code is far better than the equilibrium in which every driver is surrounded by four highway cops on motorbikes making sure he doesn't switch lanes. It's good for society to be based on our being able to trust one another because we all value our own lives.

Some airlines, before they will load luggage onto a plane, will make passengers identify their bags out on the tarmac. This ensures that no bag is unaccompanied by its owner, and we may therefore believe that no bomb is onboard. After all, who'd want to blow himself up?

Some people, apparently. It's tragic, and it occasions studies into the social causes that result in people using themselves as weapons.

It also shows we cannot simply cheer and rejoice that assumptions of selfishness and rational behavior do not hold water in real life. Sure, there are reasons for appreciating the results that have emerged from experimental economics, but there are also reasons for asking, with some concern, just how we humans actually arrive at our decisions.[12] Are we really so careless about our own lives? Or, when push comes to shove, are we selfish?

You see, without thinking about it we assume selfishness in our daily intercourse with other humans. We expect them to look out for themselves.

THE DISCUSSION OF selfishness versus group solidarity and helpfulness is not confined to game theorists and economists. It's also been studied with great intensity and fervor by biologists. Is it all merely a tale of the survival of the strong and the extinction of the weak? Or are we biologically programmed for cooperation and friendliness?

Where does our behavior come from? And where is it going?

IS IT SILLY to discuss society, cooperation, and generosity on the basis of biology's notions of selfish beings fighting for survival? Isn't it naive to want to anchor our view of humanity in such things? Well, perhaps; however, if we start with biology and assumptions of selfishness but nevertheless arrive at concepts such as fellowship and cooperation, isn't that ten times more inspiring than if we'd started by assuming that humans in the modern world have reached a stage in our evolution where we behave decently for social and cultural reasons?

We can choose between assuming that there are radical, bottomless differences between humans and animals and thereby make it clear that we humans are not base but good in some very different, elfin way. But we may also choose to study whether all the beautiful things that we (occasionally) may say about humans may be a direct effect of our actually being animals: that being animal also includes generosity: That cooperation is *natural*.[13]

Darwin I

FOLLOW THE LINE OF
LEAST RESISTANCE

IN 1859 THE British biologist Charles Darwin, working on his own, published his astonishing *On the Origin of Species,* often given as *The Origin of Species* or just *Origin of Species.*[1]

This brief title only tells half of the story with which Darwin shocked his contemporaries: namely that every living species on Earth evolved through the ages from a single forbearer.

The idea that living creatures actually evolved and were not all created at once shook the view of the world provided by the Bible: that flora and fauna were created once and for all by Our Maker, ready to go.

Darwin certainly was not the first to propose a theory of evolution: in 1800 the Frenchman Jean-Baptiste Lamarck proposed that one lifeform had arisen spontaneously and that the rest had evolved from there. But it was Darwin who was the first to suggest a reasonable mechanism that would explain how such evolution could take place. That was the second half of the shock.

The name of the mechanism can be read in the full title of his 1859 work: *On the Origin of Species by Means of Natural Selection, or the Preservation of Favoured Races in the Struggle for Life.*[2] So it is natural selection, natural choice, quality first, the triumph of the best off, or whatever you want to call it, that is the background behind Darwin's absolutely extraordinary influence on the modern understanding of life on Earth.

We'll stick with natural selection.

It is an idea that is so incredibly simple it can be hard to grasp; and it's hard to believe that anything so simple can be as important and wide-ranging as it is. Nevertheless, as the American philosopher Daniel C. Dennett so precisely put it, natural selection is "the single best idea anyone ever had."[3]

This is what the idea looks like: there is a certain variation, a tiny mutual difference between members of a species—whether they are squirrels, goldfish, or humans. Some animals within a species may be, say, a bit bigger than others, but the latter may be better jumpers. Such characteristics (size, jumping ability) are passed down from parents to children. The animals with characteristics suited to the conditions in which they live have the largest number of offspring. If jumping high is required, the high jumpers will do best—and they will also find it easiest to have many children and raise them. So we will observe that among a population of animals inhabiting an environment in which being able to jump high is important, more and more individuals will appear that are good at jumping. The ones that can't jump will not manage to breed and raise as many offspring. They will not be selected.

That's it. That's the idea of natural selection: those best adapted to the environment will have the most offspring—and so over time there will be more of them. Until the environment changes and others do better, that is.

Dennett was right, wasn't he? The best idea anyone has ever had: variation, heredity, selection lead to the evolution of new, well adapted creatures. Variation, reproduction, selection.

The best-adapted are legion because they are the best-adapted. They are adapted because they have adapted to the environment. They are adapted to the environment because they have adapted.

It does sound like a tautology (which is the philosopher's language for something that goes on repeating itself: all bachelors are unmarried, beer is beer, the wind blows, time flies, the best are the best). But it is no tautology, even though it may be hard to see such now, since this way of thinking has gained wide favor in Western minds (at least in Europe; in the United States almost half the population has more faith in the words of the Bible than in Darwin's theory[4]).

Darwin's idea is a mechanism that explains why something can evolve without a designer to control the process. The spread of technology, of course, has accustomed us to the idea of a designer: somebody wants to develop something, invents the principles for this thing, draws plans, and puts it into production. The religious picture of the world operates with the corresponding notion of Our Lord as the great designer who decides what a giraffe is going to look like.

As soon as there is a designer it becomes easy to grasp how things can take shape and also how they can evolve. The designer just becomes wiser and bolder, with the courage to constantly try out ever-more-advanced designs.

But nature? How on earth could nature design beetles and beavers?

DARWIN STARTS HIS book by writing about domestic animals and their cultivation. After all, man has succeeded in changing cows, horses, and roses, making them seem ever more beautiful and useful to us.

Variation makes this possible: when you have cows that yield more milk than others, you need only ensure that only the highest yielders have calves (or that they have more than the low yielders, anyway); a few generations later and you'll have a cow that *really* fills milk churns!

A simple scheme, then: natural variation among the cows so they have different characteristics that are hereditary; a certain amount of selection by their surroundings so that only some of them have many calves; and—*presto!*—evolution has taken place among the population, among your livestock. If you go on long enough the whole species will change. This applies to cows, horses, roses, grasses, and so on and so forth.

This scheme: variation, heredity, selection also applies to the natural selection Darwin proposed. The only difference is that horse breeders have been replaced by the environment, which consists of other flora and fauna, parasites and tapeworms, tempests, downpours and relentless sunshine, drought, inundation and night frosts, shallow waters, prairies and grottos.

At any time the environment will make life easier for some squirrels than others. It is self-evident that the squirrels that find it easiest to make ends meet will also have the greatest prospects of having plenty of grandchildren. So their numbers will grow. Their characteristics spread. Evolution occurs.

We may justifiably ask where the variation among individuals comes from, but if we assume that it exists (and that is pretty obvious if you go out there and look at flowers, beavers, and children), it's apparent that the selection mechanism will lead to evolution when the characteristics are hereditary.

What makes Darwin's idea so extraordinarily good is that it makes it clear you can do without a designer. You can have evolution without one. As long as you are patient—because the transformation of amoeba to alligator does not happen in one blow, but via many, many intermediate forms that are themselves affected by loads of teeny-weenie changes, generation after generation.

But from there . . . to the evolution of an appreciation of great art is quite a journey, all the same. We'll get back to this journey later.

N OT ONLY WAS the ire of the church roused, but many of Darwin's contemporaries in the science world thought the idea was pretty hopeless: how is variation created? How does heredity take place? What is the import of the survival of those that survive? This was before anyone knew of the laws of heredity, before genes, before DNA, before mutations, before all the other factors that make us believe in Darwin today.

Darwin knew his idea would seem reactionary. He withheld it for decades because he was not happy at the prospect of the brickbats he would encounter. It was not until 1858, when a younger naturalist, Alfred Russel Wallace, informed Darwin of a new theory that had occurred to him during a bout of malaria—exactly the same idea of natural selection—that Darwin's friends persuaded him to publish his ideas.

The fact that for more than a hundred years his theory was regarded as reactionary hangs together with the mood reflected by *On the Origin of Species*'s subtitle: "The Preservation of Favoured Races in the Struggle for Life." It sounds almost like a parody of the jungle law prevailing in young British industrial society, where social ties and affiliations were being pulled up by the roots and the working classes were hanging on by their fingertips, struggling to survive in a society where young, rich, beautiful British aristocrats ruled the roost. In society, the most favored did indeed triumph; and nature was just the same. Thus Darwin's theory appeared to be a projection reflecting onto nature a societal structure involving a desperate struggle for existence.

There was a huge difference between viewing man as God's chosen creature, on our way to a predestined Paradise, and as a beast descended from rainworms and blue-green algae fighting tooth and nail for the survival of the fittest in a brutal world of earthquakes.

The repeated criticism of Darwinism hangs together with its emphasis on the individual member of the species. If the individual is hale and hearty it can manage many offspring and its characteristics will spread among the population. This is a struggle, people say.

But it is no struggle. Any animal (including man) wants to survive and bear offspring. We all try. Not all of us do equally well, but it is not a struggle. It is just a manifestation of life.

Objectively, some do better than others. After many generations we observe an evolution. But the individual merely experiences a life of eating, sleeping, and reproducing. Defeat is not perceived in relation to others but as your own death. Only the survivors survive. Only the survivors are able to ask why they survived.

Like me, you are the latest or second from latest (or—congratulations, Granny!—the third from latest) link in a long chain of survivors: creatures that had descendants before they perished; an unbroken chain of success from amoebas and apes to Americans. Along the way, myriads of screwed-up plankton, dorks, and bad artists who never reproduced.

We are winners. If we weren't, we wouldn't be able to ask why we were.

DOES THAT MEAN we don't want to help others? That we don't care if some people are so shortsighted that they get lost around town? Or do we give them some welfare to buy some glasses, get by in life, and have shortsighted children?

Yes, we do. It is important to us, indeed very important, to help others, to stick together, to support the weak and feeble, to provide special remedies for children who find it hard to cope, and to support the childless by artificial insemination.

We help one another in society. And we are not alone. There are loads of species we can observe that similarly help their fellow members. We find altruistic behavior where some help others even if it costs them—indeed, even if it costs them their lives or in some other way reduces the number of their offspring.

Why are creatures evolved by Darwin's natural selection altruistic? *Why* do we help one another when doing so appears to run counter to the very foundations of the evolution that created us?

How could Darwin's mechanism lead to altruism?

Reciprocity

HELPING ONE ANOTHER
IS NATURAL

W OULD YOU DIVE into the water to rescue somebody who was drowning and thereby risk your own life?

This is the question from one of the most celebrated anecdotes of evolutionary biology. The answer, which was worked out on the back of a coaster in a British pub in the thirties, came from J. B. S. Haldane, one of the most notable biologists of the twentieth century, one of the founders of the mathematical version of Darwin's theory of evolution, and also a leading Marxist theoretician who devoted much of his energy to political agitation and propaganda (despite—or because of—his privileged background).[1]

Would the great Marxist sacrifice himself to rescue someone from drowning?

He would gladly give up his life for three brothers or nine first cousins, Haldane is said to have replied after scribbling on the mat for a bit.[2]

His point was that we share our genetic material with our brothers—half of it, to be precise. If we rescue three brothers from drowning but die in the attempt, we have done our genes a favor, because more of them will remain in circulation than if our three brothers died and we remained alive.

So the idea is that we are happy to rescue our next of kin, because by doing so we rescue our own genes, which can live on even if we die. But if we rescue a complete stranger from drowning we do not serve the interests of our own genes, because our genes just disappear without a payoff.

It sounds absurd, and Haldane declared many years later (in 1955) that on two occasions he had actually jumped into rivers to save somebody from drowning, both times without questioning the logic of doing so, even though it was highly unlikely he was related to the victims: ". . . on the two occasions when I have pulled possibly drowning people out of the water (at an infinitesimal risk to myself) I had no time to make such calculations," Haldane wrote.[3]

But it is an interesting anecdote anyway, because the thinking it reflects was to have enormous bearing on evolutionary biology for the rest of the twentieth century.

THE MATHEMATICAL VERSION of Darwin's theory that Haldane and his colleague drew up in the thirties unified two important biological theories. One was Darwin's theory of evolution; the other was the theory of genes, which was based on the monk Gregor Mendel's studies of heredity in pea plants early in the nineteenth century. Mendel published his genetic discoveries in 1865 but they were ignored until 1900, when people began to take them seriously. By then Darwin was no longer so popular, however, and so the unification of Mendel and Darwin into "the modern synthesis" had huge import.

After all, Darwin had not explained how the characteristics suited to a given environment were actually passed on to the next generation. He had no theory of heredity; whereas Mendel did.

Haldane and Fisher succeeded in creating a mathematical theory capable of explaining how genes were spread in a population of living beings. They were able to do so thanks to a vital distinction introduced in 1909 by the Danish geneticist Wilhelm Johannsen (who came up with the term *gene* and the two words *phenotype* and *genotype*). A phenotype is an organism as it exists in reality. We are phenotypes, you and I, formed through many factors: the interaction of genes, where we grew up, the way we were brought up, nutrition, and lack of exercise. A genotype, on the other hand, is the sum of the genes contained in an individual. It is not a given that all our genes are expressed during our lifetimes; for example, people with the same genes (identical twins) may develop differently if they grow up in different circumstances (even though it is astonishing how much similarity does remain).

So a human is a phenotype that contains a genotype. It is the phenotype that does well or badly in its specific life, but it is the genotype that is partly transmitted to the next generation. Genes can lead to an organism; the organism contains genes that it can transmit.

But in principle it is only the genotype that is transmitted to the next generation, and not the traits of the phenotype—at least those that are not genetically determined.

If a phenotype like J. B. S. Haldane is on the riverbank, he dives in without regard to his own safety, or genes, in order to rescue another phenotype. But when the same phenotype is sitting in a pub and scribbling calculations on a coaster, the picture is very different. Now, if we look at it from the genotype's point of view, while it's fine for the phenotype to dive in to save its siblings—because they share a great deal of their genotype with the compassionate phenotype—it's not too smart for the phenotype to go around rescuing strangers—because they share little related genotype.

It is a characteristic, interesting detail that in practice, Haldane the phenotype helps strangers, while upon reflection and calculation, he concludes he would only help his own close relatives.

In one sense, this is the entire conundrum of generosity and cooperation: the conclusion of any rational analysis is not to help strangers. But faced with the decision, you dive in to rescue the drowning man.

B UT THIS IS all anecdotal. The issue assumed far clearer shape thanks to a theoretical breakthrough created by one of Haldane's pupils, the British biologist William Hamilton.

After a long, extremely specialized, personally lonely period during which he sat on benches in parks and railway stations in order to enjoy at least the proximity of other humans and thereby "soften the loneliness a little,"[4] in 1964 he was able to publish one of the most utilized and quoted biology papers of modern times, *The Genetical Evolution of Social Behavior*.[5]

"With very few exceptions, the only parts of the theory of natural selection which have been supported by mathematical models admit no possibility of the evolution of any characters which are on average to the disadvantage of the individuals possessing them," Hamilton wrote, continuing, "If natural selection followed the classic models exclusively, species would not show any behavior more positively social than the coming together of the sexes and parental care."[6]

Or in other words, the mathematical version of Darwin's theory did not allow an individual to display social behavior by which he helped others to his own disadvantage: the classical definition of altruism.

Hamilton then developed a mathematical version of Haldane's calculations on the back of the coaster: if an individual, a phenotype, shares much of his genes, his genotype, with other individuals, helping them makes sense, even if it costs him in terms of his reproductive abilities.

The key is to consider it from the genotype's point of view. If "all" that matters is the survival of the genotype, it doesn't matter if a particular individual survives or not, as long as the gene is transmitted in some other way.

If we share half our genes with each of our siblings, then from the genotype's point of view there will be no problem in sacrificing our life to rescue them (if, mind you, there are three of them and we save all three), because together they contain more of our own genes than we do.

Of course, this is a slightly different way of looking at things than we phenotypes employ. Surely nothing is more important to me than my own survival? Well, my children's, perhaps, but each of them also contains half of my genes, so this makes sense in Hamilton's model.

Hamilton succeeded in composing a simple rule for when it pays to help a relative from the genotype's point of view: the payoff to your relative combined with the degree of kinship must be greater than the cost to you.[7]

Hamilton's rule was able to explain peculiar biological facts, such as the existence of sterile worker bees. So it made a huge impact on biologists. Bees, wasps, ants, and other like insects reproduce in a special way because the queen is mother to them all. The mutual kinship of two individuals from the same nest is very close: they share more than half of their genes. The entire repertoire of social behavior and self-sacrifice to be found among these insects (a bee may sting you even if it pays with its life) is a manifestation of this close kinship. But can Hamilton's rule also explain the behavior in creatures more complicated than insects?

If an act that helps a relative halves your chances of reproducing, the advantage to your relative must be very big before it pays off from the genotype's point of view.

A warning cry is one good example: a predator approaches a peaceful flock of birds that are gathering seeds. One bird spots the predator and utters a call to warn the flock. They all fly to safety, and the predator is left hungry.

Or, it does if all goes well. After all, uttering warning cries is a serious matter: you attract not just the attention of your fellows, but that of the predator, as well. By crying out, the danger of being eaten is clearly greater than if you sneak off quietly. But if you beat a discreet retreat, the whole flock will be exposed to greater danger.

What is the bird to do? Screech or beat it?

Hamilton's theory puts it very clearly: it depends on how many relatives the bird has in the flock. If there are more than two siblings it should screech. If there are more than four grandchildren it should screech. If there are more than eight cousins it should screech; otherwise it should keep quiet.[8]

The point, then, is that if you rescue more of your genes by risking your own copies, you should take the risk; otherwise, slink off to safety.[9]

This theory reveals many interesting facts. The most important, of course, is that animals living in small groups with lots of relatives have every reason to sacrifice themselves for the group, as there is a high probability that many relatives are present. In a completely Darwinian fashion, natural selection proves able to produce selflessness, cooperation, and a kind of altruism (at any rate toward your closest relatives).

So natural selection does not lead to pig-headed selfishness the way we find it, for example, in the ever selfish, cold-blooded *Homo economicus*. Selfishness of that kind is a completely un-biological and un-Darwinist idea: according to the economist's view of man, any phenotype thinks only of Number One and couldn't care less about other phenotypes. But according to the biologists, man is a phenotype who doesn't think of Number One, but of his genes. And genes are something he shares with other phenotypes.

The most naive idea of egoism cannot, then, be justified in terms of evolutionary biology. It is simply not true that we only think of Number One.

Mind you, this only applies to close family ties. A modern city dweller, who lives far from his parents in the country and his siblings in Hicksville, has practically no chance of meeting his own genes in the streets or in the briny deep. Is he meant to fish drunken Swedes out of the waters of Copenhagen Harbor, then? Hamilton's theory doesn't tell us (or more accurately, it tells us "no," but that does not explain Haldane's chivalry).

However, it was a major step forward to learn that Darwin does not leave us only with the image of lonely Barbarians clubbing one another on the head.

HAMILTON'S THINKING HAS been extended since then, not least by the keen-minded, though occasionally rather shrill, British evolutionary biologist Richard Dawkins, who published his book *The Selfish Gene* in 1976.[10] In *The Selfish Gene* Dawkins presents with dazzling pedagogical virtuosity the view that evolution is about genes, not organisms. The organism is merely the gene's way of making new copies of itself. The chicken is just the egg's way of making new eggs.

So we don't need to work out what chickens want, but how an egg turns into as many eggs as possible.

The phenotype can easily be altruistic because the genotype is selfish. A selfish genotype is able to create an altruistic phenotype that sacrifices itself for others—again, as long as they're close relatives.

This view contains quite a bit of cynicism, particularly from my point of view and yours; after all, we're phenotypes. But it also contains considerable clarity. The trouble is, though, that we phenotypes are often friendlier to other phenotypes than our genotypes are presumably interested in. We're nice to our relatives, but also to other people. We dive into the river to rescue phenotypes we've never seen before. Even drunken Swedes. Why?

THE AMERICAN BIOLOGIST Robert Trivers was a friend of William Hamilton's.[11] They worked together on their scientific theories, backed each other up and shared many ideas. In 1971 Trivers published a landmark paper on men who rescue others from drowning: *The Evolution of Reciprocal Altruism.*[12]

We are familiar with the puzzle, and it is simple: if we see a man drowning, we may be able to rescue him—but only by exposing ourselves to risk. Why should we perform such an altruistic act if we are not related to him?

Trivers's answer was just as simple: "Were this an isolated event, it is clear that the rescuer should not bother to save the drowning man," Trivers writes, taking the cold-blooded view of the genotype as his starting point. "But if the drowning man reciprocates at some future time, and if the survival chances are then exactly reversed, it will have been to the benefit of each participant to have risked his life for the other."

This argument is interesting: in isolation, rescuing strangers makes no sense, but if the situation is repeated in reverse, it's quite another matter.

If we rescue a stranger we may be so fortunate as to be rescued by him later. Trivers called this "reciprocal altruism."

Reciprocity is the key. "If we assume that the entire population is sooner or later exposed to the same risk of drowning, the two individuals who risk their lives to save each other will be selected over those who face drowning on their own."[13] Being nice to others can pay in the long run and in situations where in isolation it does not.

The legendary baseball player Yogi Berra, who was celebrated for his game but especially for his singular and not always carefully considered utterances, not unlike the flowery expressions uttered by former Danish soccer coach Richard Møller Nielsen, is credited by the American sociologist Robert D. Putnam with "the most concise definition of reciprocity," namely the immortal words "If you don't go to somebody's funeral, they won't come to yours."[14]

WILLIAM HAMILTON GAVE Robert Trivers an idea: test this line of thought against the prisoner's dilemma. We have a situation in which there is no rational selfish reason to cooperate with the other man, because if we do, and he does not cooperate, too, we will put ourselves at serious risk.

But the situation changes radically if the game is not just played once, but repeated many times. Then, cheating the other man becomes a lousy idea. Cooperation can emerge when selfish people meet again and again, as this opens up the possibility of reciprocal help—even if some time passes between one helping the other and the other helping the one. As long as they meet up again.

During the sixties game theorists, such as the psychologist Anatol Rapoport from RAND, published a series of reiterative games in which the possibility of cooperation arose. Trivers was able to draw on this experience and devise his mathematical theory of reciprocal altruism.

Reciprocal altruism generated quite different rules for the biological understanding of, for example, warning cries. Now you didn't need to have close relatives in the flock to make screeching worthwhile; as long as there are enough birds to constitute a flock, it's probable that the warning crier will benefit from another bird's cry at a later date.

Egocentrics cooperate if they meet again and again. You only benefit once from taking people for a ride.

I N 1979 THE sociologist Robert Axelrod, from the Institute for Public Policy Studies at the University of Michigan, Ann Arbor, announced a now-legendary tournament.[15] It was to shed light on a question that absorbed Axelrod as a researcher: "Under what conditions will cooperation emerge in a world of egoists without central authority?"[16]

The idea was to ask a number of game theorists to submit computer programs that could play the prisoner's dilemma. All of the programs, being, as they were, submitted by different scientists, constituted a different strategy for taking on the other players, which were also computers. The game would be repeated two hundred times to reveal which program did best. Each player (which was a computer, as I say) was allowed to recognize the other players and to remember how they had behaved in earlier rounds.

Some programs were complete hawks, always refusing to cooperate. Others were very responsive and cooperated all the time (cooperation in the prisoner's dilemma involves remaining silent and not implicating the other player). Some of the programs were very long; others, much shorter. Twenty-four programs were submitted.

To Axelrod's great surprise the winner was the shortest program of all, Tit-for-Tat, submitted by the aforementioned Anatol Rapoport, at the time a psychologist and philosopher at the University of Toronto.

The strategy of Tit-for-Tat was very simple: the first time it met another program it cooperated. After that, it did whatever the player had done last time they met. If the other player had defected, Tit-for-Tat defected too. If the other player cooperated, so did Tit-for-Tat: a form of reciprocity in which you start by being positive and continue to be so as long as the other player plays along, too. Axelrod said that the strategy was kind (never the first to defect) and forgiving (the punishment for defecting need only last one round).

The third important characteristic of Tit-for-Tat was that it was clear and simple. The other players could quickly see how its strategy worked.

But most important, the success of Tit-for-Tat showed that when the game was played many times, the winner was the player who showed the will to cooperate. "What makes it possible for cooperation to emerge is the fact that the players might meet again. This possibility means that the choices made today not only determine the outcome of this move, but can also influence and affect the later choices of the players. The future can therefore cast a shadow back upon the present and thereby affect the current strategic situation."[17]

The same point, then, as in Trivers's theory of reciprocal altruism: the shadow of the future on the present creates the possibility of cooperation.

But if the first round of the tournament surprised Axelrod, the second was no less of a surprise. The first round had been played by invited colleagues. For the second, many more were invited, partly through an advertisement in a computer journal. This second group did not just play two hundred rounds, as in the first tournament, but they also conducted an ecological experiment: the programs were all regarded as biological quantities, a population of individuals competing to see who could produce the most descendents.

After each round, the programs were awarded offspring according to the number of points won. Successful programs, thus, were given more copies for the next round. Through this device, the best programs gradually dominated the game completely, and the other players slowly disappeared from the population.

The result was that after two hundred rounds, Tit-for-Tat dominated the entire population. It continued to do so, and after a thousand rounds many of the competitors had disappeared. Cooperation pays in the long run.

Axelrod's results showed that even in an environment of players very unwilling to cooperate, a small group of programs playing Tit-for-Tat could gradually grow bigger.

There are two very important lessons to be learned from Axelrod's experiment: firstly, it shows that cooperation is a sound strategy; and secondly, it shows that once cooperation gains sway in a population it can continue its advance. Cooperation is a robust state not easily suppressed by egocentric players.

"So mutual reciprocal cooperation can emerge in a world of egoists without central control by starting with a cluster of individuals who rely on reciprocity," Axelrod concluded.[18]

And that's not bad. But of course it was only computer programs.

A XELROD'S ANALYSIS WAS greatly inspired by a decisive breakthrough in evolutionary biology. It was created by the British biologist John Maynard Smith, originally an engineer,[19] who had been taught evolutionary biology by Haldane. Incidentally, Maynard Smith contributed a program to Axelrod's little game.

In the early seventies Maynard Smith came up with a theory for the evolutionary process, based on game theory. His idea was to regard the genes as players in a gigantic game. As in Axelrod's experiment, each time a player was successful it received many copies for the next round and would gradually dominate the game after many generations.

Maynard Smith's central concept was the *evolutionary stable strategy*. This is a kind of balance in which a number of strategies form an environment for one another in which no strategy—no player—can gain an advantage by changing unilaterally.

Let's imagine a population of birds: some are hawks, others doves. They all live on the same food, which they occasionally fight for. The hawks are very aggressive and engage one another in violent fights, often to the death. The doves are peaceful and cautious. When a hawk meets a dove, the dove quickly backs off without getting seriously hurt. The hawk wins, but the dove survives. When a dove meets a dove, each threatens the other a bit and then they both go off in different directions.

Which situation is stable? A population made up exclusively of hawks? A population made up exclusively of doves? Neither.

If there are only hawks, they fight to the death. And that's that. Nobody wins in the long run because they expend all their energy fighting. If a single dove appears in this population it quickly progresses, because it's "clever" enough not to fight. The dove waits for the others to kill themselves; then it and its descendents dominate the scene.

If there are only doves, they can live in peace and harmony, yes, but the situation is very vulnerable. If a hawk happens by, it will have the game all to itself, as will a dove that mutates into a hawk.

So in a pure population it is an advantage to each bird to change its strategy. That is why the situation is unstable: no matter what the others do, a single player, a single bird, can gain an advantage by unilaterally changing its strategy.

A combination of doves and hawks, on the other hand, becomes stable if the proportions are right. A balance emerges, which means that none of the birds gain an advantage by unilaterally changing their strategy. (The precise combination for stability depends, of course, on the benefits and costs of fighting.)

Maynard Smith showed how a little model of bird strategies can be drawn up as a classic game theory problem. A hawk forfeits two points when it meets another hawk, because both get hurt in the fight, but gains two when it meets a dove. A dove gets one point when it meets a dove, which gets the other point. A dove that meets a hawk neither wins nor loses, but sneaks off and leaves the object of the fight (two points) to the hawk.

It turns out that if the population consists of two thirds doves and one third hawks, the situation is stable. No bird gains by unilaterally changing its strategy. This is an evolutionary stable strategy, a gathering of players that is in balance and will not change over time—unless a fox appears.

IT IS NO accident if Maynard Smith's idea reminds us of Nash equilibria from classic game theory. After all, they too involve the fact that there are combinations of strategies that are stable, because no player benefits by unilaterally defecting from them. In fact, they are the same thing. Mathematically, an evolutionary stable strategy is the same as a Nash equilibrium.

But there is one vital difference. The Nash equilibrium is a notion that arose to describe games in which humans use rationality and calculation to beat one another. So there is common sense, consciousness, intentions, and all kinds of other human stuff present in a game that leads to a Nash equilibrium.

But there is not necessarily any of this in a Maynard Smith stable strategy. A group of water fleas or civets that have absolutely no idea what they are doing can achieve a stable strategy. The game is not a game in the sense of chess, but an evolutionary dispute in which those who do best have the most offspring.

Missing from the biological application of game theory is any rational analysis and calculation in terms of "if he does this, I'll do that, but he knows that, so I'll do something else." Instead, we have a statistical concept: if a whole load of tadpoles do this, while a whole load of other tadpoles do that, which strategy will win? Game theory without consciousness. It has to be so if game theory is to be applicable to biological evolution—because fighting, cunning, threats, flight, and cooperation existed long before man came along with his rationality, consciousness, and mathematics. Game theory can function without conscious players.

MAYNARD SMITH'S BREAKTHROUGH was a great event not only for biology, but for game theory, because the latter could suddenly be expressed without using the rational, intellectual analysis that had always made it sound rather dry and peculiar (whether we're playing poker, rescuing Swedes from the harbor, or trying to get a stag hunt off the ground we do not consciously perform all the dry calculations game theory is so concerned with).

But it can also describe an evolutionary process in which

a large number of interactions lead to a result none of the participants imagined or wanted: a kind of collective effect.

The evolutionary interpretation of game theory is now emerging as the dominant one.[20]

M AYNARD SMITH'S THEORY and Axelrod's computer game contain a message of freedom: it can be done! It is possible to arrive at a stable state by cooperating. And not just to arrive at, but to remain there. It can be done without rationality or human intelligence. Evolution can generate creation even among selfish egoists. It is not always easy to get there, but it can be done. The recipe is reiteration, reiteration, reiteration.

It was the same recipe that lay behind the theory of natural selection: reiteration, reiteration, reiteration. Generation after generation after generation, where those who do best have the most descendents and therefore do even better in the future.

In 1981 Robert Axelrod wrote a paper with William Hamilton in which they unified the social and biological perspectives: *The Evolution of Cooperation*. It does not require wisdom and foresight but may appear among the simplest organisms. "Cooperation in biological systems based on reciprocity can evolve even without foresight by the participants."[21]

We can also put it another way: Darwin's wonderful idea of natural selection managed to eliminate the need for a designer with overview. Complicated organisms can develop merely by repeated selection. Similarly, complicated interplay and cooperation between organisms emerges without central planning or a conscious overview.

Selfish genotypes create cooperative phenotypes. Cooperation pays; especially for egoists.

WHEN THESE IDEAS and theories reached the public in the seventies they were not exactly welcomed as a message of freedom. Indeed, the first researcher to draw attention to these theoretical milestones had all the effect of a wet blanket.

Literally, too: ice water was thrown at a meeting of the AAAS, the American Association for the Advancement of Science, in February 1978. A dozen demonstrators interrupted a session on social biology, inheritance, and the environment to chant slogans at the biologist Edward O. Wilson, who was about to present a paper. In his book *Sociobiology* (1975) he had tried to show how social behavior emerges among insects and animals, not least ants, his favorite subject for research. In the final twenty-eight pages out of 575, Wilson described how some of the same laws might apply to man and human society.

"Racist Wilson you can't hide, we charge you with genocide!" the protestors chanted before pouring ice water over the speaker.[22]

That was in 1978. The intellectual climate was strongly politicized; one slogan of the day was "everything is political," and one of the leading tendencies was to seek out sociological explanations for absolutely everything. When it came to human evolution, the spirit of the day dictated that it was all environmentally determined; heredity had no bearing. Man was the product of his culture and the times in which he lived, while the biological side of the case—man as animal—played no part. Any differences in the human situation were created by society; the situation the worst off found themselves in was the product of the unfair conditions in which they had grown up.

Naturally, this attitude hung together with the belief that society could and should be changed: a belief that had very powerful wind in its sails throughout the seventies. The Vietnam War, pollution, the insanity of the arms race, the depletion of resources, indifference to the plight of the people of the Third World, female oppression, racism: there were plenty of reasons to criticize capitalism. Since 1968 a youth rebellion, particularly among students, had gone from strength to strength throughout the Western world. Freedom movements in the Third World gained sway. Environmental and gender political movements emerged in industrial countries. The demand for change could be heard everywhere. As Bob Dylan sang prophetically in 1963, "The Times They Are A-Changin'."

But there was the matter of human nature. If man is mainly determined by his genes, the problem will merely be transferred to the new, improved society—as the egoism, shortsightedness, xenophobia, and greed characteristic of man in modern society are not a product of society, but of their indelible genes. So such protests are useless.

In the seventies, therefore, being politically progressive and ready for change was equated with being of the view that environment meant everything, and heredity nothing to the human character.

This meant that people were violently provoked when a prominent biologist like Edward Wilson told them in 1975 that after decades of intense studies of ant heaps he had discovered that not only ants, but also humans, possessed social behavior and organizations that were determined (or at least codetermined) by their genes. Hey, this sort of thing led straight to racism and eugenics (discrimination on the part of society between who was allowed to have children and who was not)! This would lead to the compulsory castration of deviants, genetic filtering, and other nasty stuff familiar from Hitler's Germany.

So sociobiology ran into intense criticism from the left wing all over the world.[23] This criticism was quite irrespective of the fact that such a leading proponent of sociobiology as Robert Trivers was a friend of the Black panther leader Huey Newton, one of the heroes of the left wing in the sixties; quite irrespective of the fact that many other sociobiologists abjured racism and eugenics; and quite irrespective of the fact that Edward Wilson had played a leading part in identifying the threats to the Earth's biodiversity and life's profusion.

Today it may look a little bit comical.[24] The eighties and in particular the nineties were marked by a dramatic change in attitudes toward heredity and the environment. The mapping of the human genome and other biotechnology projects favored biological explanations. It became increasingly accepted that a very large part of man's traits are genetically determined; perhaps not in the oversimplified way we had once thought, with one gene for every form of behavior (one for eating candy, another for feeling horny), but nevertheless still in such a way that it became obvious that inherited characteristics were of enormous importance to the formation of the individual—and thereby of society and culture, too.

Was this a consequence of the fading of the left wing all over the world during the same period? And of capitalism's impressive ability to solve many of the problems that sparked the rebellion in the sixties and seventies?[25] Is there a direct link between belief in the importance of heredity and being politically reactionary (in which case the whole exposition of this book is strongly reactionary)?

The irony is that over the same period, since the eighties and most emphatically in the nineties, experimental economics, the biology-inspired game-theory version of economics, has systematically shot down any notions that, at bottom, man is a selfish *Homo economicus.*

It has at once become clear that heredity and biology in fact play a major part in the way the behavior of the individual takes shape, and at the same time that much of what we associate with the good in man is determined by this same biology.

If so, though, can the notions of natural selection from biological evolution theory explain the finds made by experimental economists?

WE HAVE SEEN that Darwin's natural selection can lead to our treating our relatives decently even if it costs us. We have also seen that reciprocity may lead to our treating non-relatives decently, because we expect them to pull us out of the river at a later date.

But can this also explain what we see around us in nature

and society? Helpful behavior toward others is not limited to relatives and people we expect to pay us back. After all, we pull tourists out of the harbor, as well, even though there is no chance they will return the favor.

Neither the Haldane-Hamilton kinship theory nor Trivers's idea of reciprocity can explain why we are so nice to Swedes.

Or, on a more serious note: the experimental economics we heard about earlier have revealed a number of sides of man. Can we understand them on the basis of these same theories? This question is currently the focus of intense theoretical argument. It must also be said to be pretty important.

"GENERALIZED ALTRUISM" WAS one of the terms Robert Trivers introduced in his pioneering article on reciprocal altruism in 1971, where the fundamental idea was that via reciprocity selfish individuals could develop "altruistic acts."[26]

Such generalized altruism would solve the problem of reciprocal altruism, which only works between two individuals who swap helpful acts with each other. In generalized altruism the same people don't necessarily give and take. In Trivers's words, people can "respond to an altruistic act that benefits themselves by acting altruistically toward a third individual uninvolved in the initial interaction."[27]

The idea of reciprocal altruism was extended in the eighties by the biologist Richard Alexander, who introduced the concept of indirect reciprocity.[28] The point is that altruistic acts are repaid by people other than the beneficiaries. The reason we may receive a helping hand from somebody we've never helped is that by having previously helped somebody else we attain social status and recognition that make others willing to help us.

The mechanism, then, is that the members of a group keep an eye on one another and award high status to those who help others. One individual feels inclined to help another if the latter previously helped a third.

Instead of Hamilton's kinship altruism—in which we help close relatives—and Trivers's reciprocal altruism—in which we swap good deeds with somebody else—indirect reciprocity involves creating a position in the group that makes others inclined to help you. You become "a good person" and so you get help. "Indirect reciprocity is a consequence of direct reciprocity occurring in the presence of others," Alexander writes.[29]

Richard Alexander thinks that this may be the reason for human ethics: good deeds give you a good image, which attracts other people's good deeds (that is, if anybody is actually watching as you help the old lady to cross the road. . . .)

In 1999 researchers from Bern, Switzerland, organized a small game with seventy-nine first-year students. The players were each given a sum of money (seven Swiss francs) to share among the others or keep for themselves. Whenever a player donated to another, the game master tripled the sum donated. During the game the players were told how the potential beneficiary had acted earlier: whether he had been generous to others or whether he had not given anything.

The result was unequivocal: donations were made more often to players who had themselves made donations. The players were most inclined to give money to those who gave money. Generosity pays.[30]

Similarly, the zoologist Martin Nowak from Oxford and the mathematician Karl Sigmund from Vienna tried running computer games with a kind of indirect reciprocity. A series of computer programmers served as players in a prisoner's dilemma game lasting for many rounds, in which they could cooperate or defect. The players assumed an image according to how helpful they were. The idea was that a good image would attract cooperation.

The results were positive: "Performing the altruistic act increases the image score of the donor and may therefore increase the chance of obtaining a benefit in a future encounter as a recipient."[31]

Nowak and Sigmund think therefore that "the emergence of indirect reciprocity was a decisive step for the evolution of human societies."[32]

But that is precisely the problem: indirect reciprocity may indubitably function in a well defined group of people familiar with one another's behavior, as in the Swiss experiment using students. But can it also emerge by itself in a less well defined group of animals without an experimenter keeping tabs on who has given how much to whom?

Richard Alexander emphasized that the idea of indirect reciprocity promoted the continual assessment and reassessment of everyone in the group. Considerable intellectual and social resources, then, are required in order to establish such indirect reciprocity.

The result is a chicken-or-the-egg problem: if you have a

community of individuals with considerable memory capacity in well functioning social groups, it's not hard to understand how indirect reciprocity can work. But how can it emerge from a non-community?

Against this background, the biologists Olof Leimar from Stockholm and Peter Hammerstein from Berlin concluded in 2001 that the necessity of the pre-existence of a fair mechanism for allocating good and bad images might prove to be a decisive problem for the idea of indirect reciprocity as the driving force that created social behavior in evolution.[33]

In practice, reciprocal altruism and indirect reciprocity have both turned out to be difficult to prove in biology. Indirect reciprocity presupposes advanced intellectual and social traits, so perhaps it isn't so surprising that we don't find many examples in the animal kingdom.

But neither is reciprocal altruism so widespread as it was thought to be. In fact, for such an important phenomenon as food sharing only two examples of reciprocal altruism have been found among animals:[34] the vampire bat, which shares blood with fellow bats that return to the nest with no booty,[35] and ravens which share information on food sources.[36]

The question isn't whether indirect reciprocity is important in modern social behavior, because it is. Experimental economics gives very powerful reasons for taking cooperation and reciprocity seriously as central human traits. The question is how cooperation and reciprocity emerged in the history of evolution. Or, to put it another way, where does *Homo reciprocans* come from?

Among game theorists *Homo reciprocans* is the name of

the reciprocally cooperative human who chooses to help others and punish defectors.[37] *Homo reciprocans* is different from *Homo economicus,* the selfish, rational human whose origins are not hard to understand.

Homo reciprocans is not egocentric, but neither is he a babbling altruist. According to the game theorist and economist Herbert Gintis, it is characteristic of *Homo reciprocans* "to come to strategic interactions with a propensity to cooperate, responds to cooperative behavior by maintaining or increasing his level of cooperation, and responds to non-cooperative behavior by retaliating against the 'offenders,' and even when he could not reasonably expect future personal gains to flow from such retaliation."[38]

THE FAVORITE EXPLANATION among game theorists for such a creature emerging by biological evolution involving the pursuit of his own interests is a variation on Darwin's theory of natural selection. It's known as *group selection.*

I hasten to point out that in the view of most evolutionary biologists, group selection only plays a marginal role in biological evolution (and I entirely agree with them). But as it is very popular among experimental economists and game theorists we need to know about it.

Classical natural selection takes place at the individual level. Individuals who do well have many descendants and so end up dominating the population.

A central achievement of modern evolutionary theory, starting out from Haldane and Hamilton, is to go one level deeper, to the genetic level, and to regard the individual genes as the egoists that drive evolution. Richard Dawkins's notion of the selfish gene is a very clear way of expressing this point of view: it shows that a selfish genotype can create an altruistic phenotype as long as the altruism is limited to members of the immediate family.

But you can take the other approach: instead of going from individual to genes you can go from individual to group. Then you can interpret evolution such that it is not individuals competing for survival but groups of individuals. The advantage of this approach—i.e., thinking in terms of groups—is that it suddenly becomes very easy to see how altruistic traits can evolve: after all, an individual who sacrifices himself for other individuals may nevertheless gain an overall advantage (to himself or his descendents) because the whole group will benefit from his sacrifice.

If we regard groups of individuals as the power behind evolution and as the object of selection, it is simple to understand social behavior—because the social aspect comes first, and the individual, second.[39]

Through much of the history of Darwinism (almost a century), group selection was recognized as a possible explanation of the origins of morality. In 1871 Darwin himself wrote, "Selfish and contentious people will not cohere, and without coherence nothing can be effected. A tribe rich in the above qualities [sympathy, fidelity, and courage] would spread and be victorious over other tribes: (. . .) Thus the social and moral qualities would tend slowly to advance and be diffused throughout the world."[40]

Darwin continues: "A tribe including many members who,

from possessing in a high degree the spirit of patriotism, fidelity, obedience, courage, and sympathy, were always ready to aid one another, and to sacrifice themselves for the common good, would be victorious over most other tribes; and this would be natural selection."[41]

So Darwin supported the idea of group selection, and indeed it lived in "quiet coexistence"[42] with the idea of purely individual selection for the next hundred years.

But in the sixties group selection became unpopular. The American theorist George C. Williams argued in an influential book that you can always "translate" a group selection into a selection for individuals,[43] that you can explain social behavior as an expression of interests that are selfish in the final analysis (in the same way that Haldane/Hamilton's theory of helpfulness to relatives shows that phenotypic altruism is in fact genotypic altruism).

Since then, though, John Maynard Smith has shown that group selection can occur—but that it is not particularly likely. The idea resembles the logic behind the passage quoted from Darwin above. If we have two groups, one of which contains many cooperative altruists and the other contains only selfish egoists, we may envisage circumstances in which the entire population, consisting of both groups, will evolve in a way that the proportion of altruists grows. The group with more altruists will do better, have more descendents, and gradually dominate.

Note that this evolution will take place at the same time that the proportion of altruists in the group containing more altruists declines. This is because within a given group, the altruists will always be on the retreat: the egoists benefit from the altruists' generosity while not contributing to the community.

So group selection has this effect: the entire population gets a growing proportion of altruists at the same time that the proportion of altruists declines in both the groups that form the population as a whole.

It sounds a bit odd, but it is an example of a statistical effect known as the Simpson paradox.[44] An example serves to explain it. Let's say we have two groups with very different compositions. In one group there are eighty happies and twenty grumpies. But more and more grumpies emerge because there is no more candy. In the other group almost everyone is a grumpy because nobody can remember when they last had any candy; so there are eighty grumpies and twenty happies. Altogether there are a hundred grumpies and a hundred happies.

If the first group grows to twice the size, which it will do because its higher number of happies causes it to be more successful, it should have 160 happies and forty grumpies—but some of the happies have become grumpy so instead there are only 150 happies and fifty grumpies. The number of grumpies has grown. The second group stays the same size, because its limited number of happies chokes its growth, but in the same period it goes from eighty grumpies and twenty happies to eighty-five grumpies and fifteen happies.

If we add the numbers from the two groups we get Simpson's paradox. We had one hundred grumpies and one hundred happies before: a ration of fifty-fifty. Now we have 150 + 15 = 165 happies and 50 + 85 = 135 grumpies. There is now a larger proportion of happies among the members of the population than before, even though the proportion of happies fell in both the groups that make up the population.

We may imagine that group selection took place the same way: the altruists are in retreat in all groups, but the groups in which they are to be found are growing. So their share of the overall population grows. That makes a little more sense, right?

As today's leading proponents of group selection, the biologist David Sloan Wilson and the philosopher Elliot Sober, put it: "Between-group selection favors the evolution of altruism; within-group selection favors the evolution of selfishness."[45]

But it is a very fragile mechanism. Neither does it explain how so many altruists got into both groups to start with. After all, individuals who sacrifice themselves will always be at a disadvantage. How then do they emerge? The absence of a sensible answer to this question has prevented group selection from gaining many supporters among evolutionary biologists. But it is not the only question to trouble the notion of group selection.

Nor does it tell us how groups maintain their borders between one another. And, in a wider perspective, this is the problem of the notion of altruism as a result of group selection: "Group selection promotes within-group niceness and between-group nastiness," Sober and Wilson wrote.[46]

If group selection is the only guarantee of the existence of sociality, altruism, generosity, and cooperativeness, there is a very serious problem: strangers. Because if group selection is so, group members must abhor non-members. Hey, their style is different! There is no reason to believe they'll cooperate! Our cooperation derives entirely from the fact that our group did better than their group during the last serious environmental crisis in the area because we cooperated! So we don't want others here!

The game theorist Herbert Gintis has shown that it is precisely crises such as famine, war, and natural disaster, in which you might fear everybody will cut and run, which may promote the groups in which there is cooperation.[47]

A mechanism like this promotes xenophobia to an extreme degree. "We're well off here; you just beat it!"

Theoretically it is not a good argument, but where attitudes are concerned it is important to realize that group selection as an explanation for altruism, however romantic it may sound, comes at an extremely high price: hatred of others.

If altruism is something that comes from within, however, from the individual, there is less reason to feel xenophobic. In this case, selfish altruism—i.e., altruism the individual exercises for his own sake—becomes more reassuring than group altruism.

But can it even emerge? Selfish altruism is surely an oxymoron.

So WHERE DOES that leave us? We have seen that man is highly inclined to cooperate. We have seen that biological evolution can be understood as the natural selection of individuals who have many descendents in a given environment. We have seen that group selection may help a tribe with lots of nice wild men outperform a tribe with lots of nasty wild men, but we have no idea how the nice wild men got there in the first place.

We have a theory of biological evolution, but it doesn't make it easy to understand what we want to understand: ourselves.

If we step back for a moment there are actually many peculiar things about the idea of evolution proposed by Darwin: we expect egoism but see cooperativeness; we expect a struggle for survival and the most extreme degree of scarcity as the logical result of natural selection, but instead we see a landscape so fertile and rich in subtleties that we are filled with wonder and profound awe again and again.

Darwin's theory of natural selection is the recipe for cultivating efficiency, cool calculation, greed, streamlining, and at a pinch, a spot of reciprocity.

But take a look out of the window! What do you see on a merry spring day? Extravagance, abundance, enthusiasm, decoration, surplus, joie de vivre, and carpets of flowers. Every single year the coming of spring marks an incomprehensible hubbub of life, growth, budding, birdsong, and buzzing. The sap rises, and anything seems possible. Mating dances are danced; nectar, lush fruits, beautiful girls, green leaves, and birds with the most amazing plumage are proffered. Nature bubbles with joy, and living creatures play merrily by land, sea, and air.

How on earth can natural selection explain all this?[48] After all, it isn't just man's generosity and cooperativeness that are hard to explain by natural selection, but nature itself! Nature is nowhere near as greedy as theory dictates. Now, surely that's a problem if ever there was one!

DARWIN COULD SEE that, too.

Yes, he had overcome huge challenges, such as explaining the evolution of the eye, that fantastic organ, which he described in *On the Origin of Species* thusly: "To suppose that the eye, with all its inimitable contrivances . . . could have been formed by natural selection, seems, I freely confess, absurd in the highest possible degree."[49] Yet he found it explicable, and the eye went on to become a classic example of the natural evolution of an extremely complicated structure that has occurred many different times in many different species of animals and insects.[50]

On April 3, 1860, barely a year after the publication of *On the Origin of Species*, Darwin wrote in a letter to one of his staunchest supporters in the United States, the botanist Asa Gray: "It is curious that I remember well [the] time when the thought of the eye made me cold all over, but I have got over this stage of the complaint, & now small trifling particulars of structure often make me uncomfortable." Darwin continued, "The sight of a feather in a peacock's tail, whenever I gaze at it, makes me sick!"[51]

But that was in 1860.

Darwin II

TAKING THE EASY WAY OUT

IN 1871 CHARLES Darwin published his second major work, another groundbreaking work that aroused indignation and sowed confusion amongst his contemporaries: *The Descent of Man*, as the title is usually given. What shocked his contemporaries was of course that the book claimed that man was descended from the apes: that we are animals that have developed into the refined, cultivated, civilized creatures we are today.

It was of course particularly shocking to the church, which believed in an image of man as Our Lord's chosen creature, elevated high above the animals in the Garden of Eden.

71

In Denmark, for example, Bishop D. G. Monrad took up the fight against Darwinism by suggesting that an ape academy be set up where apes could be transformed into humans and thus prove the theory of the origin of man.[1] Darwin's Danish translator, a botany student named J. P. Jacobsen who would go on to fame for his literary output, responded by declaring that there was no need for such an academy as "the entire Earth, since the very dawn of organic life, right up to the day the first primate emerged, has been one big Ape Academy."[2] The experiment had already been carried out: and it had succeeded.

But in reality it was not the notion that man was descended from the apes that was the most revolutionary in the book; the ape side of things was already a logical consequence of the view expressed in *On the Origin of Species* in 1859 (although not explicitly). The really novel and innovative thing, which the rest of the world spent a hundred years discovering, was *The Descent of Man and Selection in Relation to Sex.*[3]

Today this is known as sexual selection. It sounds as if it might be titillating, dirty even, but it doesn't consist of salacious, irrelevant appendices to a treatise on how the apes came down from the trees: it is, as time would tell, the very heart of the matter.

Descent of Man is a very large book: the first edition, published in 1871, is in two volumes and 898 pages. The first 250 pages contain the first part of the book, which is indeed about the *Descent of Man*. But there follows a second part of 550 pages about *Sexual Selection*. There is a twenty-page conclusion, *General Summary and Conclusion*, and the whole thing ends in a sixty-nine page index! An expansive work.

But sexual selection? What is it? Obviously something that exerted a powerful hold on the aging Darwin.

It took Darwin's biologist colleagues a hundred years to take his more-than-500-page theory of sexual selection seriously. Of course, it was also the most original of his ideas. Other researchers besides Darwin had come up with the concept of evolution and theory of natural selection; but the idea of sexual selection is quite uniquely Darwinian. Yet it was nevertheless neglected by Darwin's supporters for a century. Not until the seventies was this side of Darwin rediscovered, and it now imbues the debate on the use of the theory of evolution in understanding the human condition.

IT IS IMPORTANT to understand that there are two sides of Darwin, and that one has been ignored and forgotten. This neglect explains much of the confusion and incredulity that have surrounded Darwin, and much of the criticism leveled at his theories by evolutionary biologists.

Darwin has two mechanisms for explaining biological evolution: natural selection and sexual selection. The first imbues his masterpiece *On the Origin of Species* (1859), the other his second masterpiece, *Descent of Man* (1871). There are no inconsistencies between them, only extreme differences in perspective.

Both start out from the simple basic formula we met in connection with *On the Origin of Species*: when it is hereditary, a variation among the individuals of a species leads to the possibility of selection, and this in turn leads to evolution.

This simple formula is common to both kinds of selection.

The difference lies in what is responsible for selection. In Darwin there are three important types of selection: cultivation, natural selection, and sexual selection.

The cultivation of utility plants or domestic animals takes place when humans with desires, intentions, and needs direct evolution by exerting selective pressure on them (selective pressure might mean only planting the bulbs of the very reddest tulips, for example).

In natural selection, the environment is involved: climate, food, parasites, predators, habitats. All else being equal, the individuals of a species who are best adapted to the environment will also have the best possibilities of survival (and thereby the best chance of bearing offspring). The best adapted survive.

In sexual selection something completely different is involved; not survival but reproduction. The individuals who are most attractive as partners have the most opportunities to mate and thereby to have the most offspring. They will therefore gain ground in the population. This selection does not take place through a blind force of nature, with environmental factors culling the weakest individuals: it takes place when members of the species find certain other members more attractive than others. And so they have more offspring.

In practice, in most of the animal world by far, the males mate with all the females they can, while the females are somewhat fussier. Darwin demonstrated this fact in great detail in *Descent of Man,* but without explaining it. However, it means that since in practice it is the females that select the males they want to mate with, the males are subject to an enormously powerful selective pressure, and this in turn requires that they have characteristics that cause females to find them attractive.

The males are subjected to selective pressure in two ways: they have to ingratiate themselves with the attractive females, and they have to fight off the other males who want to mate with the same female. Sexual selection is a war on two fronts: the male must bow to the female, and the male must keep the other males away from her.

In turn this means that we may regard the male as something the females have cultivated: the male as the female's domestic animal!

The cultivation of the male by biological evolution did not happen quite so systematically or hi-tech as the cultivation of good breeding stock today. But the metaphor of the male as the female's selected creature is highly appropriate: where natural selection involves blind forces that cannot have any notion of what takes place during natural selection (what do the clouds know about the environment they create for the earthworm?) sexual selection is different. It is the result of females preferring certain males to others and finding them more attractive. This doesn't necessarily take place consciously—even among humans—but it is a mechanism that is more akin to cultivating beautiful roses than to earthquakes and collisions with comets.

ALMOST ALL THE presentations of Darwin's ideas, and almost all the criticism of them, involve the point that natural selection leads to a survival-oriented, very strict biological nature. There is no room for fun in natural selection. It's all about life and death and lack of food.

The American evolutionary biologist Steven Jay Gould, who died in 2002, was a leading critic of strict Darwinism. One of his major points was that nature is packed with curiosities, peculiar antlers, and odd colors, in which we can't see any survival value at all. Gould recognized that Darwin realized that natural selection was not the whole story, but he pointed out, with complete justification, that many of Darwin's students were unable to see beyond natural selection.

In his introduction to *On the Origin of Species* Darwin himself wrote, "I am fully convinced that species are not immutable; (. . .) Furthermore, I am convinced that Natural Selection has been the main but not exclusive means of modification."[4] Gould quotes from Darwin's last revised edition of *Origin,* which was published in 1872: "As my conclusions have lately been much misrepresented, and it has been stated that I attribute the modification of species exclusively to natural selection, I may be permitted to remark that in the first edition of this work, and subsequently, I placed in a most conspicuous position—namely, at the close of the introduction, the following words: 'I am convinced that Natural Selection has been the main but not exclusive means of modification.'"[5]

In *On the Origin of Species* Darwin did actually write a few pages on sexual selection: "This leads me to say a few words on what I call Sexual Selection. This depends, not on a struggle for existence, but on a struggle between the individuals of one sex, generally the males for possession of the females; the result is not death to the unsuccessful competitor, but few or no offspring."[6] But it was in *Descent of Man* that the theory seriously unfurled: a theory that discounts many of the objections to Darwinism made by Gould and others a hundred years later.

B UT WHAT IS sexuality? We had better take a look before we carry on with sexual selection. Why do living creatures reproduce by sexual propagation? Actually, this is the greatest riddle of evolutionary biology.[7] After all, organisms are perfectly capable of reproducing by other means.

Bacteria, which are one-celled organisms, simply divide into two identical daughter cells. In that sense, a bacteria never dies. One of its daughter cells may disappear, but as there is no difference between the individual bacteria cells, you can't say that it dies in the way a cow can die, because a cow is an individual, different from any other cow. Sexuality is therefore a precondition for the notion of death. Without sexuality, which leads to unique individuals, the notion of death makes no sense. Death is something life has invented.

In organisms that are more complicated than bacteria we find propagation without sexuality's combination of hereditary traits from two individuals. Virgin births, whereby a female bears offspring without the involvement of a male, take place among insects, snails, crayfish, lizards, and fish. There are loads of variations, loads of crazy ideas in nature.[8]

But sexuality has won the battle for life. Almost all large flora and fauna obtain offspring through sexual reproduction. Yet this is hard to understand on the basis of the theory of selfish genes and natural selection. After all, sexual reproduction is based on two individuals mixing their genes in an unpredictable way so that a new individual will emerge with hereditary traits unlike those of any other individual, including its parents. The offspring gets all its genes from the parents but combines them in a new way. This means that only half the selfish genes in an individual who reproduces sexually will be passed onto the next generation. From the gene's point of view it would make much more sense to have a goodly dollop of virgin births, resulting in natural cloning. So why is sexuality so widespread? Indeed, dominant?

There is no doubt that in the long run it is good for a population of organisms to have a wide variation among the individuals. It is a kind of insurance against future changes, because it ensures that there will most likely be individuals from the population capable of coping with changed sur-roundings. Sexual reproduction continually creates variation in the population, because the genetic cards are shuffled for every new generation. This is good for the population as a whole; but how does the individual benefit from mixing its own genes with those of another individual?

The answer is probably destabilization. There are two prin-ciple theories for the function of sexuality in the individual. One is that environmental influences continually create ran-dom changes to the individual's genes: so-called mutations. By mixing genes from two individuals you avoid giving these mutations free rein.

The other theory is known as the Red Queen hypoth-esis; it is named after the queen in *Alice in Wonderland* and *Through the Looking-Glass.* The Red Queen tells Alice to run faster, but when Alice complains that she can't move from where she is standing, the Red Queen merely retorts that in her country "it takes all the running you can do, to keep in the same place."[9] It is the concept that any movement is in order to remain in the same place that has lent its name to the theory of the origin of sex in controlling parasites.

The idea is simple: parasites are tiny organisms that invade and exploit a host organism. Parasites steal resources from the host and for that reason often make it sick. The struggle with parasites (such as bacteria, viruses, worms, leeches, fungus, and lots of other nasty things) is unequal: the parasites have a far shorter generation span than the host. A colony of bacteria may double in number every twenty minutes. This means that the host organism has trouble defending itself from the parasites. Every time the host develops a method of controlling them (via its immune defenses, for example), the parasite has many generations of selection to come up with a counterstrategy. Modern difficulties with penicillin-resistant bacteria are one example: there are so many bacteria and so many generations that emerge in the course of a simple lung infection that the chances are high that a few bacteria will succeed in surviving in an environment full of antibiotics. As soon as one bacteria cell like this emerges it will propagate at a furious pace because there is so much food available now that all the other bacteria have succumbed to the penicillin.

Parasites evolve very quickly, and so they constantly present the host with new challenges. A host organism that is to succeed must therefore continually develop its ability to respond, even if it lives in what appears to be a constant environment, in which the amount of food, rain, predators, and volcanic eruptions remains utterly constant. The parasites are tiny and unimpressive, but they are also part of the host organism's environment; indeed, part of its inner environment.

So an animal that's adapted to a particular habitat must constantly evolve in order to keep up with the rapid evolution of its parasites. For this purpose, sexual reproduction is appropriate. The individual participant in the sex game wants to constantly ensure that it has offspring with new chances of coping with the constantly changing parasitic pressure. It really does have to run as fast as it can to remain in the same environment.[10]

That is why sexual reproduction makes sense even for selfish genes that could have chosen cloning.

Sexuality is one thing; whether we understand it or not, it is very much a fact of life. But sexual selection is a theory that makes no sense unless we understand it. Why look further than the elegant explanatory mechanism inherent in natural selection?

A BRIEF STROLL IN the park will convince you that there is something requiring explanation: why are all the females camouflaged, while all the males are beautifully decorated and their colors so conspicuous?

Any drake is touchingly beautiful, any duck brown and reliable when she needs to hide in her nest. The difference is so great that when the Swede Carl von Linné categorized all known living creatures in a system of biological species in the eighteenth century he established two separate categories for two particular ducks, of which one was gray and dull, while the other was brown and blue. It has since proved that one was a duck and the other a drake of the same species.[11]

How could natural selection have evolved this difference? It makes much more sense to imagine that the females choose the males that look the most attractive. The males compete to see which has the most splendid plumage so that the females will choose them. Sexual selection.

ALFRED WALLACE DIDN'T believe it. Independently of Darwin he had developed the idea of natural selection, but he never reconciled himself to the idea that man could be a result of it. That was just too fantastic for him to imagine.

Neither did he believe in sexual selection. That is to say, Wallace believed in a variation of sexual selection, namely the mutual struggle of the males to gain access to the females: the variation of sexual selection that leads to the male arming himself with antlers and markings the better to frighten off the other males. But Wallace did not believe in the other variation, the most important in our context: the females' choice of males.[12] So he had no chance of believing that man's wonderful characteristics, such as the mind and a social life, might have evolved through biological evolution.

"Natural selection could only have endowed savage man with a brain a few degrees superior to that of an ape, whereas he actually possesses one very little inferior to that of a philosopher," Wallace wrote.[13]

Wallace's problem was that the advanced mental and other characteristics we humans possess make no sense if you only go halfway. What use is half a language, half of absolute pitch, or half aesthetics?

Human characteristics such as music, aesthetics, or mathematical sense could not have evolved through natural selection, Wallace thought. "In the same category we may place the peculiar faculty of wit and humour, an altogether natural gift whose development appears to be parallel with that of the other exceptional faculties. Like them, it is almost unknown among savages," the British natural scientist Wallace wrote. "Like them [wit and humour], too, it is altogether removed from utility in the struggle for life, and appears sporadically in a very small percentage of the population; the majority being, as is well known, totally unable to say a witty thing or make a pun, even to save their lives."[14]

Wallace's argument is an interesting one: the human characteristics we appreciate most in human culture are very unevenly distributed in the population (although the majority of Wallace's contemporaries probably had a sense of humor he merely failed to comprehend). Human mental faculties evince "an enormous amount of variation in their development; the higher manifestations of them being many times—perhaps even a hundred or a thousand times—stronger than the lower. Each of these characteristics is totally inconsistent with any action of the law of natural selection," he wrote.[15]

So, seen from the point of view of natural selection, these human characteristics are quite useless and their appearance in the population is patchy and varied, which you would not expect if they had evolved through natural selection and its struggle for survival.

Wallace concludes a major work on Darwin and natural selection with these words: "The Darwinian theory . . . shows us how man's body may have been developed from that of a lower animal under the law of natural selection; but it also teaches us that we possess intellectual and moral faculties which could not have been so developed, but must have had another origin, and for this origin we can only find an adequate cause in the unseen universe of the Spirit."[16]

Wallace converted to spiritualism in 1866 and believed in it for the rest of his life. His view of the world therefore embraced two sharply separated domains: a natural evolution that could explain the animal and human body, and a spiritual world that could explain the "human"—spirit, morals, intellect, aesthetics, and so on. A divided universe: that of the beast and that of the spirit.

This division recurs in many of Darwin's critics, who may be able to accept that the atoms of the universe might have become a silly silk monkey by natural selection, but not a singing Sicilian. They think more is required. The universe of the spirit cannot be understood through the laws of nature.

This is a point of view I have always regarded as lazy: you can't see the link between spiritual life and amoeba or aesthetics or atoms, so you merely declare that they are two different things.[17] Conversely, it is of course just as lazy to declare that man's fabulous culture and civilization is merely animal. The challenge is to understand the link between the two worlds, because one was formed on the basis of the other.

The Wallace-Darwin dichotomy continues to thrive in today's debates on biology and meaning: is there a single universe that contains both animal nature and the highest spirituality, even though we cannot yet see how? Or are there two parallel universes, that of matter and that of the spirit, with no obvious connection apart from man inhabiting both?

Observing man's fabulous abilities led Wallace to think that they could not have evolved through the natural selection of biological evolution.

So to Wallace it had to be thus: "The inference I would draw from this class of phenomena is that a superior intelligence has guided the development of man in a definite direction, and for a special purpose."[18]

Our Lord, in other words.

THERE IS AN alternative in Darwin's theory, Wallace just didn't believe it: sexual selection through the females' choice of males. If he had believed it, he would've had an interesting alternative to the notion of divine guidance: namely, another higher intelligence that has guided evolution and selected man with all his fantastic characteristics—woman.

Women are at the helm of evolution and determine its course. Women are in charge, not only in everyday life, but in the broad sweep of evolutionary history. Mankind is fantastic because women have bred and refined us! Man may provide history with its motor power, but it is woman who is at the steering wheel.

Today this kind of reverse sexism, negative male chauvinism, seems strange. But remember Darwin's day: prudish, male-dominated Victorian Britain. Darwin pulls no punches: not only are we apes who climbed down from the trees, but the men were selected and evolved according to the women's tastes: man bred by woman!

The shock of this insight was quite obviously one of the reasons why it took a hundred years before evolutionary biologists really understood Darwin's second great idea.

One of the great theoreticians of evolutionary theory, John Maynard Smith, put it thusly: "This neglect of sexual selection turned to enthusiasm during the seventies and eighties. It is tempting to ascribe this change in attitude to the influence of the women's movement. It certainly is not the case that the new research, theoretical and empirical, has been carried out by ardent feminists, but I think it may have been influenced, even if unconsciously, by the attitudes toward female choice in our own species."[19]

One of the most interesting theoreticians in the field of sexual selection, the American psychologist Geoffrey Miller, has pointed out that the large numbers of women who started studying the behavior of primates in the sixties may have played a part in the dawning recognition of the significance of sexual selection.[20] But he also indicates a succession of nonideological factors: it was difficult to come up with a mathematical theory for sexual selection, and the biological theory of evolution and animal behavior suffered from a series of deficiencies that meant that nobody could see the significance of sexual selection.[21] In Miller's view it was therefore scientific rather than ideological barriers that had confined sexual selection to oblivion.[22]

The original animosity toward Darwin's idea was rooted in the classical male role, which of course continues to play a major role today. Geoffrey Miller writes: "For male Victorian scientists it was taken for granted that young single ladies should wear brilliant dresses and jewels to attract the attention of eligible bachelors . . . they simply did not like to think of males as sexual objects accepted or rejected by female choice."[23]

It can hardly have been quite so simple. "Mogens," a short story by Darwin's Danish translator, J. P. Jacobsen, is about man as a desirable sex object, so much so that the literary historian Vilhelm Andersen described the short story as "Sexual selection in human form."[24]

THE IDEA THAT biological evolution is governed to a great extent by women's choice of men according to how good they are at presenting themselves completely corresponds to the reality familiar from human mating games on the one hand, and on the other, not at all. Because what is involved is man as a sex object, man as the object of sexual desirability or not.

Man as the one who volunteers his services and is accepted or rejected by a woman is perfectly familiar from the dance floor, where it is traditionally the man who asks for a dance and the woman who declines. We are acquainted with young men incessantly hunting for sex: the suitor who brings flowers and sings serenades beneath the window of the bride of his choice; the man who proposes; the man who asks if she'd like to come home to see his stamp collection.

On the other hand we are also familiar with the opposite: the woman putting on makeup to look more attractive; the woman spending half her spare time shopping for sexy shoes; the woman showing off her attributes come spring; the woman as a sex object for men.

How can anyone portray the history of evolution as woman's choice of man when women in the modern world so doll themselves up to please men? It seems paradoxical. But the secret is merely that human sexual selection is richer than that of most animals. There are also more firmly scientific questions to be put to the theory of sexual selection: most crucially, how is it possible? That females select attractive males is one thing, but don't you quickly end up with these sexy males developing such bizarre bodily features and patterns of behavior to attract the women that they can't live with them and die out? Wouldn't a selection that's only determined by the female's level of attraction automatically be the undoing of any offspring? After all, the poor kids would be born with characteristics inherited from the gaudy specimen their mum had fallen in love with.

Of course it is by no means certain that females are that stupid, but on the face of it, this objection seems quite valid, and there are also examples of sexual selection reducing the ability to survive,[25] and that features evolved through sexual selection have disappeared again.[26] But there is still a myriad of features developed through sexual selection that remain to be explained.

THE FIRST MATHEMATICAL theory of sexual selection was drawn up by Ronald A. Fisher in 1915: the theory of runaway sexual selection.

Fisher's idea was that females preferred certain characteristics in males: lovely blue feathers on the neck, for example, if we think of ducks. If ducks prefer drakes with blue necks, the drakes with blue necks will also have the most ducklings. So there will be more and more drakes with blue necks in the population. This is sexual selection. But Fisher pointed out that sexual selection like this could end up by running away.

The female has a gene with a preference for blue necks. Males with blue necks will therefore have lots of ducklings. If the characteristic in the female of liking blue necks and the characteristic in the male of being able to grow a blue neck are both hereditary, the result will be dramatic, Fisher says. Their joint offspring will inherit both the preference for blue necks and the ability to grow blue necks: one characteristic (the preference) will be expressed in the female ducklings, while the other (the blue necks) will be expressed in the male ducklings. The population will have more and more blue necks and more and more females who prefer blue necks. A snowball will start rolling and many drakes will grow very blue necks. Runaway.

If it also costs a considerable portion of a male duckling's energy to develop a blue neck—because the pigment is very special and requires special food—growing a very blue neck may rapidly become a problem for the male ducklings. It will exhaust them, and they will not thrive.

So the question is: doesn't sexual selection lead straight to decadence and the extinction of the species? Females prefer bizarre neck colors, antlers, tails, cheeks, whatever, and after breeding for a number of generations this preference becomes a crippling congenital encumbrance for the males. Fisher's runaway selection simply starts by females having some kind of preference, one not necessarily of any advantage to the male in terms of survival: indeed, it's a clear disadvantage. A bright blue drake with colored feathers all over is going to be more visible to predators and hunters than a discreet gray-brown duck.

At some stage, the female's preference for aesthetics will clash with the need to survive. The preferences of the female may merely reflect random properties in her sensory apparatus, but the need for survival is relentless.

Natural selection automatically takes survival into account, because it is selection with a view to the ability to survive. But sexual selection does not automatically guarantee the ability to survive; female ducks may well be turned on by characteristics quite different to the ability to survive.

So you would think that sexual selection would be no more than a fleeting phenomenon in the evolution of the species. It would rapidly evolve into decadent, perverse ornamentation that was such an encumbrance to survival that the species would succumb in transports of sexual delight; gone, dead, no more.

But that doesn't happen. Females are smarter than you'd think. The question of why and how was sorted out by a lifelong study of a bird, the Arabian Babbler. This led to an idea that may not be the best anybody has ever had, but does seem to be one of the most important ideas for understanding human life that anyone has ever had.

Researchers have put forth this idea thrice: in 1899, 1973, and 1975. A sociologist in 1899, an economist in 1973, and an ornithologist in 1975. The ornithologist was the first of them to understand just how radical it was.

Handicap

THE PEACOCK
AND HIS STRIKING PLUMAGE

T HE NOUVEAU RICHE information-technology billionaire curled his toes. Not because he was ashamed of his
extravagant motor-powered luxury yacht anchored outside
the royal palace on its maiden voyage, but because he was
freezing. Chilled to the marrow. The summer evening was
not as warm as expected and the man was in a panic. His
117 guests had been given strict orders on their invitations:
black tie and soft-soled deck shoes. The new floors and virgin
carpeting in the desperately expensively appointed saloons
could not cope with high heels beneath the gowns. The red
carpet leading to the gangplank was thronged by dozens of

party-clad information-technology people who would hardly refuse an invite from one of the world's richest men and now waited to enter the small marquis on the dockside. There, hired young women relieved them of their footwear and made most of them take off their socks as well. The partygoers had obeyed the deck shoe dictate, yes, but now the billionaire had changed his mind and wanted no shoes onboard at all. Barefoot, the guests ascended the red carpet to the panorama deck, where beautifully proportioned waitresses were waiting with champagne. The peculiar humiliation of the combination of evening dress and cold feet did not diminish their curiosity toward the ship, which looked like a computer graphic come true and had a shining engine room and an entire toy store of water scooters, catamarans, and wetsuits belowdecks. They whispered guesses as to how many half-billions a vessel like this must've cost, paid for by millions of buyers of licenses to equip their computers with an operating system.

The billionaire welcomed them and explained that having a ship like this was great. He just didn't look it, as he shivered in the cold, changed the color of his dinner jacket once an hour, and said his polite hellos. A slave to his own wealth.

What on earth did the man want a boat like this for if he didn't seem to be enjoying it?

T HE AMERICAN SOCIOLOGIST and economist Thorstein Veblen was the son of a Norwegian immigrant and is best known for his book *The Theory of the Leisure Class*, published in 1899. It contained such a piercing diagnosis of the behavior of rich Americans that the author's origins in—then—thrifty Norwegian society have been proposed as a possible explanation.[1]

Of course the behavior he was trying to understand was highly un-Norwegian: the way that rich Americans threw away their money on completely unnecessary things, such as gigantic parties and magnificent silk garments.

On one side of society Veblen identifies a hardworking class of useful people who create value efficiently and thriftily. On the other side a class of industrial magnates and urban rich who spend their money anything but effectively. Why do the urban rich waste their money?

In his search for an explanation Veblen developed the concept of *conspicuous consumption*: a consumption that clearly reveals its practitioner has money the way the rest of us have feces.

The idea behind grandiose parties, expensive silks, and excessive numbers of domestics is not necessarily that they're interesting in themselves, but rather that the poor can't afford them. Expensive clothes declare, *here comes a rich man*. There is less need for this in the country (where there is less anonymity), but in the city conspicuous consumption is the key to showing what you are worth, and thereby to status. "Conspicuous consumption of valuable goods is the means of reputability to the gentleman of leisure," Veblen writes.[2]

What matters most is its wastefulness. "Throughout the entire evolution of conspicuous expenditure, runs the obvious implication that in order to effectually mend the consumer's good fame it must be an expenditure of superfluities. In order to be reputable it must be wasteful. . . .

"As used in the speech of everyday life the word carries an undertone of deprecation. It is here used for want of a better term that will adequately describe the same range of motives and phenomena, and it is not to be taken in an odious sense, as implying an illegitimate expenditure of human products or human life," Veblen writes.[3]

Veblen's picture of society thus includes hardworking, economical, efficiency-loving people who toil and struggle to make ends meet, and the extravagant, flamboyant, wasteful, grandiose, crackpot rich men who light cigars with dollar bills and employ butlers to supervise the maids who are taken on to polish every door handle in the mansion every day.

The analogy with the relationship of the relentless efficiency of natural selection to the tendency of sexual selection to create more dissolute characteristics in living creatures is striking, but did not appear in Veblen's writings.

The fact that he is nevertheless discussed nowadays in conjunction with evolutionary biology hangs together with the logical structure of his argument: you have to do something that is *not* necessary or economical precisely in order to demonstrate how rich you are. Excessive consumption has no purpose except to show that the consumer can afford it. The good thing about an expensive item is that it's expensive and the rabble can't afford it.

As Scott Fitzgerald wrote, "The rich are different from you and me." (To which Hemingway is said to have retorted, "Yes, they have more money.")[4]

Waste and excess have no meaning in themselves, no usefulness, apart from demonstrating that you have lots of resources, which gives prestige, at any rate in the United States. Among those of us living closer to Norway it may not give as much prestige, but the philosophy is clear enough.

In the United States Veblen was regarded as a quaint Scandinavian with a penchant for Spartan living. The psychologist Geoffrey Miller writes, "Veblen's biographers often argue that his contempt for conspicuous consumption reflects the Norwegian frugality of Veblen's ancestors."[5]

The description is undoubtedly valid, but also amusing when you consider that Norway's oil has made it one of the richest nations on earth, but with a bizarre blend of screamingly conspicuous consumption in the property market and classic Norwegian frugality in the desire of society to invest. Norway has become a beautiful example of the fact that money is only worth anything if you have the courage to get rid of it.[6] After all, if money merely promotes the paranoid fear of envy and of high heels on newly laid decks, we're better off without it.

THORSTEIN VEBLEN LIVED a marginal existence in American academia and never really met with approval from economists and sociologists,[7] but he is now recognized for his writings and they are read to this very day.

Another economist achieved more recognition almost a hundred years later by resuscitating the logical structure of Veblen's argument. Michael Spence of Stanford University shared the 2001 Nobel Prize for Economics for his study of labor market signals.[8]

Spence had an interesting idea: in practice there is little point in long, theoretical degree courses if we look at the qualifications actually required for the job. Why, then, do appointments committees and human resources managers place so much emphasis on formal qualifications? (One museum director was even driven into exile from Denmark because she lied about her university degrees—and in the United States there have been several high-profile cases of people lying on their resumes.)

Spence's solution is simple: the acquisition of a long, theoretical qualification that may be of no specific significance to job performance is an indicator of the applicant's general diligence, persistence, and other qualities. It is not the degree that itself is valuable, but that it shows that the graduate is capable of completing an extensive task.

Fifteen years ago I was summoned to the newly appointed editor-in-chief's office at *Weekendavisen*. I wrote the science column but had been appointed by the previous editor-in-chief. As Schleimann, the new man, was known for his right-wing views and I for being correspondingly left-wing, I approached the meeting with some trepidation. "I can't interfere with what you write, because I don't know enough about it, unfortunately," Schleimann began, and then asked, "What's your educational background?" I explained that I was a "cand.techn.soc."—an environmental planner with a Danish degree, which is an amalgam of technological and sociological subjects with great emphasis on economics, law, and planning, and that might perhaps seem a touch irrelevant to writing about the natural sciences for the highly intellectual *Weekendavisen*. "What kind of degree you've got is irrelevant," Schliemann retorted, "as long as you've got one. Because that proves you were able to sit still long enough."

We laughed. Schleimann received no Nobel Prize for economics, but his argument was the same as Spence's: it doesn't matter that what you do is really a waste of time if only it proves that you possess a great stock of universally applicable resources.

Education is a kind of extravagance, a conspicuous, visible consumption of time that shows you are a good worker.

YES, IT DOES sound a bit far-fetched, doesn't it? A-levels prove that you're capable of doing perfectly useless things for many hours and that you're therefore qualified to be employed doing something else entirely. It doesn't exactly seem like an idea worthy of a Nobel Prize.

But consider the problem: how are we to assess whether people are any good? How can we decide whether an individual is strong or not? How do we guess the genotype from the phenotype?

In practice we have to look at the signals a person sends. An exam certificate is at least evidence that the person can get up in the morning and comb his hair.

Before you buy a secondhand car you know nothing about, it's wise to ask for a warranty. If the seller dares to issue a warranty you have reason to believe that he has faith in his car. If not, you begin to have your doubts. Only a seller with enough faith in his car can "afford" to issue a warranty; therefore, even if the warranty itself has no real value, it is a *costly signal*.

Costly signals do not have to be expensive. They are indications of quality rather than quality itself.

Costly signals matter because there are many social

interactions in which we have no direct way of assessing our opposite number's qualities; we have only the indirect method of demanding a signal that is too expensive for a weaker person to send.

THE NOBEL PRIZE for Economics sometimes seems a bit of a cinch—and it is debatable whether economics is a great enough science to supply the raw materials for an annual award at the Nobel level. It was not part of dynamite inventor Alfred Nobel's original will and testament; it founded awards for medicine, physics, chemistry, literature, and peace. But in the sixties the Swedish national bank introduced a Nobel Prize for Economics—and it has since had some trouble finding enough good candidates. Perhaps it would have been more appropriate to create a slightly broader prize in the social sciences, rather than just one for economics.

Just as remarkably there is no Nobel Prize for biology. With the enormous importance biology and biotechnology have assumed and will increasingly do so, it would be completely out of proportion if Nobel Prizes could not be awarded for biological research. Indeed they are, but it is the chemistry prize that goes to microbiologists and the prize for medicine that goes to broader biological research.

With the fusion of biological and economics research, which is taking place on the basis of the insights provided by game theory, perhaps biologists will be awarded the Nobel Prize for Economics in the future. . . .

In any case the significance of the third, *biological* variation of the idea we have now met in two economics versions, one from 1899 and the other from 1973, is far more than just economic. This message, from the Arabian Babbler, fundamentally alters the perspective on living nature—and on mankind. The messenger's name is Amotz Zahavi. He is an Israeli ornithologist and full of cheek. He calls his idea the *Handicap Principle*.

T HE HANDICAP PRINCIPLE is a splendid example of itself.

You see, it has a terrible name that evokes unpleasant and incorrect associations. It makes us think of club feet and golfers, when we should be thinking about peacocks and brilliant minds.

Nevertheless the Handicap Principle has survived, and after a decade and a half of being pilloried for its cheek it has spent the last ten years going from strength to strength among evolutionary biologists as an explanation of many important factors in existence from courtship rituals to creativity and altruism.

The Handicap Principle, in fact, is doing so well despite the considerable handicap posed by its name that it must be an unusually good idea. No bad idea would have a chance with a name like that. But it *is* an unusually good idea. Indeed, it's one of the most important anybody has ever had.

Well, just what is the idea? It's that only the very best can get by with a handicap (such as, in its case, a misleading name). Therefore, the very best pick a handicap in order to convince others of their strength.

The peacock is striking in all its plumage. The cock, that is. Extremely striking, even. The peahen is more discreet.

The peacock's grandiose tail offers a myriad of beautiful greens, browns, and blues that play in the light, changing from metallic glitter to mother-of-pearl glow. The meter-and-a-half feathers that stretch out in a fan above the bird, and in the courtship dance practically embrace the hen, can even quiver and rustle in the most amazing fashion.

The peacock comes from India, where it is the national bird. It is similar to the pheasant and other poultry, is practically omnivorous, and is pretty strong. The peacock weighs about five kilograms, the peahen about three and a half.[9] Its enemies are predators, such as the jungle cat, the tiger, or the mongoose, and in Europe, the fox. A peacock that feels it is in danger may shed its tail and run.[10]

Peahens can see peacocks' magnificence and are apparently as enchanted by them as we humans—but so can foxes. And the foxes don't feel enchanted, just hungry. So why doesn't the peacock in question get eaten?

Darwin couldn't understand why not, or at least he could not in 1860, when he had not yet developed the theory of sexual selection. Even if he had developed it he would've lacked two vital pieces.

One was an understanding of why the males have to impress the females. In our world the men crowd around the women, bowing politely at the graduation ball in the hope of winning a little dance rather than being a wallflower.

The answer did come, but with a hundred-year delay.

To celebrate the centenary of the publication of *Descent of Man*, in 1972 the anthropologist Bernard Campbell published *Sexual Selection and the Descent of Man 1871–1971* in which a number of scientists reviewed the idea of sexual selection. One of them was Robert Trivers, who had published the theory of mutual altruism in 1971. Trivers was able to solve the first problem, why females are courted by males.

The solution is touchingly simple: it requires more of the organism to make an egg than to make a sperm, it costs more to go through a pregnancy than copulation, and in many species the female invests more than the male to childrearing.

"The relative parental investment of the sexes in their young is the key variable controlling the operation of sexual selection," Trivers writes. "Where one sex invests considerably more than the other, members of the latter will compete among themselves to mate with members of the former. Where the investment is equal, sexual selection should operate similarly on the two sexes."[11]

What matters is which sex has the sparse resource. When the females invest most in their young, they're the ones who are forced to choose, because they cannot possibly have as many young as they would like. The males, on the other hand, can have as many young as they want, at any rate if they are polygamous. And in many species, they are.

The peacock, for example.

In a species with polygamous males, selection is very strong. The males compete to see how many young they can father, and in practice this means they have to compete to see which of them can mate with the largest number of hens. So the point is to seduce as many of them as possible. And that takes plumage.

In other bird species, such as swallows, dramatic, eye-catching plumage does not play such a major role. Swallows fly, whereas peacocks walk around below. So swallows cannot permit themselves such extravagant ornamentation as a peacock's tail. They still demonstrate what they are worth, but using less spectacular means. Symmetry, for example. Swallows have tails that may be more or less symmetrical, or more or less lengthy. Studies show that swallow cocks with long, symmetrical tails have many young; they have them early in the season and attract the mothers who look after their chicks best.

So birds differ. But sexual selection works all the same, even without polygamous males.

Even in species whose members all live monogamously with the same partner for life, sexual selection may play a tremendous role. If all the males want to mate with the female graced with the best genes judging by her handicap, that female will choose the best male judging by his handicap. The second-best male will get the second-best female, and so on and so forth until the male who displays the weakest handicap ends up with the weakest female as his mate. This way, the best genes meet and result in young who will manage best. All other things being equal, even if every pair has the same number of young, the pair with the best genes will have the offspring who live the longest and thus have the greatest chance of having offspring in the next generation. Sexual selection may be most apparent in species with polygamous males, but it also affects more discreet species with more stable relationships.

I T I S N O T in every species that the division of labor between the sexes is so clear that the females do the childrearing while the males rush around impregnating other females. Humans, for example. Historically, among us the men take on more and more of the childrearing while women play a far greater role in the rest of the community. So is it still only the men who woo the women? Not so. Sexual selection cuts both ways: both sexes choose each other. Both sexes are eager to display their qualities. The result, as we shall see, is huge changes.

We still lack a vital piece to complete Darwin's puzzle: why does the choice by females of spectacular males not lead to the extinction of the species?

When a peahen chooses a peacock with an exorbitant tail she chooses a male who has a major problem: a plumage like that makes gathering food and evading predators a real headache. The peahen can be quite sure that this male won't have time to look after the chicks, and that the cocks among her chicks will grow extremely inconvenient tails. In other words they will be hatched with a tendency toward a severe handicap.

What on earth would she want that for?

The answer is precisely that the peacock tail is a handicap. Only a bird that is really strong and full of resources can cope with a tail like that. A peacock able to live with a big tail has good genes. A fabulously beautiful phenotype announces that here comes an above-averagely-good genotype. Because without a good genotype you can't get by in life with just a few pretty feathers.

In other words plumage is an indicator, a declaration, a certificate of quality, a mark of proficiency: "Look, I'm alive, even with this handicap! I am strong! I am a sound individual with good genes!"

The fundamental concept of the Handicap Principle is that of the paradox: the male does something difficult to show he is strong. Just what he does is not that important, as long as the female can spot it and realize that it is difficult.

Do something difficult and the hotties of the world will find you irresistible.

So WE ARE talking about a mechanism radically different from natural selection: it involves taking the hard way out, doing something difficult, going out of your way, proving your qualities as an individual, assuming a burden.

After all, natural selection involves quite the opposite: surviving, getting by, keeping things simple, being economical, taking the easy way out and hence evading your predators.

So two different principles, two widely differing mechanisms, are at work in biological evolution. They are both based on the same conditions: variation, heredity, selection. It is only the final stage, selection, which is different. In sexual selection it is the gender that makes the greatest investment in its young that does the choosing.

Natural selection rewards the ability to take the easy way out. Sexual selection rewards the ability and will to take the hard way out.

IN THE END natural selection results in adaptation: the cat stretching her limbs, sated and sleepy, before having a little nap. She has enough to eat, she is warm enough, and she has enough kittens and enough time. She has adapted. Her adaptation is revealed by her comfort, her indolence. The natural consequence of natural selection is indolence. This is the utmost you can achieve in terms of adapting to your environment.

Sexual selection, on the contrary, is about not adapting, discomfort, and effort in obtaining life's essentials. Effort is uncomfortable.

That is precisely the problem, of course: why don't they all just die out, the species of birds and other creatures where the females chase the males who consistently take the hard way out? Is it not true, as the Danish humorist and actor Jesper Klein once put it, that "only athletes and idiots jump where the fence is highest"?[12]

WHEN AMOTZ ZAHAVI published his Handicap Principle in 1975 he was howled down by the entire world of evolutionary biology. Nobody wanted anything to do with him or his idea.

In 1976 Richard Dawkins wrote in the first edition of *The Selfish Gene,* his widely disseminated portrayal of evolution seen from the point of view of the individual gene, "I do not believe this theory, although I am not quite so confident in my skepticism as I was when I first heard it." He explained his skepticism thusly: "The handicap theory seems to contain a basic contradiction. If the handicap is a genuine one—and it is of the essence of the theory that it has to be a genuine one—then the handicap itself will penalize the offspring just as surely as it may attract females."[13]

In 1989, however, Dawkins published a new edition of the same book: "I am glad I added that 'although,' because Zahavi's theory is now looking a lot more plausible than when

I wrote the passage [in the first edition]. Several respected theoreticians have recently started taking it seriously. Most worrying for me, these include my colleague Alan Grafen [of Oxford University] who, as has been said in print before, has 'the most annoying habit of always being right.'"[14]

Alan Grafen made the evolution theorists take Zahavi seriously when he proved that the idea made mathematical sense. Since Haldane's and Fischer's days the theory of evolution had been rooted in a mathematical theory on the way genes are disseminated. The advantage of expressing things in mathematical terms is that you can sometimes show by calculation that something that is intuitively senseless nevertheless makes sense, such as when a phenotype sacrifices his life to save the lives of three of his siblings. Doing so makes sense, at any rate, from the genotype's point of view.

Alan Grafen showed that females are wise to choose males with handicaps. As the handicap is an indicator of a good genotype, she thus selects good genes even though they are accompanied by a load of trouble, much ado, and tail feathers. So in the final analysis it is better to choose a male who is able to manage despite his handicap than a male who has no handicap because he would not survive with one.

The whole point is that it's solely and exclusively because the handicap really is a handicap that proves the male has good genes. It's hard to trick your way to a handicap, because handicaps are so costly.

It turns out, too, that peahens lay more eggs when they mate with males with long tails than when they mate with males with short ones.[15]

We must not forget that peahens and anyone else who has to choose a partner are in the same boat as science was up until ten years ago: they have no way of directly inspecting the genotypes of potential partners. They cannot "see" the genes that will be added to their own during sexual reproduction. The genotype is invisible to humans (and although the DNA sequence is now visible to scientists, it doesn't mean they can assess the quality of a genotype, apart from special cases with hereditary diseases). So the female must make her choice of the best genotype on the basis of knowing only the phenotypes of the males who want her. It is this choice that the handicap equips her to make: if the phenotype possesses a costly handicap he must be a good genotype.

So females go for males who demonstrate by displaying dramatic, costly handicap they possess the resources and surplus energy to create such a costly signal. That is the whole point. If it isn't costly, it'll be far too easy to replicate, and weak males will also display it.

Costliness is the message, just as in Thorstein Veblen's idea of conspicuous consumption, which fulfills no direct need in itself but demonstrates that one can afford the best Beluga caviar instead of lump fish roe. It does not matter that you cannot taste the difference—as long as everyone else can see the difference in price.

The ornithologist Amotz Zahavi wrote in 1975, "In many species of birds the female is cryptic while the male is colorful." (In this context, that the female is cryptic does not mean that women are hard to understand, but that the female is hard to spot.) Zahavi continues, "The accepted explanation is that females cannot withstand the extra predation pressure involved in colorful plumage since they have to attend more to the nest." She does not want merely to lie there, waiting for the fox. This may explain why peahens are not so colorful, but not why cocks are. Why do the females find these colors so resplendent? "I suggest that a mature, colorful male has already proved itself to be of a better quality (than one with cryptic plumage), since it has already withstood the extra predation risk involved in its plumage."[16]

Hence a gender difference that has perhaps never been better described than by the philosopher Helena Cronin in her marvelous book on sexual selection, *The Ant and the Peacock*, 1991: "The peahen could have been designed by a hard-headed, cost-conscious engineer; her mate could have stepped off the set of a Hollywood musical."[17]

THE DISCREET, RELIABLE plumage of the peahen can be developed by natural selection. It takes sexual selection to develop something as extravagant as the tail of a peacock.

So there are two mechanisms behind biological evolution. Both are based on variation, heredity, and selection. The difference is the chooser, nature, or the mate.

There are very great differences between them: natural development optimizes, economizes, rationalizes, and ensures reliability and robustness in order to bring about the maximum ability to survive. Through handicaps, sexual selection does precisely the opposite: it reduces the survival ability of the individual by giving him a costly handicap. It is only because a handicap actually reduces the helpful adaptation that natural selection has so laboriously developed that its signal is credible.

There are two diametrically opposed principles: maximize the ability to survive, torpedo the ability to survive. Avoid risk, attract risk. Blend into the background, stick your neck out. Adapt, don't adapt.

But not all creatures are peacocks and not all species have striking males.

Monogamous species of birds such as swallows utilize more discreet means. But they still work. Swallows have tails; the longer and more symmetrical the two beautiful tail feathers are, the more attractive the swallows are to potential partners. The Danish ornithologist Anders Pape Møller has demonstrated via comprehensive studies of barn swallows how sexual selection takes place, based on this more discreet indicator. Males with long tails and a considerable degree of symmetry are healthier, have fewer parasites, etc. Developing length and symmetry is costly and difficult.[18]

Sexual selection is not only about spectacular courtship rites, but about the whole structure of the organism and the entire lives of both genders all year round. It is a vital factor in the shaping of the entire organism.

DURING PUBERTY, HUMANS develop a series of physical characteristics aimed at sexual selection: breasts, bottoms, body odors, and many other wonderful things in women; wide cheekbones, beards, deep voices, and a large penis in men.

Monkeys' penises are not as long and not at all as thick as men's. The penis is an organ developed by men to win in the sexual selection process. A thick penis is a costly signal, as are large breasts. But just as breasts can be enhanced by silicone, rendering such a costly signal cheap for the female body (but a big drain on household spending), a man can have his penis pumped up. As I wrote this chapter a piece of spam appeared in my in-box: "ADD THREE INCHES TO YOUR PENIS." Hmm.

Experience from the last ten years of intense investigation as to how the human body is shaped by sexual selection, and how our concepts of beauty are derived thereby, reveals an important point as regards cosmetic surgery: the various sexual signals are all linked.

The beauty of a woman's body signals fecundity and fertility. When men from all cultures prefer women with specific hip measurements (the waist must be 0.71 times as wide as the hips and shoulders whether you are from a culture that is into voluptuous women or into beanpoles), a certain scent, thick hair, and a good complexion, it is because these indicators are linked. They all indicate the same characteristic: fecundity and fertility.

When women from all cultures prefer the same characteristics in men—deep voices, the right way to move, a broad jaw, etc.—these things are also linked. The various attractive features in men express the same attributes: good genes.

This means that it may be of no use at all to acquire a bigger penis or larger breasts. The signal about genetic and other qualities that these enhanced sexual attributes are meant to send is countered by other statements such as build, voice, hair, and odor. So it is no good after all. It just makes you look like somebody who has had her hair dyed because your complexion reveals quite clearly that you are not a true blonde, but a redhead.

In a survey of the significance of sexual selection for human ideals of beauty the four biologists Karl Grammer, Bernhard Fink, Anders Pape Møller, and Randy Thornhill therefore predict that plastic surgery will not work. It will not make people happier or win them better mates.[19]

The four biologists propose quite a different perception of what beauty is about: avoiding ugliness. In sexual selection what matters is not so much whether one's partner really looks like a model, but whether he or she has characteristics that signal bad genes.

Symmetry is a good example. Many species, including man, use physiological symmetry, including that of the face, in assessing the qualities of a mate. You see, it is costly for the organism to develop perfectly symmetrical organs: legs of equal length, breasts of equal size, and cheeks of equal width. It can be shown that animals with lots of parasites are also less symmetrical. A perfectly symmetrical body is therefore a sign of a strong individual. It is regarded as beautiful.

In reality symmetry expresses a lack of asymmetries, which are regarded as ugly. So the ideal of beauty is symmetry, viz: non-asymmetry, non-ugliness.

If we take personal hygiene as an analogy it is immediately apparent that somebody who takes care of such matters expresses a lack of rotten teeth, ill-kempt hair, ingrowing toenails, strong body odor, and smelly feet. When hygiene is concerned it does not matter so much if your hair is dark or light, just if you are clean. Non-unkempt, non-dirty, non-smelly.

Cosmetic surgery is not alone in mixing up the sexual organs with what they indicate.

The intense obsession by our modern media culture with human genitalia, particularly in almost absurd pornographic manifestations, quite misunderstands the principle of sexual selection, which is to create the best possible combination of genetic material by choosing the mate who appears most attractive to you.

Pornography, however, is about something else entirely: showing the absurd images it does is like transmitting a chess game by only showing close-ups of the pieces, or a televised debate in which we only see lips and where the camera tries to see if it can get right under the tongue, behind the wisdom teeth, and preferably some way down the glottis, too. However deep it gets inside the throat we never arrive at what the debate is actually about.

It is not only when a partnership is entered into—i.e., the actual choice of partner—that the costly signals play a part. Love must also be present. "The development of cooperation in groups of two is no easier to explain than cooperation in large groups," Zahavi writes. "I suggest that even in collaborations of two members, a large part of the investment can be explained as an advertisement of the quality of the investor and of its motivation to continue collaborating, in order to decrease the partner's tendency to cheat or desert."[20]

In other words love also requires costly signals and that we do something for each other, because by doing so we show that we are worth keeping and have the best intentions of continuing to cooperate. Sexual selection leads to cooperation and trust between people. It is definitely not only about polygamous males like peacocks, but at least as much about the way monogamous spouses continually demonstrate their resources to each another.

However, it was a hundred years before Darwin's theory of sexual selection by female choice was taken seriously. And it took fifteen years for Zahavi's view of handicaps as costly signals to be accepted. Just look at this account by Anders Pape Møller in a book about the barn swallow:

> "The controversy over the handicap principle may also have been a clash between personalities. The ideas of the Handicap Principle were finally made acceptable to a large part of the scientific community in the early nineties by dressing them in a proper theoretical outfit. One of the major contributors to modern evolutionary biology, John Maynard Smith, who had been skeptical about the handicap mechanism during the seventies and most of the eighties, reviewed sexual selection in an address to the Third International Conference on Behavioral Ecology in Uppsala, Sweden, in August 1990. After having elaborated on the theoretical arguments about the handicap principle he formally apologized to the inventor of the handicap principle, Amotz Zahavi, for not having understood earlier the simple mechanism of reliable signaling. Zahavi stood up after the lecture, acknowledged the apology, and said that he still did not think that Maynard Smith had understood the handicap principle!"[21]

COSTLY SIGNALS ARE not only about sexual selection. In natural selection signals also play a part. In *The Handicap Principle* where Amotz Zahavi and his wife, plant physiologist Avishag Zahavi, describe the significance of the Handicap Principle in biology, they open with a description of Thomson's gazelle.

This beautiful antelope has a peculiar habit, one that has been known for years but not understood. When a lion approaches the gazelle leaps high into the air and makes lots of noise. It makes no attempt to hide or escape. On the contrary. It eyeballs the lion, jumps, glares, and jumps. It shows its rump. It jumps.

Does it not expose itself to great danger? Yes, indeed. That is just the point: it shows the lion that it is so healthy and strong that it has the temerity to indulge in a little war dance instead of making its escape. It sends the lion a signal: "You can try to catch me but you will fail, because I am healthy. We will both expend a great deal of energy on your pursuit, but you will not catch me, so it will be a waste of your resources and of mine. How about just slinking off, lion? That would save us both from an exhausting run which wouldn't make either of us any the happier."

Why should the lion believe this signal? Because it is costly. The gazelle exposes itself to considerable danger by "toying" with the lion. Because of this danger, however, the lion believes it. A weak gazelle would not dare. So the weak gazelle is the one the lion goes for. And eats.

You can't catch me! If you've got the guts to say so, you believe in yourself. If you don't think you've got a chance, you'd better sneak out of the back door before anybody notices you.

Thomson's gazelle is an example of behavior that many scientists thought had to be explained as group selection: the noisy cries of the gazelle were meant as a warning shout to warn the rest of the gazelles about the lion. Altruistic behavior by which the gazelle sacrifices itself for its herd. *Take me and let my fellow gazelles go.*

But its leaping may be explained instead as a self-afflicted handicap: I am strong enough to have the guts to do this, stay away, eat another gazelle. The costly signal is selfish: it involves the survival of the individual gazelle. It may also benefit other gazelles, but it is not performed for their sake, but as communication with the lion.[22]

THERE ARE WELL documented examples of ways in which the Handicap Principle may explain phenomena in the world of biology, but not that many: peacocks, swallows, and other birds, gazelles, some characteristics of noises uttered by humans and monkeys. Not that many more, though.[23] Biological science is making slow progress. It takes years to decipher animal behavior.

One possible example of costly signals in the living world that cannot be said to be finally explained is the color of the trees in autumn: why do the leaves turn yellow? William Hamilton, who discovered kin selection in the sixties as a young man and thereby founded the study of social cooperation as a result of biological evolution, proposed a spectacular theory in the nineties that he presented on Danish television[24] almost five years before it appeared in the scientific literature.[25] The article was only published after his death in 2000 from complications following a bout of malaria contracted on an expedition to the Congo.

The theory explains why trees expend energy on turning their leaves yellow or russet in autumn. It is not just about removing the green from the leaves but producing new colors. Why? The answer is that this is a costly signal to indicate that the tree is strong. Weak trees cannot make such lovely colors, it turns out. But to whom do the trees signal this strength? Not to tourists, but to greenflies! By assuming bright colors the tree shows that it is a bad place to spend the winter. It says, "Stay away, parasites! You'll find better food in the next tree! I am strong and full of chemical strength that will make life miserable for you!"

The theory is very beautiful and presumably true, but there are alternative explanations to the color of the leaves.[26] However, it is a beautiful example of the way a costly signal from a tree to a greenfly can give great pleasure to other creatures on their romantic strolls through the woods.

ANYWHERE ANIMALS SIGNAL to one another it is vital that their signals be credible. Costliness is a method of indicating their credibility, both as regards natural selection for the ability to survive predators and as regards sexual selection for the ability to obtain partners and ensure young (both in terms of frightening off the competition from your own gender and of attracting members of the opposite sex).

Zahavi distinguishes between two kinds of evolution: adaptation to an environment and signaling between individuals. The Handicap Principle is relevant to the latter but not the former. Obviously, signaling is vital in terms of sexual selection, but less so in natural selection, where it does, however, occur in the interplay between predator and prey. Zahavi regards sexual selection as part of what he calls signal selection,[27] but the distinction is not vital in this context. In any case the key is to do something that is difficult, something that is costly to your ability to survive. Waste, excess, danger. Not always equally graceful. Not always equally sexy.

The consumption of bizarre substances is an example. The vulture eats cow dung as a carotenoid supplement that gives its face a yellowish tinge that attracts females. There is not much nourishment in cow dung, but lots of dangerous parasites, so this behavior is interpreted by ornithologists as a costly signal. A yellow vulture is a strong vulture that is able to live with the danger of infection presented by the dung.

Of course we humans would never do such a thing, would we?

In his book *The Third Chimpanzee* (1992) the American physiologist Jared Diamond makes a thought-provoking contribution to the theory of costly signaling. "Why do we smoke, drink, and take dangerous drugs?" Diamond asks. "Why do we actively seek something we know to be harmful?"[28]

He answers: "Ten thousand years ago our 'displays' consisted of challenging a lion or a member of a hostile tribe. Today we do the same thing in other ways, by driving too fast or by taking dangerous drugs, for example."[29]

The point is that if you drink everybody else under the table and can go on dancing properly and conversing politely, you must be very strong. It is by coping with the handicap brought on by intoxication that you show your strength. Or so you think. As we know, a drunk tends to be convinced that he is walking in a considerably straighter line than he actually is.

Diamond's contribution to our understanding of our use of intoxicants is very significant: teenagers' astounding propensity to drink themselves pie-eyed in everyone's presence, inflict all kinds of damage to themselves and to their neighbors' property, and ultimately end the evening in a spectacular bout of vomiting makes sense as a kind of courtship. It's just surprising that teenage girls fall for it.

We also assume more handicaps than casual drinking and nightcaps. Any kind of derring-do or audacity may be interpreted as an attempt to impress the opposite sex or as a display of strength to members of the same sex. But don't forget: risk is only a handicap because it can go wrong.

Most of these handicap-incurring forms of behavior tend to cease once the teen years are over. Not many people go bungee jumping or get into fights in their old age. But alcohol abuse often does continue. Of course there is a decisive difference: the very nature of drinking makes it difficult for the drunk to assess whether his strategy is actually working, with the pitiful result that the massive inebriation that may impress a sixteen-year-old girl when it is borne by a seventeen-year-old youth just seems pathetic and pitiful in a forty-seven-year-old convinced in his cups that the woman seated next to him finds him and his groping utterly irresistible.

Diamond's view sheds interesting light on the phenomenon

of dependence, addiction, and abuse. Let's take his idea really seriously: let's look at cigarettes, for example. If Diamond is right, young people do not smoke *despite* the dangers of smoking but precisely *because* it's dangerous to smoke. "Look how strong I am! I've just smoked seven butts and my face almost isn't green at all!" Young people show their strength by being able to tolerate the obvious discomfort of starting to smoke. In terms of well-being smoking is a clear handicap, at least at first. But it shows you've got balls. In 1953, 78 percent of all Danish men were smokers. "When smoking was at its height in the early fifties non-smoking men were regarded as wimps," as one Danish newspaper put it.[30]

However, if sexual selection did give rise to a tendency to smoke, because smoking is a handicap that signals the smoker's strength as a potential mate, we would surely stop smoking once mating was accomplished. But in the meantime a change has taken place: not only has the mature smoker got used to the cigarettes that were so unpleasant to start with, but he has also developed a dependency on nicotine that makes it very difficult to quit.

The risk-seeking activity of youth with its obvious self-destructive features, intended to attract members of the opposite sex, turns into staid, petit-bourgeois middle-class habit and dependency. When the occasion for smoking has passed, dependency sets in. The daredevil becomes a wimp, we might say.

But isn't this all just petty philosophizing? Diamond's idea that derring-do, zany behavior and self-destruction make it easier to score babes may be elegant, but does it have anything to do with real life?

SUSAN KELLY AND Robin Dunbar from the University of Liverpool investigated a theory that "heroism persists in many human cultures owing to a female preference for risk-prone rather than risk-averse males as sexual partners."[31] Their method consisted of getting sixty women to choose among eight fictitious men described to them. The result was that women actually preferred risk-prone, brave men to risk-averse men. This was particularly true for short-term relationships.

Another characteristic they examined was altruism, the willingness to help others by making a sacrifice. For quick flings the women preferred non-altruists to altruists! However, when it came to choosing a partner for a longer-term commitment they preferred the helpful men.

The two researchers concluded that bravery is widespread because women prefer brave men whose risk-proneness demonstrates their attractive genotype.

So if you want a one-night fling don't be kind to animals: show courage and derring-do. The results match nicely with the image of the wild, excessive, ravages of teenage score behavior, while slightly more mature men who are looking for a lifelong companion are more likely to display peaceful virtues.

There is a reason why we sow our wild oats young and grow altruistic with age.

As the psychiatrist Randolph Nesse put it, "The best strategy for selfish genes is to make humans who, in certain situations, have the capacity and propensity to act in ways that are genuinely altruistic, even morally principled."[32]

7
Generosity

WHERE GOOD DEEDS COME FROM

THERE IS A remarkable similarity between two of the terms we have been looking at: altruism and handicap. Altruism is defined as behavior that exacts a price from the person who exercises it but is an advantage for others. Handicap is defined as a characteristic or behavior that exacts a price from the exerciser but is conspicuous to others.

Surely altruism is a handicap, too, then? Can we understand altruism as a costly signal that here is an individual who has the means to think of others and must therefore be equipped with very good genes? Altruism may perhaps be understood as an action the individual embarks upon in order to show that he has the means to be a good choice sexually.

But the striking theoretical quality of this analogy is one thing—and yes, it is a very beautiful idea—but whether it holds water in real life is another.

THE FIRST ATTEMPT to understand human altruism as a manifestation of handicap came from the American biologist Irwin Tessman, who suggested in 1995 that we should quite simply understand altruism as courtship. The altruistic act proclaims "the capacity and the intention of the altruist to be a reliable mate and parent."[1] Tessman pointed out that if this explanation had any foundation in fact, it raised a number of questions: "Is it really true, as anecdotes suggest, that heroes are unusually successful sexually? How widespread is youthful idealism and does it identify a reliable mate and parent? Insofar as females may be more selective in choosing mates, would males have a greater need to advertise their reliability through altruistic behavior?"[2]

Tessman quite simply suggested that courtship is the cause of human morals. We behave decently because by doing so we persuade potential partners that we are reliable. Our moral sense was developed through courtship.

In 1998 the anthropologist James Boone suggested that one could combine Veblen's concept of conspicuous consumption with the idea of handicap to explain altruism.[3] People who are able to lavish resources on others demonstrate that they can live with a handicap. This gives them greater prestige in the group, which in turn gives them greater advantages, such as power and control of resources in the future. Altruism, then, becomes a method of obtaining high status in the group.

THERE ARE ANTHROPOLOGICAL studies that have tried to demonstrate these ideas in human practice. The journal *Evolution and Human Behavior* published three studies in 2000 that claimed to be able to prove the idea of generosity as costly signals.

One study reported on fishing by torchlight from canoes on Ifaluk Atoll, Micronesia. The fishermen paddle out at the new moon, carrying blazing torches to attract fish by their light. The method is dangerous and not particularly effective, but it is an important ritual even so. This activity is watched by the women, and the researchers showed that there is a link between men who are good torchlight fishermen and men who are good at fishing in general. The will to undertake fishing by torchlight is a handicap that signals good general fishing ability. However, one argument against the sexual origins of this behavior is that many of the torchlight fishermen are not young, mate-seeking men, but happily married middle-aged ones.[4]

On Murray Island off New Zealand the turtle hunt is a hazardous ritual activity that is part of important festivities in the local Meriam culture. The turtles are pulled out of the sea via a dangerous, laborious procedure but are then shared with other people at a major feast. This is not apparently a matter of gifts that are returned in any significant way; it is pure generosity, and fits very well into the model of costly signals.[5]

A study of the Aché, a hunter/gatherer culture from Paraguay, shows that the hunters who give out the most food are also the ones who are given the most when times are hard. In this case, then, generosity is a kind of investment in future reciprocity.[6]

None of these examples provides clear proof of the theory that generosity and altruism are costly signals directed at finding a mate or increasing your social rank. However, they point in that direction, and seem to indicate that it's a fruitful field for research. Obviously, it's not easy to study human behavior; but what about the animals? Birds, for example? Amotz Zahavi also put forth a theory of altruism that is extremely interesting—even if the studies he uses to support the idea are less strong.

EVEN IN HIS first presentation of the handicap theory, in 1975, Amotz Zahavi pointed out that altruistic behavior in birds could be interpreted as a handicap. He observed that many garden birds have strong black and white contrasts in their plumage, making it easier for other individuals to see them when they have found food. "The evolution of the bright 'altruistic' plumage (. . .) is difficult to explain," Zahavi wrote,[7] because birds with more discreet plumage can keep food to themselves more easily. But the explanation might very well be that they were so good at finding food that there was enough for everyone, and so the others could join in.

The same idea was central in 1995, twenty years after his initial expression of the handicap theory (with its hint of a possible explanation of altruism), when Amotz Zahavi proposed that the handicap mechanism was simply the explanation of altruism: "Individuals invest in their collaboration in order to increase their social prestige. They do so by advertising their qualities and their motivation to collaborate. The benefit to the group is a consequence of, rather than the factor that selects for the investment."[8]

Zahavi, then, does not explain altruism and cooperation as courtship, but as means of obtaining social status (which is useful when you do go courting). His explanation of altruism is thus not as simple as Tessman's, in which it is precisely sexual selection that leads to altruism. Zahavi (like Boone) makes a detour via general social prestige.

Zahavi's central argument was an observation he'd made during decades of studying a bird named *Turdoides squamiceps,* the Arabian Babbler.

The Arabian Babbler is a highly social bird that lives in flocks of between three and twenty. The members of the flock share territory and nests. They cooperate in many ways via altruistic behavior. Perhaps this isn't so remarkable, as it may be found in many parts of the animal kingdom,[9] even though for more than a hundred years it seemed difficult for Darwin's theory to explain it. But the babblers displayed behavior that impressed Zahavi: they fought to be the first to help one another. (While sharing food, for example.) Dominant members of the flock try to prevent less dominant ones from making any contribution to the community.[10]

"Not only are babblers, by all accounts, at least as altruistic as other group-breeding birds; close, detailed observation shows that babblers actually *compete with one another* for the 'right' to be altruistic. Instead of expecting their partners to return tit for tat, they attempt to prevent them from doing their share," Zahavi writes. "The theory of reciprocal altruism cannot explain why individuals *compete* for the chance to help other members of the group, let alone why they prevent others from helping in return."[11]

Richard Conniff, writing in the scientific magazine *Discover,* reports as follows from a visit to an Israeli desert near the Jordanian border, where we meet a man named Zahavi and two Arabian Babblers named Tasha-Sham and Pusht: "Zahavi tossed a breadcrumb, and the recipient, Tasha-Sham, did not gobble it down. Instead he flitted up onto a tree where the subordinate male, Pusht, had been doing sentinel duty. Pusht saw what was coming and slipped away. But Tasha-Sham followed him to the ground. Then he held up the prize morsel until Pusht dutifully begged like a nestling, mouth open, wings quivering with sham enthusiasm. Zahavi interpreted: "The dominant says 'You'll take what I'm going to give you.'"[12]

Conniff continues: "Tasha-Sham announced his act of charity by lifting his beak and giving a special trill, like a socialite posing for an event photographer at the Red Cross ball. Watching this sort of behavior, Zahavi concluded that there are no truly selfless acts. 'Altruism is advertising,' he said. It is a handicap display, an 'unseen peacock's tail,' a bid for prestige and status."[13]

Zahavi's explanation is that the fact of helping gives an advantage to the helper (and of course to the one who is helped). Altruism is egoism at a very high level: look how clever I am! I have the means to help others!

But Zahavi's observations of Arabian Babblers are controversial. In 1997 one of his former students, the ornithologist Jonathan Wright from Wales, seriously criticized Zahavi's 1995 theory of altruism: the Arabian Babblers do cooperate and help one another, but they are so closely related that what they're really doing is just helping next of kin. They simply behave the way William Hamilton's theory of kinship selection says they should. Two birds in the flock share so much of their genotype that it makes good sense to help each other.

Jonathan Wright writes that the notion that the birds' reciprocal help is altruistic behavior that has developed into a costly signal is "a theoretically attractive and stimulating idea," but he adds that there is no data to support this notion.[14] What is actually involved are family ties.

In his 1995 article Zahavi argued that Hamilton's kinship selection and Trivers's reciprocal altruism were far too vulnerable mechanisms to explain the widespread tendency for animals and humans to help one another. It's too easy for parasites, spongers, and fakers to benefit from kinship selection and reciprocal altruism, Zahavi argued. How can you tell if they *really* are relatives or *really* are people who will reciprocate your altruism at a later date?

But kinship selection is a well documented phenomenon in the animal world, so it's hard to take Zahavi's argument seriously. In 1999 Jonathan Wright repeated his criticism of Zahavi's view,[15] only to be met with a sarcastic rebuttal from Zahavi.[16] Since then Zahavi has told *New Scientist* that a kinship study of the birds showed that they were not all related[17]—but Wright never said they were. He merely pointed out that in the same flock one Babbler is most likely related to another.

So we cannot say that Zahavi's observations prove the correctness of his idea of altruism as a handicap.

But what matters is not the Arabian Babbler, anyway. What matters is that there's a simple, elegant idea to explain altruistic behavior: it's a self-elected cost that serves to demonstrate the individual's strength and suitability as a potential partner. The idea was expressed most clearly by Irwin Tessman and later repeated by the aforementioned psychologist Geoffrey Miller who says: "Human altruism is not an evolutionary paradox. It is a sexual ornament."[18]

THERE ARE NOT many convincing biological examples to show that this is the case. But the idea is not many years old, and carrying out the relevant studies takes time.

The link between altruism and handicap seems such a beautiful, obvious idea to me that it deserves to be taken seriously, whether or not behavioral biologists have been able to prove it yet.

But, you might object, must we really interpret helpfulness and charity as selfishness in disguise? Is helping others now to be considered wrong and self-centered? Just because a bunch of babblers force breadcrumbs down one another's throats while an Israeli ornithologist is watching enthusiastically doesn't mean that we'll only help blind old ladies across the street if someone else sees us, right?

Well, what do you think? You have the advantage that nobody is checking on your thoughts: would you like other people to be watching when you do your good deeds? Are you bursting to tell your sweetheart how good you've been today?

And more principally: is it most reassuring to think that people do good deeds because in the final analysis it's also in their own interests? Or is it more reassuring to imagine that people do good deeds for no sensible reason at all? How do we sleep more soundly: if we think we help one another because it's in our interests to do so, or if we think we help them even when it isn't?

To me, the altruism-as-a-handicap idea is no less than a message of freedom: we would like to impress one another, especially the opposite sex, and now that obtaining food and getting plastered has become so ordinary, we turn to charity, socially decent behavior, and benevolence as the real proof of strength.

Reciprocity is a good thing, just as helping relatives is. It's good that we help one another if only because we'll be able to receive help later. But wouldn't it be best of all if we merely helped others because by doing so we obtain social prestige and potential mates?

It's a very elegant concept: by doing something that's difficult and costly, we show our strength and increase our chances of mating. The finest, costliest signal is helping others. The most powerful testimony to somebody's strength and power is that he or she has the means to help others.

We make an effort, we put ourselves out, we make life harder for ourselves, we go short, and we share with others; and by doing so we enjoy success with the opposite sex.

We are generous because generosity is the costliest of all signals: it shows you have the means, you have the strength to succeed in everyday life; enough so that you can give to others. You don't just cope by the skin of your teeth; you have the wherewithal and the energy to contribute a bit more to the community and the weak members of the group. This gives you greater opportunities to mate. Effort gives you success. Generosity gives you happiness.

Make an effort and you'll make out.

8
Double Darwin

WHERE ARE WE? We have taken Darwin's theory of biological evolution as our starting point. We have accepted that living creatures are imbued with the will to survive—otherwise they wouldn't be living. We have seen the almost breathtakingly simplicity of the mechanism Darwin proposed: if each member of a population of individuals is able to pass on his own characteristics to the next generation, those who do best and have the most offspring will make more of an impact on the future population than those who don't do so well. Survival is survival, and those who survive, survive. The simple basic structure of this argument only presupposes three things: variety, heredity, and choice; variation, reproduction, selection.

But we have also seen that there may be different selection pressures, different factors that determine which members will do well and which won't.

Natural selection is about the pressure that an individual's living conditions exert on the individual's ability to survive. It is a selection pressure that results in efficiency, streamlining, and dependability.

But there's another form of selection: sexual selection, which is about more than merely surviving; it's about having the largest number of offspring. If sexual selection is to be significant, those involved must have put the struggle for survival so far behind them that they have the means to undertake sexual selection. Sexual selection, then, has natural selection as its prerequisite.

But there are enormous differences in their effect: selection for survival creates efficiency, whereas selection for sexual attraction creates dissention, costliness, and extravagance: adaptation and anti-adaptation.

They both rely on individuals pursuing their own interests, but sexual selection in particular leads to this interest consisting of showing how strong you are by helping others. We have thus moved from the simplest of all hypotheses—organisms driven by the survival instinct subject to Darwinist selection mechanisms—to the existence of altruism, cooperation, and helpful generosity.

This is quite remarkable, even if some steps of the argument are still theoretical and have not yet been established from studies of animals or humans. Later on we will look at what this may mean for the future understanding of society, economics, and culture.

M AN HIMSELF IS the result of two, not one, principles of biological evolution. There are two histories to us, two aspects of the evolution that led to our becoming human.

One history is of the mechanism of efficiency and economy; the other, of the mechanism of generosity and sociality.

Natural selection gives life. Sexual selection gives meaning.

We have two sides to us, two dimensions, two aspects, two results of a natural historical evolutionary process. That is not to say that we can distinguish instantly between the characteristics in us that are created through one mechanism or the other; but perhaps we can if we try.

However, first of all let's point out the two dimensions in us: of efficiency and waste, of scarcity and abundance, of survival and experience.

We could also call them the Sun in man and the Moon in man.

The sun rests in itself and shines on its own. The sun is essential, as we know. Its rhythm is predictable because we have quite simply adapted our lives to it. We know that it always rises on time, thus demanding that we do likewise so we can get to work. The sun is vital to life: it gives food, warmth, our bearings, work, and sunshine. Sun means survival; without it we wouldn't be here.

The moon orbits something else; it only shines with the

help of another. The moon does not seem necessary to us. It seems unpredictable in its coming and going, for we do not adapt to its rhythm. Not consciously, anyway. The moon almost always comes as a gift, a present, something extra that we didn't expect. It is longing, poetry, romance, time off, moonlight. The moon is experience: without it, we would be different.

The sun in man fits with the logic of natural selection; the moon in man, with the mechanism of sexual selection.

That's one way of looking at it. But not the only one.

It is of course remarkable that the economists' notion of *Homo economicus,* an economical man who is rational and selfish, is quite reminiscent of the image of man that comes to mind if you think of natural selection (although there are also very great differences between the two). It is a different picture from the one you get if you consider sexual selection. A completely different type of man emerges: namely the giving, sharing, cooperative, creative man whom I shall call *Homo generosus,* the generous man.

This is another distinction than the one with which we became acquainted earlier: the distinction between *Homo economicus* and *Homo reciprocans*—i.e., the distinction by which we say against the background of experimental economics that *Homo economicus* is not real at all, that it is an abstraction which only very partially coincides with human existence.

A distinction between *Homo economicus* and *Homo generosus* means recognizing the existence of *Homo economicus,* the selfish, rational man who takes part in anonymous exchanges in a marketplace where consideration is given to nothing but individual interest exerted on a rational basis. This creature does exist in us and is an important part of us, but it requires anonymity and the mask that the market comprises.

But you cannot equate *Homo economicus* with the aspect of man that was created by natural selection—for one, market man has to suppress all the nepotism that is a natural consequence of natural kinship selection. As we shall see later, man really does have to don his market mask in order to become *Homo economicus.*

But we also have to recognize the existence of *Homo generosus,* the dimension in man that is generous, giving, creative, sharing, cooperative, and fantastic—but is so in an attempt to promote a selfish interest in the great sexual selection game.

Both dimensions live side by side in us. We are the result of two directions in evolutionary history, two mechanisms, two routes through the world. We contain a Double Darwin.

We don't always know who'll win, but most of our problems are based on not being able to figure out whether it's relevant to be one or the other in a given situation.

If two people interact, but each has chosen different dimensions, so that one is *economicus* and the other *generosus,* things go wrong. The giving artist is left feeling cheated by the avaricious businessman; or the solemn executive feels he's been screwed by his subordinate's blarney; or one spouse feels the other is just a bit too petty . . . or a bit too lavish.

MAN WAS BORN social in relation to others, with the eyes of others on him. We are not born as independent, isolated Robinson Crusoes on a desert island. We are born into a community, purely biologically. We are the fruit of the meeting of two humans. We evolved in and from a community. We have characteristics aimed at other people as part of our biological constitution.

Sexual selection is about making an impression on the opposite sex. Already many of our characteristics are created in relation to other people, evolved through the relationship to others. Man is fundamentally social and relates to the way others experience the world. It is not only about survival; it is also about experience—of other people.

How amoeba and earthworms could evolve into something containing intentions and consciousness has always been one of the central problems for the Darwinist perception of evolution. After all, the elegant thing about Darwin's theory is that it does not operate with teleology—i.e., explanations involving the end or purpose of a process. This makes it similar to the rest of modern science, which precisely does not explain events by saying that there was a purpose or an end to them, but solely through the causes that led to them. The Ancient Greeks thought that the stone fell to earth because it belonged there. Modern science insists that the stone falls because it is affected by gravity.

Darwin's great achievement was to create a theory of biological evolution that is not about ends or purposes. It does not say that the giraffe evolved a long neck in order to reach the leaves on the trees, but merely that the giraffes that had long necks got the most to eat and were therefore able to have the most offspring, and so in the end there were most giraffes with long necks.

The elegant thing about Darwin's theory is that there is no designer with intentions and aims involved in the explanations. But its problem is precisely that it thereby has trouble explaining the origin of the designs, intentions, and purposes that so very much imbue man and his creations.

Natural selection explains the evolution of life without the use of deliberate intent, but not the origin of deliberate intent in the evolution of life. That is why sexual selection is such a welcome help, because it involves a selector that requires intent, consciousness, intentions, and design: not Our Lord, but our lady.

SEXUAL SELECTION ACTS as a filter between the generations. Some are selected and reproduced, others not, or not to the same extent. If the filter was about selecting partners with friendly, helpful, sensitive, generous characteristics, if these characteristics were just somewhat hereditary, humanity would end up consisting mainly of friendly, helpful, sensitive, and generous people.[1] It's as simple as that. That's how well things would turn out.

Just as we can show our personal resources by being good at one thing or another—not everything, but one thing, as long as it is hard enough—it only takes one little thing, falling in love, to make us feel, if only for a while, that we can do it all, want it all, and have all the resources at our disposal.

Natural selection and survival are about being good at lots of things, but not necessarily the best. We have to be in possession of lungs, arms, good eyesight, and the ability to find food, to keep warm, to run away from tigers, and to sleep.

Sexual selection is about being good at perhaps just one thing, which, on the other hand, is so exacting that all our resources are mobilized. If you are a brilliant soccer player it goes without saying that your body works well and you're not without mental strength; you might well be intelligent, too.

In sexual selection, somehow you have to show you're really good at something, because by doing so you show that many things in you function. To be good at one thing in particular, you have to be capable of many things in general.

Survival, the result of natural selection, is about nothing but itself: it is not a signal, but merely existence: I exist, i.e., I am good at existing. I am the last in a long line of survivors. I am, therefore I am.

The costly signal, the result of sexual selection (and in some cases of natural selection as well) is precisely a signal that refers to something else: I could not give this signal if my genotype was not good. The very fact that I can give this signal proves my qualities. But in itself the signal is not interesting except as a signal of something else. I signal, therefore I am strong.

If we want to understand our world, human culture, and society, we'll be barking up the wrong tree if we try to do so solely on the basis of natural selection, as many people have done in the nearly 150 years since *Origin of Species* was published.

In the eighties and nineties a new scientific discipline emerged: evolutionary psychology. Its ambition is to understand the human mind as the result of the adaptation of organisms to the environment by natural selection.

On the face of it this seems odd. It's obvious to anybody that many of the mental skills important to survival in society are not exactly represented in abundance. We have trouble doing sums, reading for long periods, or manipulating abstract symbols, while we have a base, straightforward desire to have sexual fantasies and watch pro wrestling on television. What use is that in today's environment?

The evolutionary psychologists' point was of course that the mental characteristics we possess fit the environment as it was when we evolved from ape to man. In other words, we've evolved a suitable disposition for life on the savannah rather than life in Manhattan in the twenty-first century.

But that just raises another problem: how did early humans on the savannah find a use for musicality, aesthetics, and the ability to calculate the size of the visible universe?

It's hard to see how a mind as many-faceted and fragile as that of man could be the result of adapting to an environment, whether that of the present or of the distant past.

Nevertheless, this is the kind of adaptation the evolutionary psychologists have been looking for. To find it, they have to find characteristics common to everybody: the mental characteristics we all share even if they're not the most interesting ones. The psychologist Geoffrey Miller writes in a critique: "Genetically evolved aspects of human nature should appear uniformly across all historical epochs, all cultures, and all normal humans. Anything else must be attributed to learning, culture, or socialization."[2]

The picture, then, was that only uniformity among humans could be biologically determined. The rest evolved socially and culturally. Where we are identical it's biology; where we are different, it's culture.

The problem with this approach to the human mind is that where people are identical, we're not particularly interesting. We're different at those points that make us fantastic.

FOR MY PART, it has always astonished me why people take such trouble over concealing so many quotidian activities from others, even though these activities would not exactly come as a surprise to them. We don't like anyone watching when we urinate, take a dump, or sleep. But, there aren't any major revelations to be found there. The sides of our behavior we hide are the most common and biological of all! Yet we proudly display our peculiarities, such as stamp collections, opinions, and mental skills.

We hide the side of us that's easy to understand through natural selection. But we happily display what may only be understandable through sexual selection. But by its very nature sexual selection is social too: it's about showing off.

ONCE, AT THE beginning of the twentieth century, a German psychologist by the name of Krüger had his fortune told by a Gypsy woman and was astonished by the accuracy of her description of him. Without revealing why, he showed the description to a friend by the name of Zietz, who also thought it was amazingly accurate, although Zietz did not realize the description was of Krüger and not him. They both felt that the same description struck home.

The two gentlemen therefore arranged an experiment with members of a study group: they asked for handwriting samples and said that in a month's time they would provide each of them with an analysis of their personality based on their handwriting. A month later the participants received their descriptions and all felt that they hit the nail on the head. The Danish psychologist Edgar Rubin reports, "There were thirty-nine participants. None were displeased: a few declared that the assessment was broadly accurate, although one or two minor points were off the mark."[3]

Then the participants were assembled and told that they had all been given the same description! This inspired "minutes of merriment: we may assume that there was no little embarrassment, too, at having been fooled so easily," Rubin says.

The description given to the participants was couched in terms that are also familiar from newspaper horoscopes: a series of statements that are banally true and apply to everyone. Here are a couple of excerpts from Krüger's text:

> Deep down inside you are a sincere person . . . Among people close to you you are sociably cheerful, indeed often light-headed, and you are able to abandon yourself to the moment. There are times when you feel the urge to be alone. . . . You are no pedant or fuss-pot, but you strive to

carry out your everyday duties conscientiously. . . . There is no denying that there are certain less pleasant aspects to your character. Sometimes, for example, you can grow rather hot-tempered. . . . At the moment there seems to be some pressure on you . . . however, your personal destiny is again on a rising curve.[4]

Do you feel this applies to you? Are you like this, too? Are we all? If so, why hide it from one another? Why do we brood over our inner uncertainty like a secret when it's just as trivial as the fact that we all have to use the john and that it tends to smell when we're finished?

We are not especially interesting where we are identical. And this is really the big problem for the evolutionary psychology approach to man: it looks for all the points on which we are the same. Is that interesting?

THE CRITICISM OF evolutionary psychology came not least from biologists with political convictions. Researchers like Stephen Jay Gould in the United States and Steven Rose in Great Britain inveighed against the image of all human characteristics as adaptations that lay behind the new science.[5] You cannot understand the mind as biology, they said, in criticism that of course greatly resembles Gould's more general criticism of Darwinism, which he regarded as far too obsessed by adaptation to an end or purpose, whereas in his view biological evolution encompassed lots of random, seemingly inconvenient eccentricities.

This criticism was well founded, but it merely shows that adaptation by natural selection is not the relevant explanatory mechanism. If the alternative is a purely social explanation, it's hard to see how man evolved at all. In reality it's just a reiteration of the separation of biological evolution from the truly human that Wallace had already pointed out.

This separation is not on. There's got to be a link between the animal and the sublime in man, between necessity and freedom.

CAN *HOMO ECONOMICUS* live alongside *Homo generosus*? Can these two sides of man, each of which reflects its own mechanism in the history of evolution, coexist in an individual?

We have no trouble recognizing each of them in us: *Homo economicus* with his petty selfishness and cool calculation, and *Homo generosus* with his eager showing off and desire to play, play, play.

In love, *Homo generosus* displays all his talents from romantic candlelight dinners and artful little gifts to giddy enthusiasm for everything in life great and small, openness, abundance, exultation at a daisy on the lawn.

But it won't wash, not for long: everyday life returns, and strawberries and cream and champagne give way to porridge, oats, and diet yoghurt. You have a bus to catch and a lunch to pack. *Homo economicus* takes over with his planning and his overview.

Can they live together? Let's see who they are:

	HOMO GENEROSUS	HOMO ECONOMICUS
ORIGIN	Sexual selection	Natural selection
GOAL	Propagation	Survival
MEANS	Anti-adaptation	Adaptation to the environment
STYLE	Abundance	Efficiency
SIGNAL	Existing	Capable of something
TYPE OF RELATIONSHIP	Generosity	Reciprocity
ACTIVITY	Playing, games	Work
TYPE OF EXISTENCE	Freedom	Necessity
STATUS SYMBOL[6]	Giving	Having
FORM OF EXCHANGE	Gifts	Goods

Love is the union of the two sides of man in a relationship between two people. In western cultures a love affair starts with two people falling for each other; their generosity toward each other is boundless. But if it doesn't end, the relationship evolves into more than wondrous rejoicing at the infinite richness of existence; it evolves into a mixture of necessity and freedom.

When sexual selection has proceeded beyond mate choice and has left an indelible trace in the form of offspring, the second phase inexorably kicks in. Suddenly the law of necessity prevails: there are helpless moppets who need to be fed, changed, who need to laugh, to play, to be picked up, to sleep, to be sat by and looked after. *Homo economicus's* ability to make plans, administer resources and organize quotidian life becomes absolutely vital. But play and joy are still important.

The great challenge facing love is to unite the two sides of man: efficiency and generosity. Neither is sufficient unto itself.

Endless rows of red roses and serenades beneath the balcony just won't cut it in the long run. Common sense and seriousness are also required.

Generosity isn't enough: you need reciprocity, too.

N O FINAL, SYSTEMATIC solution to the relationship between the two sides of man is provided; only the interweaving of the two sides of human existence throughout the course of life.

But there is a law that connects reciprocity and generosity: the more you give, the more you receive; not immediately, not always from the same person, not always at all. But nevertheless, when accounts are finally settled, you get back what you give. We may call this love's law.

Admittedly it was not originally formulated as a law, but as the lyrics of a song on the Beatles' last perfect album, *Abbey Road*. To end the album Paul McCartney had written a piece of music and a short lyric (which didn't end the album, after all, because a studio technician appended a most peculiar little ballad about Her Majesty).[7]

However, the penultimate song one is still called "The End," and it wraps up one of the most creative musical stories in the history of the world, the Beatles' unparalleled career:

> And in the end
> The love you take
> Is equal to
> The love you make.

The Theory of Culture

THE FREEDOM MESSAGE: MAKE AN EFFORT AND YOU'LL MAKE OUT

WHY CULTURE? THIS question was asked in 1997 by the English musician Brian Eno. "Is there a way of understanding why humans continuously and constantly and without exception engage in cultural activity?" he asked. "We don't know of human groups that don't produce something that we would call art. It seems to be something that we are biologically inclined to do. If we are, then what is the nature of that drive? What is it doing for us? When people say, well surely this has been written about, what I say is, actually it hasn't, really."[1]

The answer seems much closer five years after Brian Eno raised the question; we humans create culture because cultural statements are "deep," they are costly to produce, and thereby signal the individual's worth as a genotype. We have developed and refined methods for expressing ourselves and impressing others. Originally these tendencies were associated with sexual selection, but they have gradually become independent and are exercised without the executor necessarily thinking of mating at the same time.

IN HIS BOOK *The Mating Mind* (2000) The American psychologist Geoffrey Miller, whom we have already bumped into, made the most extensive attempt at applying the theory of sexual selection and costly signals to explaining man's special characteristics, particularly the brain. The result is highly thought-provoking.

"The handicap principle casts a new light on the human brain," Miller writes.[2] Here is an organ that uses a large portion of the body's resources and seems wildly over-dimensioned compared to the tasks on the savannah—but not wildly over-dimensioned if impressing the opposite sex is what it's all about.

After all, doing something difficult with your brain shows that your body has the resources to both survive and allocate a large portion of its metabolism to elaborate activity. A quarter of our energy is expended on keeping the brain running.

And apart from filthy lucre what's better than profound, personal conversation, unique vocal talents, humor, the gift of gab, a good eye for the ball, cultivation, quick wit, pretty ornaments, eye-catching paintings, keeping your promises, social networks, and being up on the latest gossip when it comes to attracting the opposite sex?

It's simply very expensive for the body to keep the whole show running in its head. If you can show you can use your head, you also show you have resources. But remember that you use your head for lots of things apart from reading books: you use it when you play football, dance, fix the faucet, do the pools, walk straight, or clean the john. A powerful brain is not only a matter of being intellectual (and many will rightly argue that intellectuals don't use much of their brain capacity).

The brain is a sexual ornament in the same way that a peacock's tail is. It's an extravagant display, a cornucopia of capacity and function, apparently a huge waste of resources, which declares: *here we have a strong individual.*

It is of course important to note that not only men have big brains; both sexes do. But in the case of humans sexual selection applies to both sexes, and many of the characteristics promoted via sexual selection are inherited by both sexes. Inventories show, however, that men actually have slightly more brain cells than women: 23 billion in men to 19 billion in women, also when adjusted for the difference in body weight.[3] This fact has a natural possible explanation in sexual selection's distribution by gender.

B ut why are people attracted to humor, energy, creativity, and intelligence? Just because they're difficult to come up with? And aren't many of these characteristics useful from the point of view of survival, too?

Geoffrey Miller describes sexual selection as evolution's venture capital.[4] It's a mechanism that allows more or less peculiar eccentricities to be tested: if they prove appropriate, they may then be given a permanent place in human nature.

Venture capital is money invested at great risk. You cannot tell which small companies will make a fortune with some innovative technology or some new product. Most get nowhere and close down. So investing in them is a major risk; on the other hand, the yields can prove tremendous. Investing in big blue-chip corporations, which are stable but tend not to return the amazing gains of the small ones, is quite another matter. Venture capital, then, is for taking risks with.

Similarly, sexual selection takes risks: after all, the result won't be a matter of survival, of the life and death of the individual. Lots of innovations, such as a big brain capable of keeping track of crazy ideas, can be tested by sexual selection, and if they prove useful they can join the set of tools that ensures survival.

Sexual selection can, as Miller argues, "favor innovations just because they look sexy, long before they show any profitability in the struggle for survival."[5]

The analogy with the money market is of course bizarre, but the concept is valid enough: there is a mechanism to promote innovations and extreme skills.

Precisely because it is sexual it may easily lead to great differences between individuals. Characteristics relating to survival must necessarily be present in the majority of individuals. You don't see anybody incapable of respiration, but you do see considerable variation in terms of inspiration.

Sexual selection does not lead to uniformity but to the variety, fragility, unreliability, and self-absorption so characteristic of the human psyche.

This heterogeneity does not apply only among humans per se but also among humans compared to other animals. One of the decisive difficulties of explaining man as a biological phenomenon is that there are such huge differences in mental capacity in humans and even the cleverest animals we know. Apes are pretty bright, and whales have an enormous range of songs and behavior. But they do not manifest many of the cultural and civilizational abilities humans manifest around the world.

If it was solely sexual selection that explained the differences between humans and primates, it would be hard to locate any environmental differences capable of leading to such a huge difference in, say, brain capacity. Any evolution governed by natural selection leads to adaptation to the environment: so if the environment is merely somewhat alike, two somewhat identical creatures ought to evolve in the same direction.

But as we know, man and ape are far apart. With sexual selection as the explanation, we possess a mechanism that will *not* lead to uniform evolution if two related species evolve in the same environment. Because sexual selection is affected by quirks, strange caprices and oddball preferences in the two sexes can take evolution to surprising places. It is not about evolving the best survival strategies in a given environment: it is about seducing each other. That is why sexual selection is a far better mechanism for explaining how man has evolved in a relatively short time (a few million years) so radically differently from the primates. In the thirties Ronald Fisher's runaway theory had already showed that sexual selection could proceed very rapidly.

BUT ISN'T IT a scandalous thought? That everything humans have in common, and share with animals to a great extent, is the result of the struggle for survival: basic bodily functions, sensual organs, physiology, and base emotions? Whereas everything that separates man and occasionally fills us with an inner, quivering pride at being human is the result of the hunt for sex? Science, culture, spirituality, art, teamwork, society, morality, suspension bridges, space rockets, and the most sophisticated classical music: everything spiritual, beautiful, and wise is "merely" an aid to getting laid.

This may appear to be a brazen assertion: but instead of viewing culture and genius as tools for obtaining sex and thereby degrading them to the baser urges and instincts, we could turn the tables and say, what fantastic wealth sexuality brings with it! What a rich source for the creation of the most wondrous phenomena our attempts to impress each other is! Instead of saying genius is sex, we could say sex is genius.

The peacock's tail is still fantastically beautiful even though we know it's really just a tool for obtaining sex. After all, doesn't beauty break the bounds within which it's created?

THAT IS CERTAINLY how we prefer to think of the arts: even if we reluctantly acknowledge that culture is a grandiose example of sexual ornamentation, an endeavor to make us sexually selectable, we nevertheless insist that it has become an independent mechanism, freed of its original sexual selection roots. Culture is civilized, and thus quite different from sexual selection. . . .

Or what? Listen to the music on the radio, read novels of

the past and present, go to the theater, listen to opera, watch movies, enjoy the sculptures in the park, direct your opera glasses at the ballerinas: are these things about anything apart from sexual selection? Literally speaking: isn't every pop song, almost every novel, movie, stage play, musical, and opera, etc., only about love between two humans and all the obstacles in its path? Sure, television and movies feature quite a few men driving fast cars, shooting each other with very big pistols, indulging in pyromania, and clubbing one another on the head, but Diamond and Zahavi taught us that we may regard these things as handicaps serving as sexual selection marketing tools.

FICTIONAL ART FORMS are about love, risks, masculinity, femininity, love, making love. Fairytales reward the courage of the poor man with the princess and half the kingdom, so even while we are hearing bedtime stories as kids we learn that boldness, courage, and fighting dangerous dragons is the way to marrying the object of our desires.

And what is your inner movie house showing? What do you think about half the time? Oh, right: experimental dance theater and the last novel you read. But what was that about?

Also, why the rest of us consume art is one thing, but why do artists create art? Because they can't help it. All right, but why can't they?

Rock is one high-profile example of the way that art leads to "money for nothing and chicks for free" as Dire Straits sang.[6] Or the Beatles who helped themselves once they'd provided a bit of culture: "It was common for the Beatles to share up to six or eight girls a night," says biographer Mark Hertsgaard of their early concert period. "They swapped partners at John's command, 'Everyone change!'"[7]

Such behavior may seem bizarre and reprehensible (especially to those of us who don't have access to it). But it still illustrates the point of sexual selection's costly signals: you have to put yourself out to get what you want. You don't get sex by being engrossed by it all the time but by doing something else that engrosses other people. You have to take the roundabout route and create something that makes an impression: great music, for example. Admittedly, most of us do not possess John Lennon's talent, but on the other hand we probably make do with more modest sexual activities.

The argument, then, is the breathtakingly simple one that culture is a matter of sexual selection. Period. That is what it's about. (That doesn't mean people standing onstage shouting *ass, prick, and tits* at the audience—okay, some of them do, but not all art is that vulgar.) Most people fortunately adopt a more elegant, more roundabout approach to the matter.

IN THE OLD days the astronomers had a method they called indirect vision, which was useful when they looked at the stars.[8] Before photography and later the photo cell and CCD chip were introduced to astronomical observatories, the human eye was the most sensitive recording instrument you could put at that end of the telescope. The human eye is highly sensitive to light, but not throughout its field of vision. In the middle of the field there is an area that is very adept at seeing colors and details. At the edge of the field there is almost no color vision but considerable light sensitivity, particularly toward faint, dispersed sources of light, such as blurred, indistinct blotches. So if you want to look for nebulas or faint comets in the sky you have to use indirect vision: you direct your gaze slightly to one side of what you want to see. When you have caught sight of it, you will find it very difficult to maintain indirect vision because instinctively you want to look straight at what you are engrossed in. If you do so, it disappears, because you place it in the middle of your field of vision, which is not very good at seeing faint objects.

So astronomers in the old days, who did not have the ability of photography to collect light over time at their disposal, used indirect vision; amateur astronomers do so today.

The analogy with sexual selection is straightforward: you mustn't aim too directly for your goal or you won't get there. You must aim for the nebula at the edge of your field of vision: spirit and culture. Then you'll get what you're really after. Culture is a necessary detour to sex.

IF WE LOOK at human skills they typically have two aspects, which we may call principles of contraction and expansion.

The principle of contraction is that once we've acquired a skill we can be very good at exerting it with less and less energy consumption. A Norwegian on cross-country skis doesn't expend a fifth as much energy getting to the top of the hill as your clumsy, gasping Dane. When you master something, you do it without great effort. This form of skill development is contractive: it involves doing things with as little energy consumption as possible. This isn't difficult to understand if we consider how natural selection optimizes the way the individual economizes resources.

But that's only a tiny part of the history of man. As soon as we've learned how to get to the top of the hill with the least possible effort we want to get to the next one. We want to move on, extend our skills, expend more energy, expand our horizons. This expansive side of human skills is hard to understand on the basis of natural selection. However, it's not hard to understand the inquisitive, innovative, explorative, experimental side of man as a manifestation of the logic of sexual selection: to carry out such an expansion is simultaneously to assume a handicap, an inconvenience that will convince a potential mate of your strength.

CONTRACTION AND EXPANSION do not only apply to obviously physical activities such as climbing hills on cross-country skis. Mental activities have the same characteristics. Our brains use a lot of resources, a lot of blood sugar, when we're trying to understand something unfamiliar. But once it's become familiar and we understand it, we use far less energy. It's tiring to be at a dinner with Swedes, because you're always in doubt as to whether you got the joke (or whether it was a joke). Understanding may be described as a process that allows us to experience or comprehend something with the least possible energy consumption by the brain.[9]

Thus mental activity also becomes a field in which we find both expansion and contraction. Contraction is about understanding things as simply as possible, while expansion consists of constantly absorbing new experiences and areas of perception. Expansion, contraction; expansion, contraction: cognition breathing.

WE DON'T HAVE peacock's tails or antlers. We have breasts, thighs, beards, deep voices, and all the other features that appear during puberty: clear results of sexual selection. But is that all? What is man's special result of sexual selection? What kind of effort will help us make out?

The mind, culture, mountaineering, soccer, smiles, gallantry, wealth, cheerfulness, kindness to animals, painting pictures, traveling to the moon, saving the world, having nice shoes, having more than it takes.

The whole point of Zahavi's mechanism is that you have to do something difficult that imposes an immediate handicap in everyday life in order to show you possess lots of resources. What you do doesn't matter as long as it's difficult and others can see that it's difficult. Overcoming difficulties. Making an effort. The classic virtues.

There is no predetermined direction apart from getting away from the current state of things. What you do doesn't have to be anything in particular as long as you do it with great power and lots of resources.

This is a very important aspect of sexual selection: it's not a matter of adapting to a given environment. There is no single answer the way there is for natural selection, where the environment defines a series of appropriate characteristics. It's a well documented feature of the evolutionary history of natural selection that animals with widely differing basic structures nevertheless end up resembling one another if they inhabit the same environment. Mammals and dinosaurs are very different because dinosaurs are egg-laying reptiles. Yet we can see from the fossils we find from the Mesozoic that dinosaurs existed that were like our large mammals in physique and many of their special organs. There were dinosaurs like today's ruminants and today's predators. Later on, mammals entered the sea and became whales and dolphins, whose outsides (but not their insides) look just like fish.

The environment creates niches for particular body shapes toward which the animals there evolve despite their different starting points. An adaptation takes place in which the environment dictates the animal's shape and many of its bodily functions.

In a given environment, then, there is a single answer toward which the evolution of its animals evolves. Evolution is headed somewhere. In that sense it's not creative at all.

But sexual selection is creative to a far greater degree. There's no environmentally determined single answer here, just a bunch of opposite sex members of the same species who are difficult to surprise. You have to come up with a novelty, preferably a useless one, to make an impression. The possibilities are wide open.

So the results of sexual selection possess a very different dynamic. The spotlight is not on arriving at a particular thing but the effort to get away from the existing state of affairs. *Do something difficult!* is an order with no particular direction: all it emphasizes is the *difficult* bit. *Make an effort!* doesn't tell you what you have to make an effort to do; the effort is the thing.

I T ' S   T H E   W A Y the American science historian Thomas
Kuhn put it in 1962 when he changed the picture of the
evolution of cognition from a slow approach toward a truth
to a more unpredictable evolution in leaps and bounds. "If
we can learn to put evolution from *what we actually know* in
place of evolution toward *what we want to know,* a series of
irritating problems may disappear."[10]

Kuhn's point, then, was to regard the evolution of cognition
as the elimination of ignorance rather than an approach to a
previously given truth. If we look at the history of evolution
the same question has rumbled: is evolution unambiguously
aimed at a particular, predetermined final result in the form
of adaptation, or is it open, unpredictable, and searching?

Steven Jay Gould's criticism of neo-Darwinism was precisely that the latter was oriented toward an evolution rather
than a particular goal where it could be stated unambiguously
that some had progressed farther than others (and in many of
Darwin's students the notion is still not dead that all creatures
apart from man are just on the way down the same evolutionary axis as man: we are precocious and advanced, and the
others are lazybones). If we equate Darwinism with natural
selection, as many of Darwin's disciples do, Gould's criticism
is completely fair. After all, the point is precisely that natural
selection is a matter of adaptation to a world that is already
given, even though it changes all the time.

But sexual selection is of a very different nature. There
is no single answer. There is only the mechanism of doing
something difficult—i.e., starting out from existing reality and
challenging it a bit, giving its ears a tug. So sexual selection

doesn't lead anywhere in particular; it moves away from where you already are. It is "away from" and not "to there."

Thomas Kuhn introduced an evolution in the history of ideas that I believe will permeate almost every thought that deals with things that evolve: it is not that whatever is evolving (cognition, life, technology) wants to arrive at a predetermined result, but to get away from the existing situation. The world is open; nothing is given in advance. We are not moving "to there" but "away from." "To be continued."

THE DANISH WORD *"umage"* (trouble, effort, pain as in painstaking) is a very interesting term: it's neither merely about the person who makes the effort or merely about the object or task he makes an effort on. It's about both. *Umage* is an exertion, a form of activity, a particular attitude to the world about you. You can't say, "I am making an effort" without an object: there has to be something you are making an effort on.

Conversely, *umage* cannot be understood solely on the basis of whatever its object is. The wood that is the object of the carver's work may be the object of slovenliness or effort. One man's effort may lead to the same result that another man achieves without the slightest exertion.

So *umage* is only understandable based on a given person; but on the other hand it cannot be understood solely on the basis of that person, isolated from what he does in a given situation.

Umage is a term that tells us something about our relation to the world about us, to the way we approach it: whether we use all our resources and skills, all our concentration and attention, or whether our mind is elsewhere and we are not really involved in what we are doing. To make an effort [*umage*] you have to be there, to give all you've got, and suppress a number of inner signals that, say, it'd be very nice to have a bit of a chat with a colleague or take a walk on the beach.

We may say that the phenomenon of *umage* does not solely belong to our own world or solely to the world of those about us. It is a manifestation of our own relation to our own world at a given moment.

In this way *umage* resembles a quantity for which the legendary American author Robert M. Pirsig has been searching for decades. Pirsig's first major work, *Zen and the Art of Motorcycle Maintenance*, subtitled *An Inquiry into Values* (1974), is an account of the thoughts of a philosopher while crossing the North American continent by motorcycle. The main problem is the concept of quality: is it a property of things or of our perception of them? Is a good piece of wood a matter of the tree that created it or the carpenter who selects it for a particular job?

Pirsig's answer is that quality is primary, compared to the concepts of an observer and something observed. In other words quality has to be there first; then an observer comes along and figures that there is an object that possesses this quality. The world doesn't consist of observers and things observed who find quality in their interaction. The world consists of quality, which is identified by an observer and is thereby observed.

In his book *Lila—an inquiry into morals* (1991) in which the means of transport is a boat, it is the problem of morality that is addressed. "Quality is morality," Pirsig writes. "The two concepts are identical. And if quality is the primary characteristic of reality, this must mean that morality is also its primary characteristic."[11]

Again, to Pirsig, morality is something that is neither inside man nor out there in reality, but prior to both man and reality.

Effort involves something costly to the individual, strenuous, difficult, painstaking, beside-itself, resource hungry, but also profoundly satisfying: a step across the line between you and the rest.

Peacocks make an effort but only with feathers. Man invented generalized effort as a criterion for sexual selection.

A S A THEORY of culture, it's a very simple view to say that making the effort is more important than what you make the effort on. It tells us that there's a complete disconnection between the cultural level and the biological: biology tells us that we must make an effort. But not on what. It tells us that exertion and doing our best is an important costly signal, but it does not define a direction or content for our exertion. Biology can teach us that there are good evolutionary-theoretical reasons for man's enthusiasm to make an effort to create things great and small; but not what we want, or what is regarded as effort, exertion, or talent.

Only one thing matters: whether it looks difficult in the eyes of one other special individual.

Biology's demand for effort sets culture free to be what it pleases. The humanities are thereby set free from scientific imperialism. We cannot come up with a biologically based theory of culture that says anything other than effort is good. On the other hand, such a theory is a total theory of culture, because it tells us why we produce culture. It thus answers Brian Eno's question "Why culture?" but the answer does not help us to know how we are to produce culture, apart from the fact that we must make an effort.

THE FATHER OF psychoanalysis, Sigmund Freud, operated with the idea of sublimation, which may seem to resemble the effort theory quite a bit, but in fact they are very different: sublimation is people creating art and science because their sexual expression is inhibited and so they have surplus energy, which they channel into cultural activities. We create art because we can't obtain sex. From the effort viewpoint it's the other way round: we create art in order to obtain sex.

Effort can be exerted *online,* as something made real-time in the current situation, or *offline,* as accumulated skills (meaning that what you do here and now, however virtuoso it may appear, doesn't actually cost you anything in the current situation but involved a great deal of exertion in training; after all, practicing is also making an effort).

NATURAL SELECTION PROMOTES characteristics directed at specific factors in the surroundings: finding food, avoiding predators, etc. Sexual selection does not employ the same directional logic, for it merely involves impressing a potential mate. Sexual selection introduces an element of freedom or non-predestination into evolution. It can be anything you like, as long as the women like it.

Does that mean that the only criterion for good art is that it cost a great deal of labor and much effort? Is a scientific theory more correct because its creator worked his ass off while adherents of competing theories remained idle?

Of course not! The history of science contains plenty of examples of conscientious, hardworking researchers being overtaken at the finish by some breezy young thing who whips the right solution out from under their very noses.[12] If I tried to compose a piece of classical music it would cost me a quite unconscionable amount of effort without the result being even remotely interesting to anyone else.

Effort alone is not enough. It has to be qualified effort: you have to do something that's difficult, but it is no good doing something easy in a difficult way or something difficult in an impossible way. But we may say that without effort you can't create interesting art or good science.

In return there are loads of stuff where you can make an effort: the universe is infinite in any direction. No matter which direction you move in there are loads of details to be found. The German physicist Emil Wiechert put it this way in 1896: "The universe is infinite in all directions, not only above us in the large, but also below us in the small. If we start from our human scale of existence and explore the content of the universe further and further we finally arrive, both in the large and in the small, at misty distances where first our senses and then even our concepts fail us."[13]

The world is rich in structures and processes. There is plenty to embark on, both out in space and in the mind. It will remain possible to make an effort for eternity.

WE THUS KNOW what to demand of our artists, scientists, and indeed one another: effort. But we can't demand what they are to make an effort doing. We can ask for effort but not its content.

The great lever of Danish cinema in the nineties, *Dogme 95*, is an example of knowledge of these matters. As technological progress has gradually democratized the means of production so that anybody can obtain a camera and editing equipment for peanuts, and any special effect can be produced on a computer, the real artists have been forced to come up with obstacles to ensure that their works are actually art. They set themselves limits. The Dogme rules practically all involve not being manipulative but insisting that what the camera records be interesting in itself. That is what brings out the good story, good acting, good situations.

Dogme 95, like any art, is a choice of obstacles, the seeking out of difficulty: the insistence on making an effort.

SPOTLIGHTING THE IDEA of effort leads us into a virtue ethic—i.e., a view of the way people ought to act that emphasizes the classical virtues of good behavior, which Aristotle and other Ancient Greeks introduced twenty-five hundred years ago. For example: wisdom, justice, courage, and self-restraint (the Christians later boiled this view down to faith, hope, and love).

Virtues are not recipes for particular things we must or must not do, but characteristics we should encourage in ourselves.[14] According to this tradition, we may say that effort is a virtue worth pursuing. A succinct ethic: *Make an effort, man!*

But remember the bitter, often tragic irony in the logic of relationships: too much effort may actually cost you your mate. Not only do you have to make an effort with your cultural manifestations of courtship; you also have to make the appropriate effort with your mate. Mismatched effort may, in fact, leave you unmatched.[15]

Nobody can doubt that we do an awful lot in order to survive. We breathe, eat, exercise, and dispose of waste. But while we're doing these things we don't think about wanting to survive; we think about other things entirely. And if these necessities of survival do occur to us, we don't think about them as such: we think of breathing as the key to controlling our voices; the elegance of topping off an osso buco with a mixture of chopped parsley, garlic, and lemon peel; completing that bike ride in one hour, seven minutes despite the side wind; what on earth did I have for dinner yesterday?

We do lots of things in order to survive without thinking about survival. We have communicative feelings, such as hunger, which gives us the urge to eat without considering what would happen if we didn't, or without reminding us every time how many nutrients are actually necessary for the organism to function.

Similarly, the hypothesis that we do a whole bunch of things because in the final analysis they are directed at our having offspring does not imply that we think of it like that. We do lots of things to get laid without thinking of the costly signals required to persuade a potential mate of our qualities as breeding stock. We may hone the assertion still finer: many of the fruits of sexual selection are activities that are among the few that can stop us from thinking about sex.

If art, science, culture, and work are activities that are, in the final analysis, about making an effort in order to make out, they are precisely the kind that occasionally seem more important to us than sexual fantasies. Just as modern, genitally fixated pornography has very little to do with the behavior that attracts a mate, sexual fantasies have very little to do with the sides of the person who signals good genes.

In the picture being painted here, the point is precisely that the route to sex does not go via preoccupation with sex, but by being engrossed by all kinds of other things: intellect, risk, strength, tenderness, generosity.

But that doesn't prevent us from actually, to an astonishing degree, when we are not engrossed by anything else, thinking of sex, romance, flirting, and love.

BEHAVIORAL SCIENTISTS DISTINGUISH between the ultimate cause of a behavior and its immediate cause.[16] The ultimate cause of our eating is that otherwise we wouldn't survive. The immediate cause is that we are hungry. A human understands his own behavior through its immediate causes, not its ultimate ones, which are only accessible through deep thoughts.

The claim that what causes us to create art, culture, science, and other noble products of the mind is that we want sex and offspring involves the ultimate cause, not the immediate one as it appears in the consciousness of the practitioner.

The claim, then, is that the ultimate cause carries through into behavior via an immediate cause, an urge that the individual experiences directly. And the point is precisely that it is *not* identical with the ultimate cause. In this context we may even say that behavior that has the desire for sex as its immediate cause will not work as intended. It's not good to go straight for sex. You have to show you're attractive, and it is easiest to do that when you're not thinking about what you're after.

The immediate cause that gets people to paint, go onstage, write books, do research, and compose music is seldom—as it is in the case of Jens Jørgen Thorsen—the expressed desire to have sex. Rather, it is driven by motives such as creating beauty, expressing ourselves, understanding the world, pleasing other people, satisfying our curiosity, or because we can't help it.

The claim that culture is the result of sexual selection is not the same as saying that culture is exercised with a view to sex. The point is rather that it is these instincts—the urge to create beauty, the need to express ourselves, the desire to understand the world, to please others, and curiosity—which are the result of sexual selection.

Neither natural nor sexual selection can produce the ability to compose serial music. But they can produce the instincts and tendencies that get people to compose it.

There is a big difference between saying "I paint to get . . ." like in the epigram that opens this book, and saying that sexual selection has selected individuals with the characteristic that they have a tendency to paint or to do something else remarkable that draws on all their abilities. The assertion that we do a thing in order to achieve something particular is a psychological assertion about the motives for an act. It is quite another matter than an assertion by evolutionary theory that a selection mechanism promotes particular tendencies in individuals.

In principle, sexual selection could have led to an indestructible human urge to decorate all our utensils, conquer space, and produce seductive music quite without the people who carry out these acts ever associating these activities with reproduction at all.

But as I have indicated a couple of times, I believe that a study of our own thoughts and associations will reveal that sexuality is closer to our world of motives than we usually think. What do we want after we've done something great? What do we get when we radiate that we've done something great? We feel sexy when we've done something great: we want sex when we've been good.

"Get your frigging act together and give them some elementary leadership," a woman television producer told me while we were making a series of science programs without my having gotten used to the obvious need for supervision that arises when a camera crew is trying to put the presenter's hazy ideas into practice: "Spell out what we've got to do, and then tell them we've done it so they can straighten their backs, go home, and screw the wife."[17]

THE CLAIM OF this book is double: in particular I say that characteristics such as generosity, creativity, the will to cooperate, altruism, indeed human culture, were created by biological evolution through a selection mechanism that is sexual. But I also say, although less insistently, that the psychological impetus behind generous, creative, teamwork-oriented, altruistic, and culture-creating acts is to some extent sexual. The latter assertion, that the motive behind good deeds is sexual at bottom and aimed at finding a partner, involves a factor that we suppress in ourselves. After all, we do not consider the arts as courtship. But I assert that with a bit of thought you will realize that if paying compliments gives you a hard-on or causes a flutter below your waist, it's probably not only because you think that a couple of compliments will lead to a quick fuck, but because there's a profound, psychological link between pleasing another human and exercising your sexuality.

In reality there are three levels to the explanation:

- **An evolutionary level.** We do not make an effort in order to obtain sex. We do so as a result of the fact that those who did so in the generations before us obtained loads of sex and the offspring that resulted, who inherited their tendency to make an effort.

- **A psychological level.** We do not make an effort in order to obtain sex, but because we are curious, have a need to express ourselves, etc., which is the result of the evolutionary selection of those who like making an effort.

- **A subconscious/semi-suppressed level.** Actually we make an effort because we think it will obtain us sex, but we don't want to admit it to ourselves or anyone else, but if we're honest, we do sense it.

My view is that all three are valid and significant but at very different levels of explanation. The first level explains why we have become the way we are. The second describes how we explain to ourselves why we act as we do. The third level asks why on earth we conceal the connection from ourselves.

T HE IMMEDIATE CAUSE of cultural creations, the subjective motive, is an urge and curiosity which can be hard to understand. Perhaps we feel about cultural production the way we feel about exercise: you feel just great afterward. You feel fit and full of vitality.

Feeling in fine form, for example, is a mood or a state which may convey the link between artistic and sexual performance. You feel in fine form when you do a good job; being in good form makes you sexually attractive.

You do a good job, you straighten your back, and you radiate happiness and harmony in a way that makes people want to be with you, sexually or not.

The reasoning is that sexual selection has brought out characteristics in us that are useful in courtship and seduction. These characteristics are present in us because they have become the preferences of those responsible for sexual selection—i.e., very often women.

If we imagine women as the choosers and men as those to be chosen among, we get this mechanism: women prefer men who are good at making splendid decorations, good at telling stories, good at inventing new things, the first to discover new plants in the forest, etc. These characteristics are linked to the fact these are men equipped with considerable curiosity and spirit of adventure.

If women prefer men who discover new hunting grounds, they will have children with a slightly greater tendency to be curious and brave. These characteristics are hereditary and retained even after the hunter-gatherer culture has become agricultural or a post-industrial virtual culture. The curiosity is intact but finds new areas of application.

In terms of evolutionary history, curiosity and the urge for expression arose through sexual selection, but neither its objective nor its objective side need have anything at all to do with the context in which they evolved.

Why do we make an effort? Not necessarily in order to have sex. We do so as the result of the fact that those who did so in the generations before us obtained loads of sex and the offspring that resulted, who inherited their tendency to make an effort.

We are children of that mechanism. And when each of us exerts our effort and has such a lovely amount of sex, we have offspring who certainly can't help being created by that mechanism: they create culture for fun and because they can't help it.

Nevertheless, strangely enough if you ask a theoretical astrophysicist about one particular line of the discipline's equations, he or she is quite capable of describing it as "sexy." Scientists and artists now and then describe their products as sexy. The association is located deep within them, even though they would definitely feel insulted if you told them they only wrote their clever books to get their rocks off; and once you'd got them really boiling with resentment they'd start complaining that in any case it doesn't work!

Culture can have a sexual purpose without it following that for the individual practitioner there is a sexual motivation for creating it. But it is remarkable how strongly the subjective motives for cultural endeavor are tied to ideas of a sexual nature.

GEOFFREY MILLER POINTED out that many cultural manifestations are most powerful at the age where sexual selection is on the agenda. Painters, jazz musicians, and authors achieve most in their late twenties, when the choice of mate looms large.

You can argue whether data like this show that people perform jazz, paint pictures, or write books to get laid. There is no doubt that it *is* the cause, but may we thereby conclude that it's especially men in the most sexually active phase of their lives who do so? Vigor, vitality, the absence of kids, and the naive belief of youth that you can perform miracles might also be the explanation; if so, what explains *them*? That we are most vital and prodigious at that age because it is the way to sex.

Miller's prediction is that any publicly visible human activity will evince this profile: it is performed particularly by young men in their most sexually active period.

The sociologist Satoshi Kanazawa from the University of Pennsylvania has tested Miller's theory on scientists. By choosing 280 great scientists and identifying the age at which they were most active, Kanazawa shows that it was indeed in the most sexually active period of their lives that they were most active, which coincides with Miller's prediction. And it also turns out that the unmarried researchers continued to be productive into old age, whereas married researchers (who had passed through sexual selection, of course) let things slide a bit as they got older.

Again we may ask if married researchers stop doing research because they are no longer seeking a mate or whether difficult working conditions in a marriage are to blame. The statistical link is clear enough, however: the congruity with Miller's prediction is "perfect," as Kanazawa puts it.[18]

ALLOW ME TO present the muses: these lovely Greek tutelary deities of the arts and sciences. There were nine of them. Most of them by far belong to the domain of art and song, but there is one scientific muse at any rate: Urania, the muse of astronomy. The muses were feminine, divine, protective, and at the same time unsullied and maternal. As the *Encyclopedia Britannica* writes: "The Muses are often spoken of as virgins, or at least unmarried, but they are repeatedly referred to as the mothers of more or less famous sons, such as Orpheus, Rhesus, Eumolpus . . ."[19] The muses are a superb metaphor for what drives men to art and science: a craving to be united with the eternally virgin mother of great sons.

Men's dream of security, acceptance, and innocence.

WE MUST REMEMBER to distinguish between the situation today and the situation back in history. Thirty years ago—that's just a generation ago—women's movements were all over the world working for sexual equality. The pill, the fridge, the crèche, and many other technological and social factors realistically allowed both sexes to play an active part in society at large. Domestic chores and childcare were correspondingly divided more equally, although not entirely equally, between the sexes. Sexuality became possible without fear of pregnancy, and parental care was more evenly divided between the sexes.

The historical tradition of men going out to work and women staying at home is rapidly being dismantled. This will also mean major changes in the way sexual selection takes place. After all, Trivers's mechanism predicts that as both sexes invest equally in childrearing, women will no longer be such a scant resource, and sexual selection will be divided more equally. It also means that the cultural activity intended to persuade the opposite sex of your qualities as a mate will no longer be the preserve of men. In turn this will mean more women as practitioners of the arts, from composing to science to politics. This evolution is clearly taking place. There is every reason to believe that a more even division of parental care will also lead to a more evenly divided participation in society and culture.

But conversely, when almost the entire burden of childcare rested on the woman, men bore the entire burden of presenting themselves as good potential mates.

So there is nothing strange in the fact that the vast majority of great exponents of culture throughout history are men. That is history, and for us to understand. The future, which is for us to create, need not be like that at all.

The image of man as the suitor applies all the way into

175

sexuality, where many men try to manage the act so that the woman achieves the greatest possible pleasure. And that's marvelous, of course. But many men also complain that they lose contact in this managerial role of little engineer.[20] This circumstance will also change when courtship becomes more evenly divided between the sexes.

ONE OF THE things we regard as most important is the social status of a prospective mate. This tells us something very important: women do not have a clear shot at choosing the men they find most attractive. Social status is conveyed by the whole community, including its male members. So an attractive man is a man everybody respects. This means that women are not the only ones who govern evolutionary progress. The whole herd has a say in deciding which men are the best. But at the same time high social status is still a handicap, because it is typically attained through privation and the assumption of difficulties that only strong genotypes can cope with.

Sexual selection is not only a matter of the females' choice of males, but of the herd's choice of males and females.

We may expand our little formula: *make an effort and you'll make out* is conveyed by the mechanism: *make an effort, make a name, and you'll make out*; and more down to earth: *make an effort, make a name that makes money, and you'll make out.*

(This tongue-twister is useful as a test of intoxication.)

JUST IMAGINE: IF cogitation is something we evolved to obtain sex, perhaps it's no wonder that we constantly think about sex. Because it's in order to obtain sex that we think at all!

Just for a moment forget the earnest, adult, controlled bit about doing it to make us look sophisticated. Just for a moment let your mind wander; think of it as sexual selection, getting laid, sex.

Does anything else make us as scintillatingly happy, vigorous, self-assured, energetic, and bursting with the will of life in every fiber of our body as when we meet a mate? Does anything fill our minds more or comprise more of an untrammeled sequence of thoughts than sexual fantasies?

For a moment, forget about all the clever science stuff and regard it as self-study, self-observation, or introspection: what do you think about most, really? Soccer? All right. Girlfriends? All right. New shoes? Okay. But most of all, don't you actually think about nooky, lust, seduction, romance, sex, sensuality?

Oh, all right, you're educated and cultivated and think mostly about the contemporary symphony. Well, that's quite okay by me; but I didn't ask you what you talk about to other people. I asked you what you thought about discreetly inside.

I don't guarantee the details, but on television I heard about a survey of the thoughts and stream of consciousness in the minds of transit passengers waiting at Copenhagen Airport. It turns out that Danes think about sex, Norwegians about duty-free goods, and Swedes if they've remembered their passports and tickets. (Note to my American audience: amend these nationalities as you see fit. Or perhaps, "Californians think about sex, New Yorkers about hedge funds, and Texans if they remembered to remove their handguns from their carry-on luggage.)

IF WE TAKE a slightly biological look at ourselves it is remarkable how much room sexual selection takes up in our inner lives and the stories we tell each other over lunch in the cafeteria, in the locker room, in literature, in the movies, and at the theater. Our private inner lives, the movie house of our conscious, the television and movie theaters proper are constantly about love, partners, seduction, flirtation, stolen glances, plunging necklines, and casual touching.

There are sound reasons for taking this covert life seriously, partly because it shows per se the degree to which sex engrosses us, but especially because it also explains all kinds of other stuff: we have an inner generator constantly producing the desire to be competent on the selection market. We don't think of it as mating games; we think of it as all kinds of other things. The generator that drives us all the time to want to make an effort, be accomplished, amusing, charming sweet, clever, witty, resourceful, and successful, is perhaps the same generator that produces our incessant inner flow of preoccupation with sexual selection: a generator that drives everything generous, beautiful, wise, warm, open, loyal, lovely, and valuable in life.

Our biological evolution has turned us into creatures who reach out for each other and the world in an attempt to seize each other and the world, to capture the world so we can share it with each other through our communication with each other. A language, a conversation, and a shared experience of the world are created through an effort that arises, in the absolutely final analysis, from the urge to impress other people, particularly the opposite sex.

There is no profound contradiction between our inner, free-flying fantasies and our outwardly directed conquering of the world and the community. Both are driven by the same generosity generator.

We get to one another via all kinds of means that were evolved to get to the one and only. Communication is love.

IF WE LOOK at human communication, the most typical feature of a conversation is what is not spoken but referred to in the conversation. If you measure the information content in an act of communication between two people in bits, you find it doesn't necessarily contain much at all. A bride who answers "no" in church will arouse considerable commotion without using many bits (the minimum possible amount). Conversely, many telephone conversations contain huge numbers of bits without much sense being conveyed.

To understand communication it is no use only looking at the information, we must look at something else: namely everything the statements mean. This may be regarded as the huge volume of information in the bride's head before she gets round to her "no": "All that dumb ass ever thinks about is going bowling with the boys; I heard his last product presentation and it did *not* augur good genes; and on top of that, the guy snores; no, Chuck is a whole lot more appealing." Similarly her "no" will unleash a huge flood of information in the heads of the groom and the congregation: "She's a tramp anyway; we should never have gotten involved with that family; and what about all the food for the party after?"

The information that churns around in the mind of the

sender before she speaks and the information sparked off in the mind of the receiver was labeled *exformation* in my book *The User Illusion*: explicitly discarded information.[21]

The interesting, meaningful aspect of something that's said is its exformation—everything that is not present in the words but is referred to. Information per se is of limited significance.

By distinguishing between information and exformation we are also able to define what's costly in a costly signal; the signal itself is information, of course, which is measured in bits. But costliness was a manifestation of how difficult producing the signal was: how much it cost the organism to build a peacock tail or to write that poem. The back story, the depth of the utterance.

The idea of costly signals is thus closely related to the ideas of depth that emerged in the theory of complexity in physics and math in the eighties.[22] When this thinking was transferred to the analysis of communication, it led to the notion of exformation, which may be re-expressed as the costliness of a signal.

The physicists' notion of depth involves (among other things) *thermodynamic depth,* which covers all the energy conversions that lead to a given product, such as a living being, for example. Thermodynamic depth is thus a measure of the cost of producing something or other. This depth is therefore a measure of the costliness of a signal regarded as physiological effort, metabolite resources, or blood sugar consumption. This means that there is a completely logical coincidence between three apparently very different factors: the significance of a given volume of information is to be found in the exformation—i.e., the information that gets discarded en route; the costliness of a biological signal is to be found in the physiological effort that went into producing it; and the complexity of a physical system is measured by the amount of resources that went into its production.

In all three cases what we have to do is to probe the depths.

OUR QUOTIDIAN PROBLEM of probing whether there is any special exformation in a piece of information corresponds to the problem of sexual selection in the wild: is he a man of his word? Is there anything to his boasting? Is there depth to it?

Zahavi's handicap theory is that there are utterances that are very difficult to copy: a perfect piece of singing or an off-the-cuff joke based on something that has just happened. But others are easy to copy, because we can simply repeat what other people say, sounding cultivated and clever even though we don't understand a word of what we're saying.

These are cheap signals. Human culture is jam-packed with them. So the problem of sexual selection is how to probe to see if the signal really is costly, whether there really is depth to it.

SIMILARLY, MANY OF our social characteristics can be explained if they were evolved with a view to sexual selection. We are sweet, generous, friendly, bountiful, because these things score high when it comes to you-know-what. Being on top of things is a costly signal.

If this sounds weird, think of how we react when someone

we know suddenly seems petty, irritable, tetchy, touchy, or whining. We think: she's got a problem; something's bugging her; she's not feeling on top of things.

We know from everyday life that characteristics such as humor, energy, friendliness, and tolerance are evidence that the person evincing them has no problems in the offing. Subconsciously and indirectly, we perceive this bounciness as a manifestation of resourcefulness, indeed a surplus of energy and ability.

B UT IS THAT what we choose partners by? Why do we fall for the people we fall for? How do we choose?

In a series of major studies, the American psychologist David Buss has shown what people emphasize in their choice of partner. Buss's great achievement is the identification of a range of preferences that apply in every culture. After all, it is of limited interest to know that Danish men look for women who tolerate their watching soccer on television five nights a week.

The common denominators were simple: men want feminine beauty, and women want men with money.

This is how Buss's results are usually reported, anyhow. The feminine beauty men seek is the result of sexual selection, obviously. Breasts, butts, hips, faces, hair: all these things change radically during puberty, a clear sign that these characteristics in women are the result of sexual selection. And a number of these characteristics may be regarded as quality indicators when it comes to fertility. Broad hips and narrow waists may turn out to be associated with fertility. Big, symmetrical breasts signal fertility. So when men go for beautiful women—or in any case, women with melon-sized breasts—almost without knowing it they are going for women with good reproductive qualities.

But what about the women's choice? They want money, power, and social status. The necessities of natural selection are at stake: resources to ensure that their children can grow up in decent conditions.

Of course it takes quite a bit of effort to make a lot of money, so you might say that a high income is a kind of costly signal of an individual's quality.[23] But inherited wealth is not exactly regarded as a minus when women assess men. So some of what women go for is more influenced by the demands of natural selection than by the way sexual selection promotes men who make an effort in the cultural field.

The argument soon becomes never-ending: do women want rich men because getting rich is hard or because being rich is easy?

BUT THE MOST striking find of Buss's cross-cultural studies was another story altogether: rather than money or beauty, both sexes very much wanted partners who were intelligent and kind. This isn't so strange, because friendly people are pleasant company. But friendliness, well-being, openness, smiles and good vibes are also costly signals showing that an individual is able to rise above the basest greed and self-absorption because he or she has enough faith in himself and existence to be able to send such costly signals.

Buss's results can be reproduced in two different ways, then, and there is a reason for this, as we can see from this list of what college students from the Midwest rate most highly:[24]

THE MOST IMPORTANT
CHARACTERISTICS IN A MATE

PRIORITY	MEN PREFER	WOMEN PREFER
1	Kindness and understanding	Kindness and understanding
2	Intelligence	Intelligence
3	Physical attractiveness	Exciting personality
4	Exciting personality	Good health
5	Good health	Adaptability
6	Adaptability	Physical attractiveness
7	Creativity	Creativity
8	Desire for children	Good earning capacity
9	College graduate	College graduate
10	Good heredity	Desire for children
11	Good earning capacity	Good heredity
12	Good housekeeper	Good housekeeper
13	Religious orientation	Religious orientation

The first impression you get is that the two sexes agree to an astonishing extent on what makes a good mate. The second impression is that the choice of partner is utterly dominated by characteristics that require certain social and human wherewithal: friendliness, understanding, intelligence, personality, health, creativity, etc., are very high on the list for both sexes.

It is not until you compare the two lists that the usual picture appears, the picture we are always hearing: men think it's relatively more important that a mate is physically attractive than women do. It's third on the men's list, and sixth on the women's. Conversely, women rate earning potential (eighth on their list) higher than men do (eleventh).

So it's misleading to claim that women primarily want money while men want beauty. Both sexes primarily want friendly, sympathetic, intelligent partners with fascinating personalities. The difference is that when it comes to other characteristics, men emphasize appearance more, and women emphasize money. But neither is the most important criterion for either sex; it's merely the most important *difference* between the sexes.

David Buss is not absolved of responsibility for this very widespread misreading of his results, as he himself presents men's preoccupation with beauty and women's with money as his main result. The original presentation of his data took place in 1989 in an article titled "Sex Differences in Human Mate Choice Preferences: Evolutionary Hypotheses Tested in 37 Cultures." In the article he explains what he thinks the theory of evolution predicts men and women will want in partners. He then demonstrates that he has guessed correctly: men are more into beauty, women into money.

But the article is about the gender difference, not what people rate most highly in potential partners. This only is not apparent until twelve pages into the fourteen-page article, where Buss writes, "Neither earnings potential nor appearance emerged as the highest rated or ranked characteristics for either sex, even though these characteristics showed large sex differences. Both sexes ranked the characteristics 'kind-understanding' and 'intelligent' higher than earning power and attractiveness in all samples [i.e., in all cultures sampled]."[25]

185

In other words the result from thirty-seven cultures is the same as it is among students from the Midwest, but you have to look hard to find it.[26]

Why this confusion? Buss's presentation of the studies is heavily influenced by his expectation of what he would find. Historically speaking, sexual selection involves characteristics that differ between the two sexes (the blue drake as opposed to the brown-gray duck). This is not so strange, as gender differences are precisely what are impossible or at any rate difficult to explain by natural selection. But that does not mean it is impossible for sexual selection to produce uniform characteristics in both sexes. The model for the creation of characteristics in purely monogamous species, which was discussed in the previous chapter, does not, for example, lead to gender differences.[27]

THE CONCLUSION OF these studies of mate-choice must therefore be that on the one hand the usual version of Buss's results (that women prefer money) conflicts with the thesis of this book (that if you make an effort you will make out no matter what you make an effort on), because women want to see a particular kind of effort, namely the kind that results in money. Not all effort is equally worth the effort. But this presentation of Buss's results is misleading.

On the other hand Buss's results actually show that kindliness, intelligence, and the ability to acquire status are the characteristics men and women both emphasize most. They may very well be viewed as a result of the mechanism described above: that strong individuals find it easiest to display friendliness, energy, and sympathy and have the greatest opportunities to make an effort in their social relationships and presence in general.

But of course we cannot avoid the fact that love between men and women is not only a matter of serenades and words of praise, but very much a matter of more down-to-earth services.

Sexual selection is not only a matter of whom you choose to embark on a sexual relationship with: it is also a matter of how long it lasts. Sexual selection is not only for teenagers looking for their first kiss. All life long we have to create the trust and intercourse that provides continual reciprocity and generosity. Kindliness, openness, and an interesting personality are involved, yes, but so is human and financial security.

B UT THESE OBSERVATIONS and studies are all about what men and women *think* they want in their partners—i.e., what they consciously go for. But is what we believe about ourselves correct? Don't a number of subconscious ideals of beauty and other factors entirely, such as body odor, play a part?

It has been known for some time that smell plays a very large part in sexual selection, and that scents often even ensure that we choose mates with immune systems perfectly matched to our own, which yields a very high probability that our offspring will have good immune systems that are effective at controlling parasites.

But the most astonishing result of studies of our subconscious criteria for mate choice comes from studies of women. It turns out that their interests change as their monthly cycle progresses.

As we know, sexually mature women go through a monthly cycle of ovulation and menstruation. In the days around ovulation the chance or risk of pregnancy is great, while it is very small in the days around menstruation.

Studies have therefore been carried out to see if women emphasize the same things when they are ovulating as when they are menstruating. And they don't. Around ovulation they place more importance on masculine features that signal sound genes (a broad jaw, symmetrical features, certain body scents, etc.).[28]

This is remarkable in itself. But what about creativity and artistic talent, then? Does their value also depend on where a woman is in her cycle?

The psychologist Martie Haselton from the University of California, Los Angeles, worked with Geoffrey Miller to examine the latter's theory of creativity as courtship. They studied the choices made by a group of young women from among different types of men as they were described to them. Some men were creative and artistic, but poor. Other men had loads of dough but not much artistic talent. Whom would the young California girls prefer?

The provisional results were presented in June 2002 at the fourteenth annual meeting of the Human Behavior and Evolution Society, which was held at Rutgers University, New Jersey.[29]

Where short-term relationships were concerned there was a very clear difference as to what the women wanted. The proportion of women who preferred creative men was greater around ovulation. Among the women who preferred money to talent, most were not ovulating.

The interpretation is that during brief affairs (one night

stands or so), genes are what count. During longer relationships, or when there is no chance of conceiving, creativity does not count for as much as money or other signs that the mate might make a good long-term partner.

If these results hold true in future tests, they indicate very clearly that characteristics such as creativity and cultural skills are created through sexual selection; otherwise it would be hard to understand why the weighting of such characteristics changes during the cycle.

Studies of the menstrual cycle may well prove the key to proving the significance of sexual selection in the evolution of human culture. Another provisional study indicates that women lend a great deal of importance to a man's sense of humor: but this is when they are close to ovulation and are looking for a short-term partner. Otherwise it doesn't matter. Again the interpretation is that humor may be seen as an indicator of good genes, because being funny is difficult.[30]

If these results hold true, we'll just have to face it: men should keep the best jokes they pick up around town for when she is ovulating. . . .

IN MY VIEW, the most important thing about interpreting the human mind as the result of courtship and seduction is that it provides a direct explanation of why we are so good at reading the intentions and minds of others.

Whereas it may appear odd that having a mind arose through the intense struggle for survival by a living biology in a strange, dark universe of dead rock and extinct stars, it is not so peculiar that it arose in relation to a potential partner.

We are quite simply born "minded" and social. Biological evolution has put us into a world of relationships, opinions, meanings, interpretations, intentions, and love.

We put us there. We selected ourselves as social beings. Man selected himself. Man makes himself, as the existential philosophers say.[31] In reality, sexual selection has become self-selection. We have selected ourselves as we are. We are no longer only the result of natural selection, but just as much of self-selection.

For most people, the struggle for existence is over in our part of the world. It is not hard to feed yourself, and we only need to have a few children.

That leaves us with a huge surplus of resources, mind, and bodies evolved in order to charm the opposite sex. We have selected ourselves to live in a world bearing our own markWe have loads of talent, genius, and entertainment value. We were created to entertain each other. These days we don't have anything else to do, either.

Man is his own pet.

But will that really provide a living? The question used to be biological: can you obtain enough food for you and your next of kin? But in the modern world it is a question of economics: can we make enough money? We thus move into the world of economics again, but we will start in a different place, one that is unusual for economists: the gift economy.

10
Commodities and Gifts

THE MARKET MECHANISM
AND THE HUMAN FACE

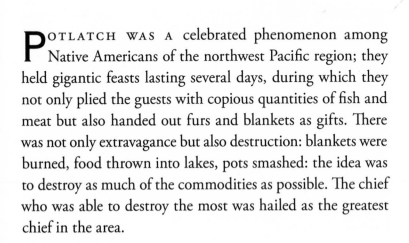

POTLATCH WAS A celebrated phenomenon among Native Americans of the northwest Pacific region; they held gigantic feasts lasting several days, during which they not only plied the guests with copious quantities of fish and meat but also handed out furs and blankets as gifts. There was not only extravagance but also destruction: blankets were burned, food thrown into lakes, pots smashed: the idea was to destroy as much of the commodities as possible. The chief who was able to destroy the most was hailed as the greatest chief in the area.

Potlatch is thus an extreme example of the extravagant consumption Thorstein Veblen described among rich, white Americans. Potlatch is just much older.

But we are unlikely ever really to find out what the original potlatches were like. The first researcher to study them was the anthropologist Franz Boas, who followed the Kwakiutl Indians in the 1890s, at a time when white men were already in full swing with the destruction of the social structure of the Native Americans of the northwest Pacific region.

But the phenomenon is genuine and to be found in many cultures. It's simply a matter of displaying strength by wasting resources: a kind of social handicap.

THE FAME OF the potlatch phenomenon is due not least to the French anthropologist Marcel Mauss, who published his celebrated work *Essai sur le don* ("The Gift")[1] in 1924, which was a watershed in the understanding of the significance of gifts in building societies not as organized as those of Western industrial nations. Mauss describes potlatch as "the purely sumptuary destruction of wealth that has been accumulated in order to outdo the rival chief as well as his associate." An extreme version of the gift economy.

Marcel Mauss found examples of less dramatic gift economies in many cultures, the Nordic among them. He starts his book with a lengthy quotation from *Hávámal,* part of the *Edda,* the Old Icelandic poems of the thirteenth century (or earlier) that comprise the nucleus of Old Nordic written culture:

42: One must be a friend   *skal maður vinur vera*
    To one's friend,   *og gjalda gjöf við gjöf.*
    And give present for present; *Hlátur við hlátri*
    One must have   *skyli höldar taka*
    Laughter for laughter   *en lausung við lygi.*
    And sorrow for lies.[2]

So reciprocity is what it's about: good for good—gifts and laughter—and less good—loose talk—with lies. Pure reciprocity. Tit-for-tat.

More surprising is the content of another of the stanzas that Mauss quotes:

47: Noble and valiant men   *Mildir, fræknir*
    Have the best life;   *menn best lifa,*
    They have no fear at all   *sjaldan sút ala.*
    But a coward fears   *En ósnjallur maður*
      everything: *uggir hotvetna:*
    The miser always fears   *Sýtir æ glöggur við gjöfum.*
      presents.[3]

What does the last line mean? The first three are obvious enough: you are best off if you are generous and brave (as Zahavi has already taught us), and being cowardly makes you fearful, of course, as we also know. But why does a miser fear presents?

Marcel Mauss's great achievement was to cast light on precisely this fact, which also explains the potlatch phenomenon: being given a gift costs you. Not in the form of money, but in the form of something quite different, for which Mauss found a term in the Maori culture. The Maori are the aboriginal population of New Zealand, who migrated from the many islands of Polynesia in the Pacific Ocean.

The term Mauss came across in Maori was *Hau*: "the spirit of the gift." *Hau* is "the spirit in things, particularly in the forest and the wild animals there."[4] Even if you give an object to somebody else as a gift, the object will still have its *hau*, which wants to go back to where it came from.

Through *hau* the giver has a hold on the recipient: the spirit wants to return. It resides in the object and means that the giver is not out of the picture. As the giver he has become part of the recipient's world because his *hau* is in the gift. The *hau* always goes along too.

So if you're given a gift by a Maori you have a problem: you also get his *hau*. How can you get rid of it again? By giving him a gift in return. "*Hau* is the force," the American anthropologist Marshall Sahlins writes, "which explains why gifts are repaid."[5]

When you give a gift you also equip it with a spirit that wants to return. This enables many aboriginal cultures to regulate their economies via the exchange of gifts, in which a variation of *hau* ensures that you give something back at some stage.

And even more important: when you have given a gift to somebody, with *hau* and all, you establish a relationship to the giver. A bond has been formed, a connection. Gifts give relationships.

It is this connection, this non-anonymity, which the miser fears. And you don't need to be Old Norse to feel this way.

"I'd rather go Dutch," we say when we can tell that the guy who has asked us to lunch wants to have some control of what you write about him and his company or his research.

The radical difference between gifts and commodities is that when we exchange gifts we have a handle on each other; when we sell commodities to one another we pay what they cost and we're in the clear. In principle we're done with each other (this time round).

With gifts something sticks. It was put most beautifully by the Norwegian social anthropologist Thomas Hylland Eriksen: "Even in our society, in which gift exchange is far less important than in almost every traditional society, if we look we find traces of the *hau* of things. In most Norwegian families giving money for Christmas is regarded as an emergency solution. (. . .) If usefulness had been the only relevant aspect, nobody would have questioned money as Christmas presents. Naturally, getting rid of items one has received as Christmas presents is morally problematical. Even the most hideous vases and ghastliest neckties are kept for a long time before their *hau* finally seeps out of them and we are at last able to give them to the boy scouts' flea market."[6]

In our modern society of abundance, in which the exchange of Christmas gifts is a meaningless ritual because we really only buy things on one another's behalf, we still sense the power these gifts possess. We incur misfortunes if we "re-gift" something and pass it along. The gift is a costly signal that we want a relationship.

Gifts build relationships. In societies without market economies, gifts build society.

BUT IN THAT case is a gift a gift, or is it just a disguised kind of exchange? Does the giver expect his gift to be reciprocated at a later date?

In traditional societies gift-giving is the very backbone of the structure of society; it establishes the institutions, morals, and relationships of that society. The French anthropologist Clause Lévi-Strauss, who carried on and developed Mauss's work, emphasized that the moral commitments we make when we take part in the exchange of gifts creates the very foundations of society. "*Hau* is not the ultimate explanation for exchange; it is the conscious form whereby men of a given society, in which the problem had particular importance, apprehended an unconscious necessity whose explanation lies elsewhere."[7] This unconscious necessity is the very structure of society. The gift is a means of creating society. The spirit of the gift becomes the soul of society.

In such societies, gifts are very definitely something you reciprocate. The *hau* of the gift ensures that you dare not do otherwise.

So we may ask whether gifts are gifts at all. Aren't they just a kind of advanced barter?

This is a question quite analogous to the difference between reciprocity and generosity. Reciprocal altruism, after all, is just an exchange of helping hands. Real generosity is not evinced in the expectation of getting something back (but in the hope that *she* will see it and yield). Is gift-giving reciprocity or generosity?

Are gifts gifts, or things we swap? The French philosopher Jacques Derrida pointed out that gifts are an impossibility.[8]

Because if a gift is a gift you have to return in kind, it is not a gift, but the commencement of an exchange. And if it's not a gift, but just free of charge, it's not a gift either.

The French sociologist Pierre Bourdieu tried to solve the problem by pointing at the time factor: "Mauss described gift exchange as a discontinuous series of generous acts. Lévi-Strauss defined it as a reciprocity structure that transcends the individual acts of exchange, and where the gift refers to the gift that is given in return. I pointed out that what was missing from both these analyses was an awareness of the decisive role the interval between gift and counter-gift plays. Neither of the analyses deals with the fact that there is an unwritten rule in practically any society that you do not immediately return what you have been given, which would be the same as a rejection," Bourdieu writes. "The function of the interval was to shield the gift and counter-gift from each other, and to give two thoroughly symmetrical acts the opportunity to appear as unique acts with no link to each other."[9]

At Christmas perhaps we swap like with like (but we are most embarrassed if we give each other exactly the same thing); apart from that, we carefully pretend that any gift is a one-off. You get gifts on your birthday, I get them on mine.

But our Old Norse misers had good reason to dread gifts: they build up a society round his ears and this creates a tacit expectation that at some stage, but not too soon, he will give something back.

Gifts mean we have a hold on one another. We enter into relationships with one another. We owe each other something—in other words, we share a future. We bind each other together.

THIS IS VERY different from the market economy we are used to, in which the commodity is the central means of exchange. Exchanging commodities means a very different notion: namely anonymity. It doesn't matter who you are as long as you pay what it costs. And the price is the same whoever you are.

We are indignant if anyone obtains something for a favorable price just because he or she has the right business or political connections, or is related to the right people. We regard it as corruption or nepotism. And we shrug our shoulders when we meet sidewalk vendors in southern climes who shout, "Special price for you only!" as we pass them by.

The exchange of commodities is anonymous; it is a completed act, and afterward we don't owe each other anything (apart from what it says in the guarantee). So you cannot build relations between people or build society on the basis of the pure exchange of commodities. The exchange of commodities means that in principle people don't know each other apart from the way they act in the marketplace.

E-commerce is the ultimate anonymous act; in it, only the postman can have any sense at all of what we buy and what the parcel conceals. The rest is computers and warehouse employees on other continents who don't even know you exist. Similarly, modern supermarkets are experimenting with ways of getting customers to scan the prices of the commodities they buy as they leave the store. This creates a comfortable anonymity where nobody knows the trashy freeze-dried fast-food product you (only now and then of course) sneak into your shopping bag.

Actually, e-commerce and self-scanning at the supermarket are less anonymous than you'd think. Even though you don't have to look anyone in the face you're quite thoroughly scrutinized. Because every transaction is recorded electronically, the store manager can register your purchasing patterns and offer you special deals accordingly. A new kind of non-anonymity is emerging via digitized trade, where we are recognized not by our faces but by our digital identity. Our biological mechanisms for telling whether we are under surveillance have been rendered null and void. Anonymity is an illusion. We have a relationship with our shopkeepers . . . but it is digital.

Even so, anonymity has become a comfort to modern man, who would rather not owe anyone anything. How embarrassed we are by the voluble greengrocer who asks what we want those tomatoes for (embarrassed, even though it's actually highly relevant if he's to select the kind of tomatoes we need!).

B UT IT RAISES a very fundamental problem: if the reciprocity of gift-giving creates networks of relationships that grow into a society, how do relationships and societies emerge in a modern market economy where everyone hides behind the anonymity we may dub *the market mask*?

If hyper-automated modern commerce on the web and in stores using hand scanners permits the total absence of interaction, how can society continue to exist at all? And what will become of all the reciprocity, generosity, and helpfulness if nobody knows whom they're dealing with?

We can even go a step further and ask: if the market economy can't create society, and yet we very obviously live in one, are we actually living in a disguised gift economy that we know as little about as the Maoris know about their social structure disguised as *hau*?

KARL POLANYI WAS one of the leading theoreticians of the twentieth century in the history of economics. His principle work, *The Great Transformation* (1944), describes the way man administered his material supplies in the past and how the huge transformation of industrialization created the industrial market mechanisms we live in to this day.

But the springboard is the gift economies, in which the necessities of life are distributed without the use of a market. All exchanges take place concretely between a sender and a receiver, who exchange reciprocally: such societies are characterized by reciprocity.

The next phase in the development Polanyi describes is a society characterized by redistribution, where commodities are assembled in a central pool and then redistributed into society. This may involve a chief, a priesthood, or, in our day, a state. The distribution of commodities is no longer through direct exchange from man to man, but via superior regulation.

Finally, the economy of the marketplace emerges, in which products become commodities to be exchanged with one another in terms of their price in money. "The most startling peculiarity of the system lies in the fact that, once it is established, it must be allowed to function without outside interference" Polanyi writes.[10] The market has to regulate itself.

This is radically different from the situation of distribution based on reciprocity and redistribution. When reciprocity is involved, the exchange of commodities is part of a social, cultural, and familial context from which they cannot be isolated. The exchange is based on and underpins other sides of society. Similarly, redistribution reinforces the structures of society, as long as it is perceived as legitimate and fair.

But the market ignores everything around it. The individual transaction does not define itself, either. The market assumes the same function as the concept of a field has in physics. In physics we can study how two particles or two planets directly interact with each other. But in practice it makes it much simpler if we see how the planets create a gravity field together, which affects each of them. We sum up a whole bunch of individual interactions between planets or electrons in the idea of a gravity field or an electrical field. Then we can take each particle or planet and look at how it interacts with the field. When we want to plot the course of a spaceship on its way to the moon we don't think about the fact that the spaceship has a gravity interaction with the earth, the sun, and the moon. Instead we think about the field of gravity in which the spaceship will be moving.

Similarly, the economic theory of markets and prices is based on the notion of a field, the market prices, with which the individual commodities and consumers interact.[11] We don't think about the fact that a farmer has bred a cow that gives a bit of milk that is sold via the dairy to the supermarket and then to me, who pays for it. The farmer thinks about the market; the dairyman, the shopkeeper, and the consumer think about the market. The price, which is the amount of money we have to pay for the commodity, is a property of the commodity in the marketplace, not of the buyer or seller.

In a market society the rest of society is present in the exchange of commodities, yes, but this is manifest in only one way: namely the price.

On the face of it this may seem a strange claim. I once worked with a young economics student who had a part-time job as a foreign-exchange dealer at a bank. When I asked him out of politeness how the dollar and the Swiss Franc were doing or whatever else I could come up with in my extreme ignorance of foreign-exchange rates, I received a protracted, expert response with loads of stuff about what was going on in the Soviet Union at the time and confidence in the politicians in Brussels. Slowly it dawned on me that foreign-exchange dealers inhabit the same universe as the rest of us. They keep just as much abreast of the arts, the state of society, and environmental problems, because when push comes to shove these are what determine the worth of a national currency. If Argentina loses an international soccer match, this affects its already nose-diving currency.

A foreign-exchange dealer is interested in precisely the same world as I, but sees it through an extremely narrow slit: the exchange rates. All that information about Russian peasants, German metal workers, Japanese robots, and the success of grass-root movements in combating environmental crime is boiled down into a single figure: how many dollars can you get for a hundred-kroner note?

The price of foreign currency, other countries' money, reflects the global situation, expressed in a single figure, purged of anything else.

The market is a gigantic abstraction, a looking-away-from, a reduction, a purification. Where reciprocity and redistribution involve all kinds of traditions, friendships, family ties, royal caprices, and papal bulls, the market is pure and anonymous. There is no kin selection here. External factors play a part but only by affecting the price, roughly like an invisible planet that hurtles through the solar system and disturbs our gravity field a tad.

IN HIS MAJOR work, *Das Kapital,* Karl Marx provided an analysis of commodities that is still very informative (whatever else you may think of Karl Marx's political theories).

The starting point is that people need products made by other people (unless they are totally self-sufficient). A product has a specific use-value to you because you can eat it or use it to hammer nails. But when you want to sell your product in the marketplace you look at another aspect of the product, its exchange-value. This expresses how much the product is worth compared to other products: you give me six chairs and I'll give you an oak table.

This exchange-value is more abstract and peculiar than its use-value, which is immediate and specific. It is a property of the product as a commodity and not of the product itself. It is only in the specific context of other products in the market that it possesses an exchange-value.

Instead of saying "two pigs for thirty chickens," a common measure of exchange-value is introduced: money. Money originates from products with their own use-value and is therefore able to serve as a kind of universal use-value. Gold is good as an intermediary, for example, because it's a product with a universally accepted use-value as the raw material for jewelry but is also imperishable and rare.

Gold serves as the commodity we exchange all other commodities for: we sell our pair of pigs for eight gold coins, which we may then use to buy thirty chickens. The price is the expression of how much gold we can exchange our commodity for. In practice gold is represented by a symbol: paper money, for example. But the players in the market are confident that the symbol is good and in principle can be converted into gold.

By introducing money, people avoid having to stand around comparing one another's products and their value: "Are my two pigs as valuable as your thirty chickens?" Both parties can consult a price list that shows what their products are worth. And they can buy and sell without ever talking to or meeting each other. The money is the intermediary.

Commodities exchange is about prices and concealing other factors. This way society "hides" in the price, which is of course determined by technological progress, consumer power, the harvest in Central Asia, fashion, the weather, fortunes of war, and all kinds of other things that are not present in the marketplace but are nevertheless expressed in the price.

So Karl Marx talked about commodity fetishism: that the commodity is like a totem pole or other tangible object in so-called primitive cultures, to which spiritual characteristics are ascribed. People think that gold itself possesses the properties revealed by the strange moments of the money market. Via its price the commodity contains a reference to the state of society as a whole.

The point of Marx's analysis is to point out that on the one hand the commodity appears as an object with a price, in isolation from everything else, but in reality, part of society is expressed in the price. Similarly, commodity exchange, trading in the market, is really a social act but merely looks as if it is little old me scanning a tube of toothpaste that has nothing to do with anyone else. If I think a bit I can see that the price reflects the conditions for producing titanium dioxide coloring, labor conditions at the toothpaste plant, and the pricing policy of my supermarket chain, but I usually just see it as a tube with a price tag; indeed, nowadays even the price tag is a row of lines in a bar code that only my scanner understands.

The market is apparently isolated from the world about it. I don't appear to be trading with people but with things and bar codes. The portraits of the dead political leaders on my cash is about as close as I can get to another human.

There are no conscious agents picking up each other's tricks like in game theory. Just me and a field of prices that I need to tune to my needs.

The market mechanism has absolutely obvious advantages: all the strange considerations you would otherwise have to pay to your cousins and to the fact that you refuse to trade with redheads and you can't stand that guy Walter simply evaporate. There is no sentimentality, no consideration. It is a cold, clear, anonymous mechanism that causes commodities to be moved around society so that whoever will pay most for them gets them.

We may say that we put on masks of anonymity when we go to market, market masks that make us forget any sentimental considerations and look solely at price formation.

It's important to remember that many of the characteristics of man that the market mask is meant to conceal are fruits of natural selection: nepotism, for example, is a consequence of kin selection. So it's not the case that there exists a rational, cold *Homo economicus* born unintegrated through natural selection, because this would promote nepotism and other intrusions into the free play of the market forces. We have to don our market masks to hide our humanity as developed both through the nepotism of natural selection and the generosity and altruism of sexual selection. We pretend we're indifferent to one another. We play a game, a role as *Homo economicus,* which we actually believe in to such an extent that we are surprised when experimental economics shows that we don't always react as coolly as we'd expect from the description of our role.

We put on our market masks and ignore any feelings or considerations. But only to a certain point. We don't pursue our own interests right to the line. The ultimatum game shows that we're willing to punish ourselves in order to punish others whom we think have acted unfairly.

As the economist Robert Frank points out, we have feelings for one another: feelings that prioritize relationships and solidarity more than narrow self-interest; emotions that bind us in cooperation and prevent us from plundering one another mindlessly in ways that may yield short-term gains but leave us worse off in the long run. We do not act as our selfish reason dictates. We have human faces we don't want to hide.

We can't keep our masks on.

KARL POLANYI DREW attention to the fact that the market economy can only exist because the market is always embedded in a society. "Embeddedness" is a term he probably derived from geology,[12] which describes the way coal deposits are embedded in less interesting strata. The term describes the way the market is always part of a society, embedded into its other activities. The market may appear to be a self-regulating entity, but without courts of law to lock up anyone who uses counterfeit money, without police to catch thieves, without environment regulators to ensure that there are still natural resources to make money from tomorrow, without the tacit rules of society that ensure that market operations can take place, the market will not work.

The market always requires the existence of confidence in society, the will to cooperate on fair exchange: a kind of Highway Code for commodity transactions.

You can have societies without markets. But you can't have markets without societies.

THE PROBLEM IS then that where societies can create markets, markets have a much harder time creating societies, precisely because commodity exchange is anonymous and does not involve the building up of networks and relationships the way gift-giving does, for example. The same anonymity that grants the markets their efficiency also means that they lack the ability to create their own reason for existence, a society around them.

We must therefore ask what it is that enables societies to hang together, and for there to be enough trust and cooperativeness for the market to work.

One answer may be the gift. To a much greater extent than we think, we still live in a gift economy. The market is a game we play, a masquerade.

IF WE COMPARE gifts and commodities as methods of distributing goods in a society, we get this picture:

GIFT	COMMODITY
Personal	Impersonal
Hau	Terminal action
Relationship	Anonymity
Face	Mask
Network	Market
Sharing	Owning
Giving	Having
Superfluity	Scarcity
Redundancy	Necessity

How much of our everyday lives is really characterized by what we see in the right-hand column? Quite a bit, of course; or maybe not.

Whenever we say to each other, "Oh, thank you so much, you really shouldn't have . . ." we enter into the state of gift recipient. We've received something we weren't entitled to or had no right to expect: a big surprise or a small one that makes us happy. It may be an object, in which case it really is a gift, or a favor. In either case what is involved is superfluity, "unnecessariness," a giveaway; redundancy,[13] to use a fine word for it; more than was necessary; something that was not necessary.

There are huge swaths of society that are quite outside the anonymous market of the commodity economy: first and foremost our personal, family lives, where we don't sell meals for money, after all! Perhaps we do expect somebody other than the cook to clear the table afterward, but apart from teenagers we don't operate with payments for household chores. Within our households pure reciprocal economics or gift economics prevail.

Friends, neighbors, relations at work: these are other areas where there is no market, but personal relationships, the exchange of favors, and helpfulness.

Network is now a buzzword in business: people want good networks. Business magazines describe top executives' personal networks of business pals. But network is only another word for relationships that are not due to the market but to reciprocity.

The black market is prevalent in societies like Denmark. It is not only a matter of punitive income taxes and the fact that many services are taxed. It's also a matter of networks, of neighbors helping one another, of the relationships that subsequently develop.

Colleagues who help one another even when they are employed by different companies are no rarity.

Shopkeepers help by giving you bits of advice without any payment. They build up confidence, customer relations, image, or brand.

Corporations invest a great deal of money in their brands; it's a kind of marketing but also a kind of relationship with the customer.

Christmas presents, chocolates left when you pay polite visits, postcards, flowers for the hostess: there are loads of quotidian gift-giving.

The British anthropologist John Davis has tried to show that reciprocity and gift-giving are not restricted to traditional societies, that the market does not absolutely prevail in western industrial nations. In rich countries, too, the market is embedded into a wider economy, he argues. He has tried to put a figure on how much of the economy has to do with gifts, and arrived at a figure of around 4 percent.[14]

But the economic importance of gifts only comprises a tiny proportion of their importance in our lives. When we act helpfully, lend a hand, or offer a cougher a lozenge, it's not money that is involved.

It's actually impossible to calculate how much of the economy has to do with gift-giving. The British anthropologist Mary Douglas wrote in the foreword of the American edition of *The Gift* by Mauss, "I myself have made an attempt to apply the theory of the gift to our consumption behavior, arguing that it is much more about giving than the economists realize." But she soon gives up: "Much of the kind of information I needed about what happens in our society was missing from census and survey records."[15]

Economic statistics are all designed to record economic activity in the market, and not reciprocal exchanges between citizens. So they cannot tell us how much of our lives relies on these reciprocal exchanges, anthropologists such as Douglas conclude.

So I PRICKED up my ears even more than usual when the Dutch economist Wilfred Dolfsma declared during a lecture at a conference in the Netherlands on the Internet and economic value among other things, that the UNDP (United Nations Development Programme) had shown that "half of everything that is produced is gifts."

Dolfsma's source turned out to be the 1995 edition of the UNDP's annual Human Development Report.[16] The report tries to calculate the value of women's work in order to determine how much of the work in the world is done by women compared to men. But the problem, of course, is that the bulk of women's work does not involve production for a market. They don't receive wages and they don't sell anything; they do household, chores which don't appear in systems of national accounts (SNA). So the UNDP did two things in order to get an idea of the importance of the women's contribution.

Production in society can be calculated even if it isn't work included in a market economy and measured by wages and sales revenues. The UNDP defines work as anything somebody else could do for you. That is to say: brushing your teeth in the morning is not work and never can be (even though brushing your children's teeth may be work). Sleep and eating meals cannot be done by anybody else, and so they cannot be defined as work, either. But preparing meals can be work, the same way it is for chefs and cooks. Childcare, cleaning, shopping, house maintenance, gardening, and so forth are all activities we can buy our way out of. So they are defined by the UNDP as productive activities. These productive activities can be divided into those that are market-oriented and thus included in the economists' statistics and those that are kept outside the marketplace. The point is, of course, that the latter can be paid work but happens not to be. (The UNDP quotes the pioneer of welfare economics, Arthur Cecil Pigou, who explained at the start of the twentieth century that the national income falls every time a bachelor marries his housekeeper.[17])

If working hours are calculated this way, the result is that women supply 51 percent of the work in industrialized countries, while men are responsible for 49 percent. In developing countries the division is a little more pronounced: women supply 53 percent to men's 47 percent.

But the really big difference consists of the proportion of each gender's contribution included in the market economy. Of men's working hours, two thirds are spent on market economic activities, that is, "work" in the traditional sense, with wages and commodity sales. A third of their contribution goes into activities that are not market economic, such as work in the home or the community. In the case of women the exact reverse is true: they spend two thirds of their working hours outside the market economy, and only a third inside it. These figures apply to the industrialized countries: in developing countries no less than three quarters of the men's activities are market economic.

"As a result," the UNDP writes, "men receive the lion's share of income and recognition in society for their economic contribution."[18] The men get all the money, because they put their efforts where there is money involved. (Of the countries surveyed, this discrepancy in the SNA component of work between the sexes was smallest in Denmark, where men only account for 58 percent of work in the market.[19]) Incidentally, the figures show that working hours have fallen over time and become more uniformly divided between the sexes, most likely because women are working less in the home.

The other measure of the importance of non-SNA activities for society that the value of this work equals if not exceeds SNA work: "Clearly, the value of non-SNA production in industrial countries is considerable, whatever the standard. It is at least half of gross domestic product, and it accounts for more than half of private consumption."[20]

So we have suddenly been given a figure for how much of industrial society's production is not included in the market economy: half of it. Non-commodity-production is half of all production. Or, as Wilfred Dolfsma put it, half of all production is gifts.

Half! We live in a market economy yet it only accounts for half of what we consume. In other words, the market economy is highly overrated.

We could claim with equal justification that we live in a gift economy with a market economy embedded in it: the latter allows men to earn money with which to impress women.

213

IT'S PRETTY CLEAR that our lives would not be much fun or particularly efficient if *everything* was subject to the market. This is not intended as a political statement for or against the market. It is a statement of fact.

Perhaps precisely because the market today is the object of general acceptance and popularity right across the political spectrum in almost every country in the world, it has become possible to spot the fact that it is an illusion to believe that everything is "market."

We may choose between two starting points in order to understand society. One is that in reality we are all *Homo economicuses,* selfishly and anonymously pursuing our own interests but now and then giving in to a spot of self-indulgence. The other is that in reality we are generous, sharing creatures who have realized that it is a mighty fine idea to use the market in a mask, because we thereby increase the volume of wealth for ourselves and others. But we can't stand wearing our masks the whole time. We want to get home from work, take off our jackets, and play with the kids.

The market is a great activity to have running as long as we don't mistake it for society. And as long as we don't insist that it has to be capable of everything.

Experimental economics shows that beneath the mask a living creature is hiding who finds it hard to suppress his feelings.

THE MOST CELEBRATED example in the history of economics and social philosophy of the notion that self-interest ultimately leads to benefits for everyone came from the Scottish economist Adam Smith, who published the idea of *the invisible hand* in 1776.

His idea was that if everyone pursues self-interest, an invisible, almost divine hand will ensure that everybody gains nevertheless. The market will make everyone work in everybody's interest by pursing self-interest. But against the background of experimental economics and the importance of relationships created by the gift economy, perhaps we should consider a new version of Adam Smith's invisible hand: the invisible hand consists of the fact that humans look each other in the face.

"**B**UT SOCIAL INTERACTIONS, even in economics, are not restricted to impersonal market contexts," the economist and game theoretician Herbert Gintis writes.[21]

The health sector is a good example. On the one hand it is an important, expensive part of the economy of modern society. On the other its product is primarily the care and relief of sick people (it does happen, though not so often as the doctors preach, that medical science actually cures them, too). Care and human contact are supplied not via market economic mechanisms but by inter-human mechanisms: what is involved is relationships, generosity, and attentiveness.

The Norwegian nurse Kari Martinsen, who is a professor of nursing science at the University of Tromsø, described the purpose of nursing as "promoting the sufferer's love of life."[22] To give another human more love of life, you must give him a care and attention devoid of ulterior motives.

Kari Martinsen applies the idea of Danish theologian and

philosopher K. E. Løgstrup that "man must only give in order to give—and not for any other reason," and that morality is a service rendered with no ulterior motive.[23]

Good nursing, then, is generosity incarnate: the abundance that due to the very nature of its abundance helps another human to win back his love of life and thereby the desire to heal himself (with a little help).

JOBS LIKE NURSING, teaching, and the priesthood are traditionally characterized by *the call*: you help others because you have been called, often in the form of a divine revelation that you have a job to do in life. The idea of a call is of course terribly old-fashioned and is met with skepticism by employers and trade unions alike, which are constantly arguing about pay and conditions. But in practice it's very difficult to use contract work to regulate jobs that are all about care and tenderness toward other humans. If you do, the result is very likely to be that your nursery staff or health care operatives insist on their coffee break whether the kids are yelling or not.

The market, including contract work, is a rigid, anonymous way of regulating people's working hours. This is clearly revealed whenever it involves other people. In reality a not inconsiderable portion of the proudest results of the Danish welfare state—health and education—has been loused up by over-administration that treats everything as contract work (employers and trade unions are both to blame here). Nurses, teachers, and other heroes of everyday life are entitled to decent wages; of course they are. But this only covers a very small portion of reality. The bulk of the activities in these professions involves relationships between humans, where the vital thing is that you give without wanting anything in return as a pure and unadulterated *simplicity,* as Løgstrup put it: "Giving in the creative, simple sense, where not only the gift, but also the good deed of giving the gift is given to the other person."[24]

But not many hospital executives listen to that kind of theological philosophizing.

INCIDENTALLY, IT IS remarkable that the female professions about whom men most often have sexual fantasies are precisely those involving nurses, airline stewardesses, and other generous creatures in uniform. We have known this for ages; however, the explanation is perhaps not the mystique of the uniform but rather the mechanism for sexual selection that tells us that other people's generosity is enticing.

It's also remarkable that these same professions, particularly that of airline steward, were among the first to become the objects of experiments by behavioral scientists to find out how to create satisfied customers by teaching personnel about artificial smiles and other cheap signals.[25]

BUT ARE GIFTS reciprocity or generosity, then? They're both. To a great extent in traditional societies, gift-giving forms the foundations of society, and the existence of *hau* ensures that gifts are reciprocated. But at the same time gifts are used as status providers in potlatch and in other cases where resources are conspicuously wasted.

This is the equivalent of the commodities of the market

economy that are used for meeting genuine, incontrovertible needs for food, clothing, housing, and the like, but are also used for luxury, boasting, and bragging, the way Veblen described.

There is a big difference whether it is commodities or gifts that drive the pumps. Vital activities in modern society in addition to those we have already mentioned are poorly served by being turned into objects in the market economy.

11
Creativity

BEING GIVEN AN EXPERIENCE

"A WORK OF art is a gift, not a commodity," the American essayist Lewis Hyde wrote in *The Gift,* his perspective-rich book published in 1979. "Or, to state the modern case with more precision, works of art exist simultaneously in two 'economies,' a market economy and a gift economy. Only one of these is essential, however: a work of art can survive without the market, but where there is no gift there is no art."[1]

Lewis Hyde describes the gift as something we receive free of charge; something we obtain with no effort. And the point is that the artist and the audience both receive something. We describe talent and inspiration as gifts; indeed, we say people are "gifted" when they are bursting with talent and ability. Artists describe the way they get their ideas as a kind of revelation: gifts from outside.

The Beatles song "Yesterday" is one example of the kind of giveaway in which the artist simply registers a completely finished work. Paul McCartney, who wrote the tune, says "I had a piano beside my bed and I . . . must have dreamed it, because I tumbled out of bed, put my hands on a few different chords while I had the tune in my head. It was all there, a complete song. I could hardly believe it."[2] Of course not all songs come about like that, and they are not necessarily of the same quality, either. But "Yesterday" is perceived as a gift by the listener, to remain in Hyde's analysis. It is not only the composer but also the listener who feels he is being given something for free, a mood, a way of looking at his emotions that he didn't have before, a vent for the painfully sentimental feeling that he has thrown it all away.

"That art that matters to us—which moves the heart, or revives the soul, or delights the senses, or offers courage for living, however we choose to describe the experience—that work is received by us as a gift is received," Hyde writes.[3] He describes the way a familiar landscape suddenly assumes new colors because we've been to an art exhibition, or, how music lends us new ears.

Great art is a gift. But more than that. After all, we have to pay.

"I do not maintain that art cannot be bought and sold; I do maintain that the gift portion of the work places a constraint upon our merchandising," Hyde writes.[4] He thereby announces a major theme not only of our own times but probably, for reasons we will examine shortly, of the future, too.

THERE ARE GOOD reasons that products like works of art and other fruits of creative processes seem like gifts. Characteristic of the human organism, particularly its central nervous system, is that it processes enormous amounts of information: both because lots of information enters via the senses and leaves via body movements (including speaking and singling), but also internally, in the brain, quite astronomical quantities of information are constantly being processed. An incredibly small proportion of this information flow is accessible to our conscious control of our bodies and our thoughts. We are unaware of most of what goes on inside us and between us and the people around us.

We can put a figure to it and show that a million times more bits—the unit for measuring information—enter and leave us than we realize. And a million billion more bits are processed in our minds than we realize.

So we cannot be aware of what we do or what sparks us into action, particularly if these are things that draw on many of the resources of our brain. When we synthesize a wealth of experience and many years of intense digestive effort to understand something or other, it's quite obvious that we cannot possibly be aware of what is going on; there are so many bits in circulation that it cannot be something of which we have sufficient time to gain awareness.

After I had presented this information-theory analysis of man's mental abilities in *The User Illusion*,[5] the Danish philosopher and writer Villy Sørensen remarked that this was of course something that the Danish language already knew about. In Danish we say "Jeg har fået en god idé"—"I've gotten a good idea." The natural question is, "And whom did you get it from?"

According to your temperament you may answer "divine inspiration," a dream, or the unconscious Me. The fact is that you acknowledge that you did not create the idea yourself: it was given to you. In this context "you" is the same as your conscious, active, decisive I.

The genuflection to something greater than you that is implicit in your acceptance of having been given something beyond your conscious control is a property of creative work that is described universally—and, as Hyde points out, also of its reception.

Revelations.

MIHALY CSIKSZENTMIHALYI IS a good example of the Handicap principle, for the same reason as the principle itself: despite a name that is unusually difficult to read and even more difficult to pronounce (he says it should be pronounced "chick-SENT-me-high"[6]), the Hungarian-born American psychologist has won a huge audience for his theory of flow, which he published in the book of the same name in 1990.[7]

The idea is that when you do something you are especially good at, particularly if it is creative, you enter into a state where everything else is excluded, time seems suspended, and the work process just flows in an even stream. Subjectively speaking, this state of flow is very pleasant, and objectively speaking it is highly productive. Flow is familiar from lots of occupations and hobbies: researchers, philosophers, artists, athletes, and all kinds of people are familiar with the state, which characterizes our happiest, most satisfying moments. To use the language of *The User Illusion,* these are the sublime moments in which we're unconscious of what we're doing and simply do it.

But it's characteristic of the state of flow that we don't submit to control by the conscious will as we do in many other life situations. We are brave enough to stop monitoring ourselves, precisely because we are well prepared and trained. We may say that flow is experienced as a kind of reward for immersing ourselves in creative work (which of course also means depriving ourselves of much ordinary social traffic). Similarly, as users of the products that emerge from an artist's flow we may feel that very same state of flow; for example, we completely forget time and place as we immerse ourselves in a good book or an engrossing movie. (It's in the bad books and bad movies that we're always aware of how much time has been spent on the experience—and how much time is still left to go—sorry!)

CREATIVE WORK IS best when it's carried out in the flow state. But that also means that it cannot be controlled via a deliberate act of will. For that very reason the result is a gift we simply receive and say thank-you for. An important part of such work is learning how to have the courage to let go and let the process flow: you can edit and select afterward, but in the meantime you must remain open and accept what comes.

It's about having the courage to accept gifts. With all that

that implies. Sometimes, after all, it means learning something about yourself that you didn't know before. And sometimes you even show it to other people who are looking at your work or watching you perform. In improvised performance—theater, music, lectures, etc.—the problem is very pronounced, because you reveal your inner self to an audience in a way you cannot control.[8]

The same goes for the audience: having the courage to receive is difficult. Movies, theater, music, books, dancing: they arouse feelings in us that we may not have known and would prefer not to know. We can say afterward that we thought the work was lousy, but sometimes, without knowing, what we really mean is that we discovered a lousy trait in our personality.[9]

WHEN WE MAKE an effort to create or do what we think will win the favor of our one and only, we're in the flow, unconscious of what we're doing. When we come to present what we've created or done to our one and only, we're nervous and shy, and only all too aware of ourselves.[10]

THE PROBLEM FOR the performer and the audience is postponing judgment: postponing the time when we judge what is being created or experienced for as long as possible. As soon as we begin to judge, to be aware of, to put into words, to categorize, we have already lost part of the experience.

But it's extremely hard not to judge. A very large part of training in creative work consists precisely of having the courage to refrain from judgment, from seeing things through an imaginary eye from without ("I wonder what they'll think about what I'm writing?").

Not that we should never assess things from the outside, through other people's eyes, but it must wait till afterward, when we edit the copy or work. Until then we must simply remain open and take whatever comes by way of gifts, *hau* and all.

The designer Jacob Jensen, celebrated all over the world for his Margrethe bowl, Bang & Olufsen stereos and many other unique pieces of industrial design, has described how he assesses a cardboard model of a potential product that he has made during his working day: "In practice, what happens is that I put the model I want to judge onto a table, put a spotlight on it, and leave. The next day I step into the room, look at the item for five or seven seconds, and write down what I see: for example, 'too dull,' 'sloppy proportions,' 'too tall,' 'needs to float more,' 'illogical,' or 'not surprising enough.' The important thing is that I only look at the thing for a few seconds. Otherwise I compensate: 'It's not *that* dull,' or 'Tall, yes, but not very,' etc. I stick to whatever I write down, and then I start making changes. A new model, the light, five more seconds the next morning, the same business all over again. And again. And again. Laborious? Yes, but I know no other way."[11]

So Jacob Jensen is able to postpone his verdict for five to seven seconds. Then consciousness and considerateness begin to interfere. Honesty stops. The impression is no longer something you're given, but something you form. And then it's too late.

A N INDUSTRIAL DESIGN can be created through a creative gift of charity. And it can be perceived as a gift of beauty.

But it's also a commodity, which has a price. What is the relationship between these two aspects of an industrial design?

This question has a precursor in the question of the relationship between science and industry. Over the centuries science has enjoyed huge success and laid the foundations of colossal economic growth. But it's not governed by the same laws as the economy that builds on it.

TRADITIONALLY SCIENCE IS organized as gift economy. For years, the sociology of science, which studies behavior in the scientific community and relationships between scientists, has compared the scientific community with the gift economy of traditional societies. This is because scientists don't buy and sell their results, but give them away to their colleagues as a contribution. In return for a contribution of original knowledge the scientist receives the acknowledgement and respect of his colleagues. This acknowledgement can be converted into permanent tenure, good research conditions, fine prizes and medals, etc.

It was the science sociologist Warren Hagstrom who pointed out most clearly that science is organized like a gift economy; that was in the mid sixties.

A crucial characteristic of a gift economy is that in it you cannot buy your way to commodities, precisely because it is a gift economy and does not operate with money as a measure of value.[12] You can't buy an ingenious new idea or acknowledgement by your colleagues. The scientific community's insistence on keeping money out of it (apart from salaries) is a major explanation of this community's ability to operate autonomously in society and to challenge authority.

It's no accident that many of the founders of modern science, such as Charles Darwin for example, were wealthy individuals who were able to enjoy the independence that made great discoveries possible. The economist Thorstein Veblen described science as an idle curiosity, which he compared to the games animals and humans play, particularly young animals and young humans.[13]

Science, understood here as basic research, is very strongly characterized by its lack of a single purpose. Its practitioners try to understand things, to explore them, because these things arouse their curiosity or because not having a handle on the organization of living nature—or whatever it is—bugs them.

So science is an activity of plenty, a fruit of curiosity, play, and seeking—a kind of intellectual generosity, a display of effort-making. From a narrow, shortsighted, economic point of view science is waste: a handicap only wealthy individuals or societies can afford to assume. Like the arts, science is an expression of life that announces the presence of gifted individuals: in other words, an attractive choice of mate.

A scientist gives the scientific community his newfound knowledge, receives his peers' acknowledgement and their desire to be part of his game. The most reliable way of finding out what the others are up to is to make a contribution. If you contribute something important the others will feel like telling you what they've figured out.

If you have something to offer you'll make playmates. Make an effort and you'll make out: though in this case you'll mainly make science, not love.

BUT WHETHER PLAY and curiosity are the motivators or not, the achievements of science have proven almost shockingly effective where more practical matters are concerned. The original unfettered quest for knowledge is increasingly giving way to the well organized, deliberate pursuit of particular ends or solutions. This is known as applied science.

As science has continued to grow dramatically in size— perhaps society has realized that it's a source of an endless stream of useful discoveries—the free, playful element has receded into the background while the cooler overview and modern human resource management have come to the fore. The transition from playful, free research primarily conducted by wealthy individuals like Darwin to large-scale industrially organized research is usually dated to World War II, where the atom bomb project convinced the authorities that well organized research could change the world completely.

Today, sociologists of science describe how science has moved from one mode to another—*Mode 1* to *Mode 2*—where the first was dominated by curiosity-driven basic research while new science is dominated by applied research, state subsidies, industrial patents, secrecy, and cool calculation.[14]

In other words, science is leaving the domain of the gift economy and becoming increasingly dominated by the logic of the market economy.

This is a problem for many reasons. Researchers are also humans, so they behave the way they have to if they want to get paid. But curiosity and independence of the authorities vanish as a result. The playfulness evaporates and science becomes work. The cultivated, wealthy lepidopterist is a dying breed.

BUT THERE IS a problem for the forces that are trying to integrate science into the market economy, in which it has hitherto made up a pocket of gift economy similar to the family and neighborliness: science produces knowledge, not material objects.

Knowledge consists of information: bits. Bits are very different from the material goods are made of: atoms.

If I have a few atoms that make up a salami on rye that I wouldn't mind eating, and which I bought at a deli, you can't have it once I've eaten it. It will be gone, swallowed, digested. In time its atoms may get turned into fertilizer, which will nourish plants, which may be eaten by pigs, which fatten up into something we can turn into salami. So a few years from now the atoms from my salami on rye may end up as part of your salami on rye. But if we ignore the ecological context, which is in any case only a remote possibility, when you are standing there envying my salami on rye, well, it's you or me: only one of us can eat that sandwich.

Atomic goods, material things, are exclusive: if I've gotten it, you can't get it too. Atoms can only be in one place at a time, so what's mine cannot be yours. If we want to make a copy of that salami on rye, we'll have to make a detour via a pig and a field of rye first.

Bits are completely different. They can be copied till the cows come home. Newton's law of gravity doesn't become less useful to me if you use it; more like the other way round. If it doesn't cost anything to copy information in practice, and that's the case with digital technology, there's no reason at all why you shouldn't get what I have gotten—and vice versa.

An ancient Chinese proverb puts it very simply: if I have an egg and you have an egg and we swap, well, each of us still only has one egg. So there isn't much gained there. But if I have an idea and you have an idea and we swap, suddenly each of us has two ideas.[15]

So there is plenty of logic in regulating knowledge via the gift exchange and not the commodity exchange we use for regulating atomic products.

The problem with scientific knowledge is not so much obtaining it as finding it. Having somebody to point it out is very useful. It's a gift.

A S SCIENCE HAS grown and come to cost more and more, there is an increasingly urgent need for the private companies that fund research to convert their knowledge into a commodity: i.e., to render it exclusive so that you can only obtain it if you pay for it. This runs contrary to its nature precisely because information is not exclusive. But patents, secrecy, provisos, user contracts, and all kinds of other legal gimmicks nevertheless attempt to solve the problem by forcing knowledge into commodity form.

The problem is that knowledge is generated with the help of knowledge. You need to know what other people have figured out if you are to generate new knowledge. So if all knowledge is kept secret it will become extremely difficult to generate new knowledge.

Shared knowledge, like natural laws, is a shared good that everyone benefits from everyone's having. Shared knowledge is a *common area,* to use the term for the shared pastures peasants kept jointly, separate from their own private land, for their cattle to graze on.[16]

The more knowledge is kept secret the harder it becomes to generate new knowledge (which you will be able to keep secret). So everybody loses if the individual acts selfishly and keeps his knowledge secret.

Our research policies today are characterized by this dilemma. Science has become so expensive that whoever pays the most gets to keep it, but it's only really useful if we have it in common.

The commodity form has difficulties where knowledge is concerned.

It's no accident that knowledge, the arts, sport, culture, childrearing, care of the elderly, and many other activities in society are traditionally organized as gift economies. But capitalism today is characterized by the fact that more and more areas of society are having the logic of the market economy imposed on them. Privatization, patenting, and pricing are going on all the time. One sanctuary of the gift economy after another is disappearing into the logic of the market.

But at the same time the foundations of the market economy are moving. Whereas the wheels of the economy used to be turned almost exclusively by products consisting of atoms, they are increasingly being turned by products that consist solely of bits. The economic substratum increasingly consists of bits, not atoms.

So a twofold movement is taking place: the commodity form is spreading into every area of society, and meanwhile the substratum of the commodity economy is increasingly made up of bits and information, which used to be regulated by a gift economy.

Art and culture have generosity, gifts, and shared experiences as their dynamo. But they are increasingly being integrated into the economy.

In the twentieth century it was science that underwent the difficult process of obtaining power, honor, and funds by giving up some of its self-regulation and its privilege as a pocket of a gift economy amidst a market economy. This century it will be the turn of the arts and cultural production as information technology and biotechnology put messages, meaning, significance, understanding, and communication at the center of technology and, from there, the economy.

Cooperation between the arts and big business, which is increasing all over the world nowadays, is hard to get to work in practice, because in it gift-economic and commodity-economic traditions meet. Very different conditions are required for each of them to thrive. Common denominators are hard to find. Culture workers function in a gift economy where you give whatever you can and get something given to you in return. The petty bottom line is an emotional insult. Conversely, the artist seems irresponsible, annoyingly uncontrollable, and impossible to adapt to modern management systems. Being open to each other is tough.

12

Openness

THE MANY ADVANTAGES
OF SHARING EVERYTHING

PICTURE THE FOLLOWING sequence of events: people are suddenly given a brand-new way of talking to one another. A new technology for communication is discovered. It can link everybody's computers together so they can send text, images, sound, and a great deal else to one another, practically free of charge. Information can be exchanged between continents, grassroots groups all over the world can share their experiences, cultural expression, and hobby clubs proliferate. People can communicate.

Once the system has spread to universities everywhere and perfectly ordinary people start to use it, it's suddenly discovered by a new, young generation of capitalists. They see huge opportunities for making money, which will rapidly make them richer than the richest people on the planet. They declare a complete business revolution and are soon worth more on the stock exchange than the old guys. Shouting, whooping, boasting, and absolutely not in neckties they take over society's attention and declare everybody else to be old-fashioned. Turnover is enormous and gigantic investments in the young studs lead to the exorbitant consumption of all kinds of status symbols.

A year or two later it turns out that there is no quick killing to be made on this new technology. The brash young capitalists have spent billions on hot air and withdraw despondently, giving humankind's new conversational tool the bird. "There is no business model for the Internet," they said. Bits were too easy to copy. The signal was not costly in itself. Money could not be made. And they bailed out. Maybe that's not so remarkable. What is remarkable is that everyone else bailed out of the Internet, too. Yet it can still be used to put people in touch with one another. And it's being used by almost a billion people.

THE INTERNET EMERGED from a gift culture. Maybe that's not so surprising. For many years following its infancy in 1969 the Internet was only used by the military and academics. After all, both exist far from the efficiency of the market economy: society regards their work as so important that plenty of funding is given without anything in particular being demanded in return. So the military and academic communities are internally imbued with a considerable element of free cooperation between individuals spread all over the world. The Internet is quite ingenious for this purpose.

So the Internet spread rapidly amongst academics in the eighties. It wasn't till the nineties that commercial interests began emerging for real; dot-com fever began to rage in the closing years of the century and collapsed immediately in the new millennium.

The market was not that enthralled by the digital technology of the Internet after all. It crashed head first into a wall built of gift logic.

The Internet manages to move bits around the globe in huge quantities and at a furious pace. It costs practically nothing, and the original is just as good as copies, precisely because things are digital. Any kind of message (text, sound, images) is boiled down into a row of zeros and ones that are easy to move about and duplicate.

But because it doesn't cost anything, the exclusiveness has vanished. This is good for consumers but lousy for the bottom line. And to make matters worse: not only has the exclusiveness vanished but it clashes with the interests of the consumer! For a moment, let's return to the industrial era and its status symbols and conspicuous consumption.

A red sports car! Vroom! Look at it go! Beep beep, here comes one of the guys who's got what it takes! Complete with sunglasses and a blonde at his side! Isn't he just a marvel? His sports car impresses the mob because they can't afford one. The cool thing about a sports car is that it's too costly for the uncool. So anyone can see that the guy in the Ferrari has got talent.

It's characteristic of the status symbols of the industrial society that they're exclusive and financially unattainable for the masses. Conspicuous consumption.

But what's the picture in the communication society, the information society, the network society, or whatever we call the society that's not based on heavy industry, but on fiber optics and teeny-weenie interconnected electronic gadgets that handle learning, research, art, culture, and business transactions?

A fax machine! A bunch of atoms costing a few hundred dollars that permits the transport of photocopies via the phone line. What can we say of the first man to buy a fax machine when they emerged in the sixties? The guy was a real dummy. Because he had nobody to send a fax to. He owned the same bunch of atoms you can buy today, and may even have paid the same amount for it, but it was completely useless since nobody else had one.

As soon as more people got fax machines our pal's machine came into use, as well. That very same bunch of atoms grew more and more valuable as more and more people got one.[1]

When you have access to a communication network the network becomes more valuable to you the more users there are. This is known as Metcalfe's Law, after one of the pioneers of Internet technology, Bob Metcalfe. His law states that the value of a network of people using a network increases with the square of the number of participants. Among economists it is known as network externalities: the more users, the more possibilities there are of finding somebody to talk to.[2]

This is the opposite of exclusivity: the more people who use the Internet, the more enjoyment I may get out of my Internet connection.

This is good for man, but a pain for Steve the Stud in his sports car. He can try waving his sparkling silver cell phone with its inbuilt video recorder, but if he's got nobody to talk to, all the glitter is a waste of time (apart from its value as conspicuous consumption).

In an industrial society status derives from having and using something other people don't have. In a network society status derives from having and using something everybody else has, too.

The more people online, the more fun it is being online. The more people you can share with, the more fun that what you have to share becomes.

That's a very different logic from that of a value society. Sharing everything is what counts.

W E'RE FAMILIAR WITH this in many aspects of life: what is common to everyone is what is most valuable to the individual.

Language, for example: if everybody had his own word for "Hello" or "A grilled foot-long hotdog" language wouldn't be worth much. There may be variations and quirks in different regions, but fundamentally language is a shared resource. Nobody owns language, but everyone uses it. The greater the number of people who can use it, the greater the value of being able to use it.

If only a few people owned language or parts of it, it would not be worth anything to its owners or to the rest of us.

But you can own a single word of a language: trademarks, for example, which nobody else is allowed to use in commercial contexts. Artists are entitled to protect their own distinctive linguistic concoctions from abuse by others. But this only goes for a few words in specific contexts. I can kick up a fuss when the umpteenth travel agent wants to use the phrase "Mærk verden"—which was the original title of my *The User Illusion*; it translates literally as "feel/notice the world"—as a slogan in an advertising campaign, but I can't make a fuss when people use the phrase in everyday life; on the contrary, I am thrilled.

Language is language because it's a common area. Without language we'd be left cocooned in our own little world of experience, brooding over our thoughts.

KNOWLEDGE HAS THE same nature. Nobody owns the laws of nature. They are common to all mankind. But somebody can own more specific knowledge, such as the best way of casting concrete so the bridge doesn't collapse. Specific knowledge of concrete casting can be private, but it's still worthless if it cannot be compared to the law of gravity.

A very important facet of common ownership of the laws of nature is that an absolutely decisive reason for my believing in Newton's laws of gravity is that so many people are familiar with them and have used them for centuries. When I apply Newton's laws I benefit from the fact that many other people have applied them, too. The laws have survived the test that many people have used them in many situations and discovered that they hold good (apart from a few very special situations in which Einstein's theories take over).

If Newton's laws were owned by somebody who didn't want to explain what they were about but was prepared, if I paid him enough, to apply them to my bridge, I'd be up the creek. Not only would I have to submit my bridge blueprints and pay the owner of Newton Law, Inc., to calculate whether the forces of gravity would be too much for my bridge, I'd also have much less faith in the law. After all, Newton Law, Inc., might be full of bad apples.

Because the laws of nature are public and accessible to everyone, they also show that they possess a great strength: they've survived all kinds of attempts to disprove them. Openness means that the laws get tested as much as possible. When the laws of nature are common to everyone, it proves they must be very strong. It's a costly signal for a law of nature to be public—shoot me down anyone who can!—therefore, I prefer to use information that is in the public domain, because this increases the likelihood that it has been tested and approved by many different people in many different contexts.

If the laws of nature took the shape of commodities they'd be less valuable—to their owners, too.

THESE DAYS WE often hear the opposite: if knowledge can't be owned, nobody will develop it. If it's impossible to patent an invention nobody will invest money in making it: pharmaceutical companies won't bother to develop new drugs, biotechnology companies won't bother to splice genes, and the computer industry won't create new software.

But this argument comes up against several serious problems. The first, and most serious, is that if the fundamental knowledge of the world, as contained in the most important scientific discoveries, is not generally accessible, the question is not whether anybody will want to invent things but whether they'll be able to do so at all. It's roughly similar to if grammar were privately owned: all argument would cease.

The other problem is that it's simply not true that inventions and technological breakthroughs only occur if there's a prospect of a patent and subsequent commercial success. The great discoveries and inventions are very often due to a very different motivation: recognition to the researcher from the scientific community.

This mechanism is about the scientific community reciprocating the generosity of the individual with a good image within that community—a mechanism that is more in line with the way sexual selection operates than with natural selection. But, we may ask, who is going to pay the researcher's salary? A corporation? A university? A state? Why should they, unless they can cash in on the right to use the research results? They should, precisely because their efforts will be reciprocated.

A good researcher with good results attracts attention from other good researchers with other good results. So a nation or a corporation that invests in a pool of good researchers gains a window on the world. Good Danish researchers secure Danish society access to the results produced by researchers the world over because the good ones swap knowledge and insight the way kids swap marbles and baseball cards.

The only way you can buy the attention of the international science world is by buying your way into a pool of good ones. If your own researchers can't publish their results they won't be able to attract the attention of researchers in other countries either.

A country the size of Denmark has researchers who produce about 1 percent of the world's research. The probability research necessary or useful to a Danish company happening to be created in Denmark is therefore about 1 percent. A new discovery that may raise vital new issues for a Danish company will have been made in another country with 99 percent certainty. So it's more important to Denmark to be completely open regarding its research so that it will be provided with a window into the researchers in other countries—that window is far more valuable than it would be to patent or keep secret the 1 percent of the research done in Denmark. The same applies to every other country in the world; even the United States, which looms so large in the scientific landscape but nevertheless produces less than half of the world's research.

It's better to share with the other countries than to keep everything to yourself.

SCIENCE AND TECHNOLOGY are fundamentally about generosity. Great discoveries can change the world but they only very seldom do so overnight. Years, indeed usually decades, pass from the making of a discovery to our being able to exploit it in practice. And even longer before it really becomes economically significant.

So science is an investment, a hand offered to the world, which occasionally leads to huge economic gains. But you can't tell in advance. As is true of any form of generosity, including reciprocity, you have to give something without knowing whether you'll get it back, and if you do, when that will be.

Research is useful to *Homo economicus,* but is exercised by *Homo generosus.* If it were up to *Homo economicus* to decide what should be researched and how, he'd shoot himself in the foot. Because it's only through the latitude and generosity that allows researchers to pursue unlikely paths that the pioneering results, upon which whole new industries may be founded, may be achieved. Inquisitiveness is good business, but business is seldom inquisitive enough.

THIS ALL SOUNDS lovely and romantic, but real life is tough: research is increasingly being conducted only when those behind it are sure they will benefit from the results. Or is it?

The most recent example demonstrating that it's not true that research is only done if the rights to exploit the results can be secured is computer software. The vast majority of the software that makes the Internet work, for example, is not commercially protected, but open and free. The very structure of the Internet relies on things being open and shared. Only because there is a foundation of common knowledge and common software can a level of commercial exploitation of the Internet be built on top.

But this does not mean there are no forces working to make things as privately owned as possible. There are plenty of them. The richest man in the world, for example.

Bill Gates is the greatest businessman of our time. Through prodigious cunning and intelligence he has created a global near-monopoly of the most valuable asset of our day: operating systems for personal computers. His company, Microsoft, dominates this market completely and has outdone competitors by the dozen. The price of this monopoly is partly that it costs the consumer a lot of money, but particularly that it creates a monoculture. There is no variation, competition, or difference. It's easy to spread viruses, and difficult to create innovation.

But worst of all, from the consumer's point of view, the heart of a Microsoft computer program is concealed from the consumer. You may have paid a lot of money for the product but you can't have the code for the software, also known as the source—i.e., the deepest level of programming, which speaks the language the machine can understand. It's this code, a seemingly endless row of zeros and ones, which makes it possible to change the program if you want to, to identify and sort out bugs, and to make improvements.

But the code is secret when you buy a program from Microsoft or similar software firms. You cannot move backward from the program in your computer and calculate the code for yourself. So it's a closed, inaccessible system you can't repair. You only possess the phenotype, but you don't know the genotype.

It wasn't always like this with computer programs. The computer was invented during World War II[3] but didn't really get off the ground till the sixties when a series of companies produced their own makes of computer, using their own operating systems. It was very difficult to exchange data and programs between computers from different manufacturers, because computer networks like the Internet had not yet been created and because there was no basic common language or operating system.

Early common languages like ALGOL and COBOL were augmented by UNIX in the late sixties: UNIX was developed at Bell Labs, a research unit of AT&T, the telephone company. UNIX was an operating system that could run on any machine, a common language that was given away. This made UNIX very valuable, because the more people who use a common language like it, the more valuable it becomes to the individual user.

But it was not idealism or insight into the logic of the gift economy that persuaded AT&T to give its operating system away. The reason was that the telephone company had agreed with the United States federal government that it would not enter the computer market; its monopoly in the telephone market was too great for that. So AT&T was quite simply not allowed to sell its operating system; on the other hand it had a powerful interest in UNIX's continued existence, because the company used a huge number of computers to manage the American telephone network and found it extremely annoying if different computers could not talk to one other. So the only option open to AT&T was to develop an operating system that could be used on any computer, give it away, and hope that it would be used as much as possible, because this would make it more valuable to AT&T.

This compulsory visionary generosity lasted until 1984 when AT&T was divided into many smaller companies that were no longer prevented from selling computer software. UNIX was no longer free.[4]

The United States academic community reacted strongly. UNIX had been born at AT&T but precisely because the program was open and accessible to everyone, computer scientists at United States universities had contributed to developing the language. It had become a kind of standard for programming in that world. Many had contributed, but suddenly the fruits of their labors were no longer publicly available.

One UNIX developer, Richard Stallman from the Massachusetts Institute of Technology, started a movement to develop a new language, GNU (a funny name that's actually a recursive acronym for *G*NU's *N*ot *U*NIX), which would be common property. Stallman invented the term "copyleft" as an alternative to the copyright that limits other people's right to use and develop programs the way they want. The fact that the term "copyleft" includes the word "left" as in "left-wing" was no coincidence. Stallman's organization, Free Software Foundation, worked to make programs available to everybody, and to ensure that all future programs based on programs with copy protection would also be in the public domain and usable for free.

Stallman and his colleagues developed a series of programs

for GNU, but something was lacking: the core of an operating system that would make it really useful.

It was the young Finnish computer science student Linus Torvalds who put the solution onto the Internet in 1991: an operating system called Linux, which was freely accessible to and could be modified by any user. Linux spread like wildfire and became a serious alternative to closed programs, such as Microsoft's. Programmers all over the world began to contribute to the development of GNU/Linux. The more people who used it and contributed to its development, the stronger it grew.

It is a decisive characteristic of an open system that many people have the opportunity to check out its functionality. Just as a law of nature has to be investigated through many experiments that try to disprove it before people seriously begin to believe in it, programs must be run again and again on computers before people begin to think they're stable. Brand-new programs have hosts of bugs that stop them from working properly. In practice these bugs can only be revealed through tests. The more people running tests, the more is learnt about the weaknesses of the program. When private companies develop closed code, they cannot let people test it and fix the bugs, because the code is secret. So they can only do a limited number of test runs before the program is released. In practice this always means that far fewer people have tested the program than will have to use it. The bugs won't be found until the program has been shipped.

As a result, open software is often far more efficient than closed software, because many more people have tested it.

In 1997 Stallman's highly political movement was continued by more moderate forces in the Open Source movement, whose members wanted source code to be freely accessible but were not necessarily against commercial exploitation.

The result is that today much of the software that runs the Internet was developed as Open Source, which is in turn part of the explanation of the Internet's almost miraculous ability to grow and grow without breaking down.

Linux has been adopted by many corporations, including IBM, because it makes them less vulnerable to insuperable problems associated with software by, for example, Microsoft.

IN OTHER WORDS it's the same story we already know from the world of science: openness gives robust, stable results because lots of people can perform tests and discover mistakes. Science produces knowledge, whereas computer programmers produce codes, but both are mental constructions that get tested in practice. The difference is the superficial one that science is conducted at universities, whereas computers are developed within corporations. The difference is superficial because computer giants, such as IBM and Xerox, and telephone companies, such as AT&T, have research departments that often enjoy at least as much freedom of research as the universities; partly because universities today are not particularly free of commercial interests.

In both worlds the gift economy, openness, and the sharing of knowledge are instruments for ensuring strong products.

B^UT WHY, THE economists ask in amazement, do programmers take the time to develop a language they can't make money on? How can huge cooperative projects with hundreds of contributors be possible when there are no time sheets, clocking in, or bonuses for long and faithful service?

The Finnish philosopher Pekka Himanen tried to explain the phenomenon by calling these programmers hackers. "Hacker" is originally the term for a furniture maker, but in the computer world it has come to mean someone with a high degree of computer skills who enjoys exploring computer programs and stretching their potential to the utmost.[5] The press has come to apply the word to people who break into others' computers without authorization, but in geek language such people are known as "crackers." Hackers just love to program and they do so for fun, roughly like lepidopterists, amateur astronomers, and the guy who gets home from work and tries to master Rolling Stones' songs on his guitar.

Himanen defines "hacker" as "an expert or enthusiast of any kind." The point is that the hacker's attitude toward his work is imbued with enthusiasm and passion, unlike the wage slave. The hacker's work ethic is "a general passionate relationship to work that is developing in our information age."[6]

The hacker ethic involves being happy to toil away and happy to share your knowledge and results. A kind of modern vocation.

Himanen's point is that this attitude toward work is nothing new. Prior to industrialization, for example, craftsmen took great pride in their work and approached it with great passion. The academic world is based on the same meticulousness and zeal. Artists are imbued with the same attitude toward work.

The point is that hackers represent a modern version of a showdown with the so-called protestant work ethic typical of industrial society. The protestant ethic is a term derived from the great German sociologist Max Weber, who published an analysis of how the emergence and development of capitalism was typified by work becoming a duty rather than a pleasure.[7]

So hackers make freely accessible computer programs for the same reasons that scientists make science and artists make art: because they can't help it. But why can't they help it?

An important indication is to be found in the clashes between the inventors of programs like GNU and Linux. Practically nobody among the general public has heard of GNU, but lots of people have heard of Linux. But Linux is based on GNU and developed to be part of it. So why don't we say "GNU/Linux"?

"I've received more heat about this issue than about any other I've discussed in this book," the lawyer Lawrence Lessig writes in his otherwise pretty controversial book *The Future of Ideas*. The reason, of course, is that squabbling over who invented what is pretty widespread in the hacker community. Lessig quotes one of its denizens as saying, "Where Linus gets far more credit than he demands, Richard demands more credit than he deserves."[8]

The squabbling is widespread; and this is perfectly in line with the situation in the academic world, where intense personal conflicts about who came up with an idea can pollute everyday life.

These conflicts are a clear signal that the hackers are not only motivated by inner passion and the joy of play, but by the recognition they think they merit. The respect of others and high social status in their community are vital goals.

Just as scientists swap new knowledge for recognition, hackers swap good programs for recognition.

This factor has reassured the economists: it's not altruism, but my self-interest that keeps the wheels turning. Just as researchers get jobs on the basis of the discoveries they've made, an Open Source contribution can land a programmer a job in the future.[9] Contributions to projects like Linux may thus be regarded as costly signals announcing that the sender is somebody with considerable resources and the talent to generate important results. Costly signals that can lead to good jobs.

Many of the people who started the Free Software movement and the Open Source movement also mention nobler motives, such as the desire to create a better world.[10] There is no doubt that these motives matter to the individual and that they are a decisive factor in creating the gift economy, the logic of sharing, and the openness that power Open Source.[11]

But as we have already seen in other contexts, there is not necessarily any contradiction between doing things for others and doing things for ourselves, because altruism can be a form of enlightened egoism.

The personal, individual motivation may well be powerfully egocentric, as it is (for example) in much scientific research conducted by people with extreme personal ambition and correspondingly extreme cynicism and brutality toward others, but which nevertheless may result in improved conditions for huge numbers of people and sublime insights into the wonders of the world.

The impassioned, inwardly motivated creator of great works can be of great value to the community, even if in the final analysis his or her motivation is the pursuit of social standing and, ultimately, the pursuit of the opposite sex.

The decisive factor is not the personal motivation but the objective function: openness, sharing, and cooperation create better software than introversion, property rights, and autocracy.[12]

The point of Open Source is not that it's well meaning, but that it creates well functioning software. That in the final analysis Open Source is economically rational merely proves that generosity pays.

SIMILARLY, THE PROBLEM of copyright, patents, and property rights as regards to knowledge is not so much that they're an expression of egoism and evil, but rather that they're a poor long-term strategy. You can make quick bucks, and Bill Gates has made plenty of them, but in the long term it doesn't work.[13]

Openness and sharing create greater innovation and more progress.

When western pharmaceutical companies refuse to allow their drugs to be copied in poor, undeveloped countries that cannot afford to buy them at full price, they may generate short-term profits for themselves, but in the long run it's bad business. Because if they donated a bit of AIDS medicine to the poor countries of Africa, where the condition is widespread, they would advance the time at which the population will be sufficiently back on its feet to create an economy that'll enable them to buy other, expensive drugs.

We are contemptuous of pharmaceutical companies that don't want to help the poor, not so much because we think they're evil, but because we feel contempt at their narrow mindedness and shortsightedness.

Openness is a superior strategy.

We know this from our own lives, in which open exchange with other people is the way to creating a stable mental inner life. If we never share our thoughts and feelings with others, we're easy victims for ghosts and paranoia.

We know it from science, where openness leads to robust revelations shared and tested by many.

We know it from societies where openness between people and between people and the authorities creates the possibility of stable and well functioning communities. You can't run a high-tech society as a dictatorship because it requires too many people prepared to work on too many tiny details for a dictatorship to be realistic.

Openness is the ultimate costly signal: there is nothing to hide, no ulterior motives or hidden agendas. The big challenge is to understand that we need a common sphere, a common area of knowledge where everybody can graze.

When economies were especially powered by the trade in atoms, it was obvious that it was to the advantage of the misers to conceal their hands. But when the economy is powered by trade in bits, things are different. Common knowledge is more fertile than private knowledge.

EVEN SO, THE trend is for patents to spread into bio-technology; for universities to be run like corporations; for vital, fundamental knowledge such as the structure of the human genome to be privatized. It's part of a double strategy, whereby economies are becoming increasingly dependent on the output from sectors of society that generate knowledge, messages, and meaning, while simultaneously wanting to lasso them into a market economy alien to their nature.

In many ways it's today's great debate: openness or not? Private knowledge or common knowledge? Share or horde? If we gaze into society beyond the horizons of innovation, the question appears to be even more ominous: Communality or not? Welfare or not? Society or not?

IT'S LIKE THE stag hunt of game theory: together we can kill a stag, but only if we work together and don't run off after the first hare that hops past. Establishing trust is the big issue, especially if the amount of meat on a hare is almost as great as the individual hunter's share of the stag.

Today's pursuit of quick killings through the privatiza-tion of knowledge and technology actually lead to the rapid accumulation of wealth by a few individuals. But what is lost as a result? What great discoveries and beautiful technological systems thereby become impossible to create? What stakes in network technology are made impossible by private greed?

Sex and sexual selection are perhaps not the only mechanisms that can ensure the spirit of cooperation gets a chance: if you don't get laid for a hare but venison makes the right impression, won't that be an incitement to cooperate?

I F WE TURN for a moment to the decline of information-technology visions after the dot-com collapse, the most surprising thing of all may be that after a few years during which the raving young capitalists dominated these new technologies, any mention of civil society, decentralization, and user control vanished from the network-technology debate. After the dot-com collapse, the visions also ceased, often, what's more, with the rage of self-loathing that derives from feeling you've been too naive.[14] But the visions were not naive. It is a technology that can be shaped and used if that's what people want. There is nothing naive about that. The naiveté was solely the belief that people would quickly and resolutely seize the technological chance to rule over their own lives. It takes time.

So although dot-com is over, the huge potential of network technologies are most definitely not.[15]

There are loads of perspectives. One good example is protocol 802.11b. (Yes, that's its name even if it sounds cryptic.) In this case, wireless networks are reinforced the more users there are.

Today, Internet access is predominantly by cable. The telephone companies and other Internet service providers run the networks that give the individual user access to the global network. It's often not the best technological option that is offered. In Denmark you can only obtain access with a bandwidth (the capacity to move information) too low to send video to another computer or receive high-quality television signals via the Web.

Since 1997 I've been arguing that it would be good for the Danes and Danish society if everybody could download and upload large amounts of information on the Web, by giving everybody access to a bandwidth of 11 million bits a second.[16] This is precisely the amount of information man can absorb from his surroundings.[17]

But this vision has not come about, partly because it's expensive (but it *is* expensive to build society, with all its roads, libraries, and other infrastructure), and partly because the existing telephone companies would like to make more out of the infrastructure they already own. The copper wires of the telephone system do not allow users to achieve a full bandwidth of 11 million bits a second.

But 802.11b could change this completely. It's a "communication protocol," which enables us to connect a computer to the Web via a wireless connection. At the end of a cable with access to the Internet you attach a small box—it's called an Airport if you're an Apple or Mac user. By using radio waves this Airport can receive and transmit 11 million bits a second to and from any computers within a radius of fifty meters. You can install a gadget like this at home or in a workplace, and all your computers can use the connection, whether they're desktop or laptop. This cuts out a whole forest of cables, but from society's point of view that's not the point.

The point is that if I have an airport at home, my neighbor, and the guy driving by outside, can also use my link if they want to, and if I let them. If I let Jensen use my network when he's near my place, he might let me use his when I'm in his neighborhood. We'll simply swap wireless connections.

If everyone in the world goes along with this, something remarkable happens: we swap links with each other, and everyone can access the Web wherever he or she is. The more people who use the system, the more locations you can access the Web.

If there is a significant number of computers in action in an area they can amplify one another and help move the bits between themselves and the Web. You'll therefore have Internet access throughout all of society if you carry your laptop around.

The telephone companies will still be able to make money, by conveying the bits to the individual user's Airport. And we'd want them to supply the full bandwidth to it, because it can't expedite more than it receives.

But from that point on, people help each other by creating a wireless network. The more people who use it, the better it works.[18] Metcalfe's law in operation.

When you're dealing with information, which has the wonderful property that you can share it without losing it, you've just got to be generous. The more you give, the more you may get.

Share everything.

THE GENERAL OUTLINE for evolution is that in the future the only scarce resource will be attention. Man's attention. There will be plenty of information, and material goods, too (even though it will probably take most of a century to get global welfare organized).

We will live in a society in which the atoms are not scarce, but attention is. The value of a commodity will be determined by how much human attention has gone into it. The price of a commodity will be determined by how much attention we're prepared to dedicate to it. The absurd battles over copyright and the extortionate prices charged by telephone companies will give way to a society where a product is paid for by the attention we give it.

Electronic payment and intelligent technology will make it realistic to pay in teeny-weenie doses for things we use, whether they are media products or hair dryers. A thing's value will derive from how much attention I dedicate to it. The value of my work will depend on how much attention others dedicate to it.

The economy of the future will be a much simpler one:

You pay for what you pay attention to
You get paid from those who pay attention to your work.

Public Spirit

WELFARE PAYS;
GLOBALLY, TOO

"THE CONSIDERABLE SUPPORT for the modern welfare state even among the well-to-do constitutes the most significant case in human history of a substantially voluntary egalitarian redistribution of income among total strangers," the economists Samuel Bowles and Herbert Gintis write in an analysis of the welfare state in light of the results of experimental economics.[1]

We have already met Gintis and his work on game theory. He and his colleague Bowles of the University of Massachusetts, Amherst, one of the most socially oriented universities in the

United States, have been trying to explain modern society for years in light of the experiences of human nature given to us by experimental economics.

Could the existence of a will to cooperate and a will to share resources as documented by game-theory experiments explain the existence of a welfare state? And could it also explain why the welfare state is under attack all over the world?

After all, it's not only the traditional features of the welfare state that are in trouble: the very idea of society as we know it is under attack.

THE GLADSAXE TRANSMITTER is a very tall tower on a hilltop north of Copenhagen that broadcasts television signals to a whole metropolis. Not many years ago, all the television signals in Copenhagen came from that tower. Everyone watched the same television news, and so everyone completely agreed on society's agenda. Only the most advanced viewers watched the Swedish television news programs and showed off by quoting superior foreign affairs analyses provided by the latter.

Today television is broadcast by whole forests of towers, transmitted by satellite, through cables, and soon by solid-state and wireless Internet connections.

Nobody watches the same television news program anymore. Nobody asks in the cafeteria at lunchtime, "Did you watch what was on television last night?" Because everybody watched television, but nobody watched the same thing.

So does society still exist?

TRADITIONAL SOCIETY AS we know it is under threat from above and below: from above because globalization is marginalizing the existing nation states that provided the framework for society for centuries; and from below because the institutions that ensured the perception that there was a common agenda are breaking up. The common newspaper, the common television channel, parliament, local bars, the family, workplaces, togetherness, and traditions: they're all more or less slowly disappearing. Instead, legions of media choices, television politicians, Seven Elevens, therapists, voluntary visitors, remote workplaces, and virtual friendships are on the advance. What makes all these things hang together?

The Internet symbolizes the dilemma: on the one hand it's the greatest gift of national and international contact between humans, ideas, information, views, creative works, and connections the world has ever seen; and on the other, it represents remoteness and distance, the abolition of everyday physical functions and human contact.

The Internet heralds the epoch in which the role of "headquarters" in human society will become less significant.

THERE WAS ONCE a king, and he was society incarnate. "L'état, c'est moi," the Sun King, Louis XIV of France, is supposed to have said: "I am the state."[2] That was pretty straightforward. Society was tied together by an autocrat who controlled the army, the currency, the police, the workhouses, and tax collection. Nobody could be in any doubt as to what kept society and the nation together.

But it's not like that anymore. Not only the king, but also company presidents, television channel owners, and trade union bosses are losing ground and influence. Society no longer has obvious power centers and places where decisions are made; instead, it has representatives who, despite fine-sounding titles, such as prime minister, chairman of the board, and chief of staff, have very little influence on power. Whereas the revolutionary movements of yore were able to demand with considerable justification that the people be given power by the king/landlords/factory proprietors, today this demand is absurd. Because it's hard to identify who has any power that you can demand of them.

Sure, the presidents of big corporations do as they please with the lives of thousands of employees, but only until the day the board decides there's not enough on the bottom line; and the board itself gets ejected when the shareholders get uptight; and the latter run around investing haphazardly while the stock markets shoot up and down; and one financial scandal after another rolls across CNN's financial news crawl.

Who is really in charge? The populations of almost every industrial European nation complain about European Union red tape and the massive immigration from societies at stages almost infinitely remote from their everyday lives. The political leaders spread their arms and explain that their little country can't make all the decisions in the European Union and that immigration and the refugee quotas correspond to what the country committed itself to accepting when it signed the relevant UN conventions.

Nobody seems to have made these decisions; nobody is willing to say, "I did! Vote for me or kick me out!"

Society no longer has a ruler or a center. There is no *Dinosaurus Rex* (Denmark's main radio station) to keep everybody's attention. But is there a future for societies nevertheless?

THE ABOLITION OF headquarters via the Internet involves the dissolution of an organizational form—the pyramid with headquarters that rules the riff-raff—and its replacement with another form, in which obligation, the network, reciprocity, concreteness, and self-organization are at the center. But can society emerge from below, or can it only be created from above via a regal ruler or a television channel president who installs people in a society under his control? This question is linked to another, namely whether humans create societies and treat each other decently because it is our biological nature to do so, or whether we do so because we have slowly evolved via a laborious process of civilization lasting millennia to the stage where we are nice, cultivated people who don't resort to fisticuffs but argue politely for our cause and obey the laws the king has decreed, despite our biological characteristics.[3]

The last few decades have apparently been about the way the market has totally taken over power from the rest of society. People wear their market masks everywhere, while virtues involving reciprocity, relations, and cohesion recede into the background.

THE CLASSIC ECONOMIC argument as it shaped up in the middle of the last century was about the clash between market and state. Karl Polanyi, whom we met earlier, was one of the great spokespersons in favor of a decisive role for the state in order to ensure that society hangs together and the economy works. More liberally inclined economists, such as Frederick Hayek, argued that the market would solve everything if it was left to do so free from interference by busybody politicians of all kinds.[4]

Today most people would agree that the market and the state both have their limitations, which can compensate for one another to some extent. The market creates a harshness and inequality that is inexpedient, because it creates social discord and harms productivity, but inequality can be moderated via state compensation. The state, for its part, creates a bureaucracy and autocracy that is kept in check by the market.

But there is a third factor with its very own logic: the relationships of civil society, by which I mean all the relationships, networks, and connections that are created through the exchange of objects and services.

Traditionally, the cohesiveness of civil society has only involved the stuff in the private sphere: family, friends, the neighborhood, the sports club. But things are changing.

THE SPANISH SOCIOLOGIST Manuel Castells, whose great three-volume work *The Information Age*[5] has positioned him as the sociologist of network society, points out that the role of the networks changed with the breakthrough of information technology. The network played a role way back in history, but thanks to information technology it has become more widespread.

Earlier the networks played a role in people's private lives: among their family and friends. But information technology means that the network can now displace the hierarchies and pyramids that used to dominate corporate life and state bureaucracies. "Networks . . . had considerable difficulty in coordinating functions, in focusing resources on specific goals, and in accomplishing a given task," Castells writes. Challenges such as these used to call for a strong person at the top of the hierarchy capable of imposing direction and focus on the organization.

"Networks were primarily the preserve of private life; centralized hierarchies were the fiefdoms of power and production," Castells writes but adds, "Now, however, the introduction of computer-based information and communication technologies, and particularly the Internet, enables networks to deploy their flexibility and adaptability."[6]

Whereas in the past civil life was characterized by networks between people who entered into direct relations with one another without control from above, while the world of power and production were characterized by control from above, the networks are now becoming vital organizational forms even in the "serious" world.

The logic of the networks thus becomes vital to our working lives, too: personal relations that create the possibility of flexible cooperation matching the job in hand. In the language of this book we may say that the *hau* of the gift economy and concrete personal relations of civil life have been transferred to the working life (which used to be the preserve of the impersonal hierarchy and people wearing market masks).

The civil organizational form, the concrete connections between humans who coordinate one another without chiefs, the distributing organization, has its archetype precisely in the Internet: it was created against the background of the experience of biology in the robustness of "flat" networks, which are superior to fragile hierarchies. For hierarchies are never stronger than their most vulnerable point: the top. If the top is eliminated nothing can function. Networks, on the contrary, can be self-organizing and can adjust to a much greater degree. The original vision behind the Internet, which we owe to Paul Baran,[7] was precisely the recognition of the strength of the network in the face of centralization.[8]

But networks are not always flat. The Internet, for example is not flat, but very irregular: some points are more connected than others. One central experience from network research in the last ten years is that many networks are completely dominated by a small number of hubs linking innumerable points in the network that themselves don't have many connections.[9] Just as there are some people who are social with a huge number of other people, whereas most of us are social with only a few, there are network hubs with many connections. A network structure is no guarantee, as such, that the system will be flat, but it creates the possibility.

IT'S WORTH NOTING that the extension of the network into the sphere of power and production introduces a third factor into the traditional debate on society. In the past, people argued market or state and how the two should relate to each other. The overall political and ideological argument in society was between proponents of more market (liberals and conservatives) and proponents of more state (socialists and communists). The Scandinavian social democrats developed a kind of synthesis between the two points of view with the mixed economies of the welfare state, in which a very powerful state controls half of society's economic resources but uses them to create the best possible conditions for the private sector.

But in relation to the networks, the market and the state are on the same side of the fence. Power and production are in contrast to the self-organized and voluntary relations of civil society that create networks.

So instead of a debate on society that is about market or state, the right to own the means of production, or whether society should control them, liberalism or socialism, right or left, the debate today is on the threshold of a completely different set of problems: network or hierarchy, concrete human relations or anonymous organizations. *Hau* or money.

THIS CLAIM MAY sound weird all the while that civil society is reportedly beating a violent retreat in relation to the market and social control. And isn't the Internet just a way of demolishing the final bastions of private life to surveillance by Big Brother and the market's dream of turning the meeting of all human needs into commodities: picking your nose can surely be turned into a commodity somehow too, and become something we have to pay for?

The decline of civil society has been charted by the American sociologist Robert Putnam from Harvard in a work vividly titled *Bowling Alone.* One of the favorite American pastimes used to be bowling with a gang of your buddies, as I probably don't need to tell my American audience—or perhaps I do, since I imagine the closest many of my American readers come to a bowling alley is when they drive by on their way to the ballet. In any case, more and more people are now going bowling alone, Putnam says, but he doesn't quite mean it: people merely bowl in informal groups rather than proper teams.[10] They have fewer meals with pals, take less part in clubs and societies, fail to respect highway signs, spend less time on voluntary work, and spend a hell of a lot more on watching television and on other forms of cocooning. Putnam dates the switch to this "home life"—away from seeing friends and going to places of public entertainment—to 1970.[11] American civil society has been on the retreat for over thirty years, a whole generation.

Putnam labels the value of civil life for the well-being of society and the well-being of the individual with the rather unfortunate term "social capital." The idea behind the label is all right, but the name isn't (another case of our special handicap principle when it comes to naming unusually good ideas). After all, capital is *things, money,* not *relations.* In Danish the somewhat more fortunate term *sammenhængskraft,* "cohesion," is used for the same phenomenon.

The more networks of civil activity and voluntary connections between people society reflects, the more trust, willingness to cooperate, and desire to function sensibly you will find in that society. The point is that social capital is a good for the individual and for society alike: people are more productive and function better if they have good social networks. We work better, create more wealth, and feel better as people. So it's good for the individual and society if we care for one another.

It's also self-reinforcing: the more trust there is between people, the more you feel like showing trust. It's easy to get cooperation moving in societies where people trust one another and know one another.

The American sociologist Francis Fukuyama, known for his controversial idea, the End of History, following the fall of the Berlin Wall in 1989 (there is nothing left to fight for; capitalism has simply won), has since drawn up the thesis that the countries with the most trust also do best economically.

IT MAY SEEM peculiar that Castells claims that the network organization of civil society is spreading into the sphere of money and power, while Putman claims at the same time that civil life is disintegrating where it used to be strongest, namely, beyond the sphere of power and production.

But really this is just a reiteration of the double movement we observed earlier when it comes to the relationship between commodities and gifts: on the one hand, every activity in society is increasingly being turned into a commodity; and on the other, the substratum of the economy is increasingly becoming the bits and ideas that used to be regulated by a gift economy. Translated into hierarchies and networks, this says that on the one hand, technological progress is dismantling many of the civil, social networks between people that used to carry society and culture; and on the other, technological progress is increasingly making it possible for hierarchies in the world of power and production to be supplanted by networks.

The Internet makes it easier for people to talk to one another—irrespective of distance—socially, geographically, linguistically, or scientifically. The Internet makes it easier for people to live their lives all alone, in isolation, obtaining their experiences without having to interact directly with anyone else.

The good news regarding the Internet is that it enables the individual to pursue his dreams and goals without being dependent on the understanding or appreciation of the people around him. The village idiot can study his moons of Saturn and birdsong from the Andes quite independent of any help from his immediate surroundings.

The bad news regarding the Internet is that it enables the individual to pursue his dreams and goals without being dependent on the understanding or appreciation of the people around him. The village idiot can study his Saturn moons and singing birds without ever having to ask to borrow the storekeeper's moped to run down to the library.[12]

THE PROBLEM REMAINS: what does it take to create trust, the will to cooperate, the will to share, and to get society to cohere? If we assume that hierarchies aren't as efficient as they thought, that it was not headquarters that created the society around it, that Louis XIV was not the state at all, but only thought he was, that kings, company presidents, prime ministers, schoolteachers, lecturers, and all kinds of other people who feel they're the bee's knees are perhaps not at all as vital as they thought, but that the society around them is built up from relationships between people rather than relationships to headquarters, then we can try to pursue the ability of concrete relationships to build society.

EXPERIMENTAL ECONOMICS AND game theory have taught us that we need not regard humans as isolated islands of selfish rationality reluctantly dragged into cooperating and sharing. Humans are willing to share and willing to give something up in order to develop sound customs in a group.

Bowles and Gintis summarized the experiences of experimental economics in the expression "strong reciprocity": this is when humans evince the will to 1) be generous to strangers; 2) share what they possess, especially if it was given to them; 3) contribute to common goods and common projects; 4) punish people who go it alone and freeload on the community, even if punishing them costs something; and a final aspect of strong reciprocity is 5) that these positive attitudes to others apply all the more strongly the closer the relationships between people are.[13]

Bowles and Gintis therefore consider it understandable for people to want to help the poor and support the weak, but only if the poor and weak make an obvious effort to help society, too. "We think that people support the welfare state because it conforms to deeply held norms of reciprocity and conditional obligations to others."[14] Something is given, something is demanded. Both ways.

But what's it all about, then, this demand that people must do something for themselves and others before we can be bothered to help them?

In reality we might say it's about *hau*, the spirit of the gift.

If we look at Scandinavian welfare society we may regard it as a purely egoistic construction in which the rich members of society give away some of the cake to those in trouble, but also demand something in return: public spirit.

The widespread equality and care for all that imbues Scandinavian society creates extremely well functioning societies if we look at the figures for crime, violence, and aggravation in the streets. By ensuring that nobody has to fight to avoid starving to death, that people in difficulty can hope for help, and that there is a point to trying to make sure your children live good lives, we suppress the desire to spoil society for others.

A kind of social contract is entered into: nobody is seriously deprived, but nobody gets in the way of anybody else. The well-off make sure they can live happy lives without continual fear of crime or disturbance.

Viewed in this light, welfare is a gift accompanied by a social *hau,* the expectation that the recipients will feel like a constructive part of society. Gratitude is not what is demanded, but the will to lead good lives. Help to help themselves; mutual solidarity. Self-interests cooperating.

A DECISIVE SHIFT IN the fundamental structure of welfare society took place in Denmark when the welfare legislation of the seventies began to operate with the idea of entitlement. You no longer merely had a right to help: you had the right to insist on it. The change was made with the best intentions but removed the reciprocity inherent in society's insisting that welfare recipients show public spirit. The result was "clientification."

The problem grew even worse when extensive international solidarity led to immigrants' and refugees' being given considerable welfare payments with no counter-requirement that they make an active contribution to society. Whereas countries like the United States have always tacitly expected immigrants to be more patriotic and American than the Americans, European countries did not expect this of their immigrants. After all, refugees in particular had a need for help that could not be met while simultaneously insisting that they merge constructively with Danish society.

The gift was not accompanied by a *hau* spirit insisting that when you receive welfare you are part of society and have to prove that you feel as such.

The problem was not helped by the lack of a reasonable answer when the population asked why so many refugees and immigrants should be admitted. The politicians simply referred to "international conventions."

As a consequence, immigration is not regarded as the result of deliberate, transparent, democratic decisions, but as federal decisions—i.e., decisions made by government representatives in a closed forum with no democratic debate in their own countries. The very significant transformation of homogenous countries, such as those of Scandinavia, to strife-ridden multi-ethnic societies took place without ever being perceived as a democratic decision (roughly the way the European Union appears to be a federal collaboration between governments and not the result of a democratic process throughout the area).

The populations are giving gifts, but without *hau*.

273

Immigration to western Europe means enormous advantages for the receiving countries. Resourceful, enterprising people arrive who revitalize its shops and restaurants, expand its cultural horizons, supply valuable labor and forge links to distant nations in just a few decades. These are definite goods that we Europeans have reason to appreciate. Unfortunately it happened without any feeling of co-responsibility from the original populations.

Democracy is a very expedient form of government for society, not so much because democracies necessarily make the best or most correct decisions; on the contrary, many of them are undeniably affected by kowtowing to the electorate and mood swings among the populace. But democracy is effective because it gives legitimacy to the authorities: you may not agree with the decisions made, but as a citizen you feel jointly responsible because they're the result of a democratic process. The authorities are legitimate. You don't resort to Molotov cocktails.

The way forward is therefore a stronger emphasis on reciprocity, demands, *hau,* and public spirit. You can't love people if you don't demand anything of them.

THE PROBLEM OF the aversion to immigration on the part of the people of Western Europe cannot be solved by insisting that they ought to love immigrants unconditionally, but by acknowledging that they contribute to the community.

Experimental economics has not only indicated that man is a *Homo economicus,* but that he is *Homo Parochius,* a human who favors members of his own group as opposed to others.[15]

The propensity to support your own kind rather than others is deeply rooted in the problem of reciprocity: the price of reciprocal altruism is that we distinguish relentlessly between members of the group who return our altruism and those who don't. The feeling of "us" and "them" is deeply rooted in the tradition of reciprocity. The cost of such reciprocal altruism is group egoism.

So there are sound reasons for focusing on pure generosity.

A WELFARE STATE INSURES the entire population against starvation and poverty, and as a result the productivity of the whole of society grows. This kind of development has taken place in much of the world, with the Scandinavian countries to the fore. But the same process will probably soon be on its way globally. Here comes a prediction:

The people of the world will see that poverty is too expensive. This will not be a shift in mood engendered by sentiment, but because it will be obviously true and in everybody's interest, including the rich countries.

Will we then create global welfare, which can be established in just a few decades if that's what we want, out of charity and moral obligation? No. We'll do so out of pure and utter egoism. It's not a question of morality. It's a question of simple common sense.

In a world that invented the airplane is it just too stupid to imagine that we can live safe and sound at one end of the world while our fellow men die of contagious diseases at the other? We all belong to the same biological species, and so we catch the same diseases. As long as a considerable portion of our fellow humans live in poverty and deprivation, disease has an easy time of it. As long as there are airplanes, epidemics will spread across the globe. So it makes simple common sense to help all our fellow species to eliminate starvation, poverty, and poor sanitation.

In a world that we have finally acknowledged is one world, with one ecological system of life and climate, it is fundamentally idiotic to believe that we can remain indifferent to the poverty-stricken people on another continent. Their need forces them to use the last remaining twigs for fuel, so deserts spread and farmland turns to dust. Their poverty is our poverty because they're forced to exhaust the earth's resources. We live on the same globe with the same climate in the same atmosphere. We can't afford to let them starve.

In a world inhabited by thousands of cultures, each with its own language, folklore, history, music, cuisine, and dress, it's pretty poor to imagine that we must make do with Coca-Cola, Elvis, and bad English. With technology being about communication and the exchange of cultural content it's foolish to think we'll be better off if the others don't have this technology. It's in our interests for everyone to become wealthy enough to be able to send their legends and myths, music, and manifestations of humanity across the global network. We have an interest in their joining the communication network. Because they've got stuff to say.

Helping the poor escape from poverty is not a question of being morally superior, compassionate, magnanimous, or heroic. It's a question of not being stupid anymore.

A hundred years ago we abolished death by starvation and poor sanitation in our part of the world. The result was not only better lives for the worst-off, but absolutely for the best-off, too. Diseases receded, beggars diminished, violence lessened, and members of society were able to concentrate on generating welfare.

The time has now come for the same effort to be made worldwide. There are six billion people in the world today. The UN estimates that about a billion have plenty: economically and nutritionally. Correspondingly, a billion people live with starvation every day. The remaining 4 billion get by, but not at our level.

How much will it cost if each and every member of the wealthy billion pays to ensure that there is enough food for at least a single member of the poor billion? The amount is shocking: each of us wealthy people will just have to pay 16¢ per day to provide food for one of the poor.[16]

Sixteen cents per day! The cost of not paying is more environmental destruction, more infections, and a poorer culture.

Honestly, it so obviously makes sense to pay this tiny amount that it's, frankly, immoral not to.

The next question is how this help should be provided. It isn't enough to ensure that they can buy food. The food must also be taken to where it is to be consumed.

And that's where the problems start: there are aid organizations that need a slice of the cake for administration; there are local governments that never release the food; there are highwaymen who rob the trucks; there are poor who refuse to accept charity.

It isn't easy, especially when everything is organized as foreign and emergency aid. It corresponds to the poorhouse or the workhouse prior to the advent of the welfare state.

Neither is it made any easier by the fact that many of our corporations make a lot of money helping developing countries to spend their foreign aid. Or by the armies of aid workers in those countries who live the good life compared with native residents. Corruption, cronyism, and greed sully the picture in the wealthy donor nations and the poor countries themselves. So perhaps the classic kind of official foreign aid may not suffice. There are reasons why the people of the wealthy world should take matters into their own hands.

The day we recognize that the problem is actually no bigger than this—that for each poor person, one person needs to be wealthy enough to provide food without even noticing, that there is enough food on the planet, and all we need to do is distribute it—well, perhaps something conclusive will take place: A billion people from the wealthy part of the world will demand that their contribution to alleviate poverty will actually benefit somebody, that cronyism and corrupt local rulers be removed, that real efforts are made to distribute communication technology that will enable cultural and commercial contacts across the globe, that we open up to the rest of the world.

People everywhere will realize that we can do to the whole world what we have already done with our part of it: eradicate poverty and all its dreadful consequences.

We will all grow wealthier when the poor are given decent lives. It makes so much sense that it's immoral not to take it seriously.[17]

World welfare is an agenda that has become inescapable. The Scandinavian dream of everybody being part of society, with everybody participating and contributing, being listened to and respected, has been good business for the Scandinavian countries.[18] The more members of the population who take part in and contribute to society, the richer their lives and our purses. Fellowship pays. Welfare leads to wealth.

B UT STARTING THIS process isn't only common sense: it also means esteem, respect, and sexual selection.

Global generosity is like any other generosity: it's the ultimate handicap demonstrating the strength of the individual. Purely selfishly motivated behavior yields great benefits all around. In the final analysis it is aimed at obtaining the prestige to be gained by behaving decently: prestige in the eyes of the opposite sex in particular.

Once upon a time prestige came from obtaining money and resources for oneself, food for the kids and two automobiles. Soon such things will no longer give prestige because they'll be a matter of course when robots do the hard work. We are moving from a society dominated by the problem of survival to a society dominated by experience as a problem. We are moving from the logic of natural selection—survival—to the logic of sexual selection—convincing others that we're worth having fun with.

We humans will end up like Zahavi's babblers (or at least like he says they are): we will end up fighting for the chance to do good deeds. It's urgent. Soon, world welfare will have been implemented and global generosity will be boundless.

There will no longer be any sex appeal in fast cars and big boats. What will matter is being able to say that back then, you helped to save the world.

Conflict solving will be a matter of doing your utmost, making an effort, and showing how good you are; the fight between nations and races will take the form of subtleties such as producing the most delicious little pies;[19] women will go on sex strike to end wars,[20] corporations will compete in the do-good stakes.

Right now it's mostly individuals, young and cheerful, who are attempting to save the world. In the course of the century we have just embarked on, it will become increasingly clear to companies and states that the only way to prestige in the modern world is through generosity.[21]

IT MAY SEEM cynical to emphasize so highly the significance of the fact that we practice generosity and philanthropy in our own interest. But it is important to relate to it. And it will become even more important in the future.

Philanthropy and voluntary work for good causes are remarkable in many ways if we regard them as social activities.

The givers are seldom especially interested in whether the money actually gets there, so the poor get something to eat, or whether it all ends up being spent on administration and luxury apartments in Florida. If reciprocity were what it was about, or at least the well-being of the recipients, surely we'd spend some time checking out who needed most help and whether the money actually got to them. But no. What is involved is giving for your own sake. It makes you feel better and you may even be able to tell your girlfriend.[22]

The recipients are not always interested in receiving the money. They feel humiliated and mocked. "I worked for some years in a charitable foundation that annually was required to give away large sums as the condition of tax exemption," the English anthropologist Mary Douglas explains. "Newcomers to the office quickly learnt that the recipient does not like the giver, however cheerful he be (. . .) the whole idea of a free gift is based on a misunderstanding. There should not be any free gifts. . . . A gift that does nothing to enhance solidarity is a contradiction," Douglas writes.[23]

The givers are often interested in showing their generosity via big parties, badges, plaques, and things to tell their friends.

Charity makes you feel all warm inside. But does it provide warmth on the outside, too?

Is this an argument for ceasing to be charitable or to support good causes? Not at all: but perhaps members of the opposite sex ought to make more of insisting that the money actually end up with the poor, the sick, the suffering. It's great that there's sex appeal in supporting a good cause, but it would be even greater if there were sex appeal in ensuring that the aid actually made it.

But is it naive to think that the future will be characterized by massive philanthropy and ambitious attempts to create global welfare? Aren't we merely moving toward egoism and every-man-for-himself-ism? Is it not the case that the world's leading nation when it comes to development aid to poor countries as a percentage of its national product, Denmark, is currently divesting itself of its leading role and hastening downward among the ranks of countries that demonstrate stature? Yes, indeed. But the kind of generosity exercised by the state may not be of primary importance in the future; perhaps what will be important will be the generosity of civil society: individuals getting together to sort out a global predicament that's embarrassingly distorted and perilously unstable. As our government reduces the priority it gives to healthy global common sense, we may see popular movements emerging. *Decent Danes* could be what we call ourselves the day we feel our nation has become too much of a disgrace and we decide to take matters into our own hands.

The Coming Flood is the title of a report from the visionary Global Business Network (GBN). Its subject is philanthropy in this decade.[24] Its main point is that in the next few years vast amounts will flow into charity work in the United States. It may well end by a total sum donated to charity in the present decade exceeding the total sum given in the last quarter of a century, even measured in fixed prices. The GBN estimates that charity in this decade—i.e., from 2001 to 2010—will amount to between two and three trillion dollars a year. So a considerable proportion of the economy of the decade will go to charity. Why?

The demographic development, more particularly the composition of the population by age, is the explanation: very large generations of very wealthy Americans are approaching retirement age and are writing their wills. The entire celebrated generation of 1968 has to divest itself of its wealth without the money ending up with Uncle Sam. So a wave of charity has begun, and it's continuing despite the economic downturn of recent years.

As one of the largest benefactors, Thomas B. Murphy, says to the *New York Times*: "The amount of resources that are emerging, despite the current blip in the economy, is sufficiently large that the way the money is ultimately allocated will have significant effect on what our society will look like."[25]

A series of reports from the Social Welfare Research Institute, of Boston College, indicate that newly rich millionaires will donate huge amounts in the next few years.[26]

But that is in the United States, where tax legislation rewards philanthropy to a very high degree. The underlying cause—that demographic development means that very large generations of people will either hand their wealth to the IRS or to charity—will affect the whole wealthy part of the world. So there are reasons to suppose that there will be more money for philanthropy in the future.

The GBN actually warns us that there may be trouble if there are not enough qualified organizations to administer these funds.

It's important to emphasize that the anticipated flood of fortunes seeking tax exemption is the result of factors that have nothing to do with generosity as a handicap. It's a consequence of the way society's wealth is distributed and how the population is made up in terms of age—a large generation is retiring. On top of these factors comes the thesis of this book: that in the future, generosity will be the only convincing way of displaying your wealth.

Where our equivalent of the peacock tail used to be conspicuous consumption, in the future it will be conspicuous generosity (where the really neat thing will be to give all your gifts anonymously).[27] Prestige won't be in having, but in giving.

There is a very big difference between what yields prestige in a society imbued by scarcity and a society imbued by superfluity. We are on our way to a society imbued by an enormous superfluity of material goods and information. This will change the rules for displaying our strength:

DEMONSTRATIONS OF STRENGTH IN TWO KINDS OF SOCIETY

SCARCITY SOCIETY	SUPERFLUITY SOCIETY
Having	Giving
Owning	Sharing
Cocooning	Opening out
Excluding	Inviting
Knowing	Telling

But does all we have discussed mean that man is selfish or that man is altruistic? Our genes are selfish, and man is altruistic—sometimes.

Thirty years ago the philosopher Thomas Nagel put it this way: "To say that altruism and morality are possible in virtue of something basic to human nature is not to say that men are basically good. Men are basically complicated."[28]

W E H A V E T O learn to distinguish between what we can call concrete and abstract altruism.

Abstract altruism involves the individual sacrificing to himself something, well, abstract: an idea, a cause, a religion, a class, a race, a people, a society. In my view this leads very easily to terror and torture, boundless evil, and suicide bombing.

Concrete altruism involves the individual's making sacrifices, because he wants to achieve something very concrete: desire on the part of his one and only. We make sacrifices but only in order to go on living and to reproduce. We make sacrifices, but we don't sacrifice ourselves.

Concrete altruism is to say "yes" to man, to say "yes" to life on Earth. It is an investment in sticking around and having offspring. Abstract altruism, on the contrary, promises virgins in paradise.

I F W E H A D N ' T realized it before, this became very clear on September 11, 2001: we are all participants in a gigantic ultimatum game here on Earth. Some of us are wealthy, others poor, so the roles are defined in advance: it's obvious who's going to make the first move and is able to offer to share, namely, those of us in the wealthy part of the world.

How much do we want to give? How much of our wealth are we prepared to share with those who have too little? How much are we prepared to help in order to include everyone else in global welfare? How much are we prepared to give to the environment of our planet?

Shall we be greedy and take as much as we can for ourselves, and just hand out a few alms so they won't fly into our skyscrapers? Shall we keep our expensive life-giving pharmaceuticals to ourselves and protect our farmers from competition? Shall we burn all the coal and race around in our automobiles, even if it changes the climate so our kids can't go tobogganing in the winter?

Or shall we look to the future and invest in making a healthy world and a richer world? Shall we be generous and visionary or greedy and shortsighted? What is best for our own interests? What's the most human?

If we offer too little, none of us will be given anything at all in the long run. Overpopulation, mass migration, environmental collapse, and infectious diseases will pollute our lives and make our wealth meaningless: it will slowly disintegrate.

If we offer enough to reverse the trend and create global welfare, a cornucopia of human creativity and generosity will welcome us wherever we go.

So what are we prepared to give? Which do we want?

WE NEVER DID settle our ultimatum game. What are you prepared to give me? And me, you? And can you accept what I offer?

How about fifty bucks each? Because you're human, too.

14
The Future

"WE CHOSE TO go to the moon . . . not because it is easy, but because it is hard," President John F. Kennedy said in a celebrated speech at Rice University on September 12, 1962.[1]

The previous year Kennedy had told Congress that he wanted an American on the moon before the decade was out.

"Why choose this as our goal? And they may well ask why climb the highest mountain," Kennedy asked at Rice University and answered: "Because that goal will serve to organize and measure the best of our energies and skills"—i.e., to create new knowledge and technology, and, as Kennedy's final argument went, to create new companies and jobs.

As we know, it worked. Not only did a dozen men visit the moon, but there were spin-offs, too, such as Teflon frying pans, computer chips, satellite navigation, and space food. And perhaps most important of all: the image of Earth viewed from space, a tremor of epochal significance in the history of science and thought.

Kennedy could not have predicted the kitchenware, computers, or the concept of Spaceship Earth, but he had the courage to believe that doing something difficult would lead to something new.

Doing something easy doesn't lead to anything new, of course. Because facility comes precisely from knowing how to do it. Difficulty comes from the opposite: from moving in unknown territory.

Denmark shares exactly the same experience as a nation. Several times in its history it has gone for something difficult and strange.

In the sixteenth century Denmark was a great power in astronomy and benefited for centuries from the scientific community then created. The cooperative movement started by its farmers elevated Denmark into an industrial society. Free universal health care in our welfare state led to flourishing industrial companies. And twenty-five years ago popular demand for sustainable energy, trashed by practically all the experts, became the Danish wind-turbine industry, which now has the global wind in its sails.

You have to set almost impossible goals. When you go for

them you learn a lot on the way. And you're rewarded with spin-offs nobody ever dreamed of.

Take the hard way out—and you'll reach the moon.

JOHN F. KENNEDY'S reason for going to the moon was a grand example of a costly signal. At bottom the reason was military, of course: the Americans were scared stiff at the prospect of Russian domination in space science—and hence space itself—and, in turn, the world. To show the Russians they needed to respect the Americans, the United States sent the costly signal of putting a man on the moon. This is entirely within the logic of the handicap principle: if you can do that, there's a hell of a lot else you're capable of, too.

The journey to the moon is an archetypal example of a costly signal, a burden you assume to show your strength. At the national level it's a kind of generosity: we're doing this out of our surplus resources for everyone's benefit. "We came in peace for all mankind," as the plaque on the first moon-landing craft, the Eagle, from Apollo 11 read. It was pure and unadulterated national selfishness, but utilized itself in the common interest. Which indeed it was, too, or it would not have served the nation's selfish interests. It was by doing something that impressed everyone and could be seen by everyone as magnificent, that the Americans showed how strong they were.

The moon landing is not only an example of the way our own interests can be promoted by costly signals in everyone's interests, but also of the way the logic of generosity brings effects in its wake that exceed the selfish interests of the original motive and the general interests that made the costly effort an interesting signal.

Because, of course, the most important lasting effect of the moon landing was not to frighten the Russians or conquer space, but something quite different: the sight of Earth from without. This spin-off, the shockingly beautiful sight of a blue, blue planet against the blackness of space, unlike anything we humans had ever seen in the skies, became an emblem of environmental awareness and responsibility on our planet: an infinite insight into the fact that we humans are traveling companions onboard a spaceship, a teeny-weenie, tender planet orbiting in the light of a star in a universe dominated by darkness.

The technology surpassed its original horizons; self interest led to a magnificent act that led somewhere quite different from the itinerary: not the conquering of space but the discovery of Earth.

Unfortunately, there's no reason to suppose that every technological investment will lead to such benign surprises. On the contrary, there are reasons to be concerned about technological progress this century, precisely with respects to sexual selection and man's propensity for behaving socially. As far as I can see there are at least two reasons.

THE ULTIMATUM GAME shows that we are more willing to share the cake with another human than with a computer. We are prepared to accept lower offers from a computer than from another human because we can't be bothered to train a computer. We don't take offense at a computer's greed.

When conducted with players in brain scanners, the prisoner's dilemma showed that there was less cooperation when the human player thought he or she was playing a computer. The cooperation that led to activity in the reward center of the brain when the opposing player was human did not result in the same pleasure when the counterpart was a computer.

So on the one hand we've learned from experimental economics that man is no *Homo economicus*. We're by no means as selfish and rational as the economists think we are. On the other, we have learned that *Homo economicus* does exist in its pure form: there is an opponent that's cool and rational, and that we treat accordingly, without compassion, empathy, or indignation. Ironically, this *Homo economicus* is the computer.

All the coolness and common sense we erroneously think we possess exists because we created it through the cool, rational design of a machine. We created the computer in our own image. The fact that the image is false does not stop the computer from working.

But it raises a serious problem.

THE COMPUTER IS far inferior to man today. It is stupid and expensive and not very good at very much of any interest to us. Its ability to process information, its processing power, is way below that of the human brain. But it won't last. Robotics scientists nearly all predict that by the year 2030 (when your house is paid off) the processing power of the computer will exceed that of the human brain.[2]

In a generation—i.e., thirty years—robots, computers, communications networks, and many other entities will be controlled by processing power similar to our own. We will be surrounded by robots, agents, network butlers, and gadgets capable of amazing things. There can hardly be any doubt that many of the activities that send us off into society today will be carried out on our behalf by agents like these. Classic examples of their functions are precisely those—such as comparing prices, purchasing goods, sorting out insurance matters, and so forth—which come within the sphere of economics. Much of our interaction with the economy will be brokered by these quick-thinking technological agents. A huge relief when it comes to struggling with train timetables and store catalogs.

But, and this is where the problem arises: how do you negotiate with a robot? Will it involve all the feelings of cohesion, loyalty, fairness, reciprocity, and largesse with which experimental economics has shown man meets man? Will the feelings of reciprocity and obligation, which the economist Robert Frank pointed out as the decisive reason why something so apparently heartless and anonymous as the market economy can function, still be there when we haggle with a computer?

Today our image of ourselves is that we're always wearing our market masks; but we have seen that this only works because there is a human face behind the mask that restrains us from the very stupidest kinds of automatic rationality.

But now we've spawned technologies that can make the notion of *Homo economicus* a reality: namely, what we may call *Robot economicus*. What will this mean to society? Will cordiality disappear? Will involvement in other people vanish?

Will we end up living in a social environment dominated by machines, and thereby lose our ability to empathize? Will we begin to regard everyone else as cynical machines for whom we are not prepared to sacrifice anything in order to turn them into decent partners?

This set of problems is not way out in the distant future. Interfacing with artificial agents will become an important feature of our social lives. It's high time that we realized why and how our society operates. If it's true that the market can only function because it's part of a society that in turn can only function because it's sustained by an extensive civil network of personal relationships confirmed by a gift economy, can we build functioning technology without equipping it with the feelings that sustain civil society? Computers and robots will have to learn about *hau,* about generosity, and in the final analysis, about sex.

It's an enormous task. Not only because the people who direct the development of this technology come from a background in engineering and economics, with its demonstrably incorrect image of the way man and his society operate, but because in the present decade most western welfare states are giving a lower priority to the parts of society's care for its members that lead to healthy humans: schools, nurseries, the arts, communities—all these are being dismantled at present.

But nursery schools are probably the most important strategic resource in the development of a robot technology not based on pure notions of *Homo economicus.* The nursery school is a nation's secret weapon in the global economic competition. And I say this for a reason.

WHEN WORK BEGAN on artificial intelligence in the six-ties, scientists ran into a problem: as they tried to extract the rules for intelligence and knowledge from humans in order to give them to computers, they discovered that it didn't really work. It's hugely difficult to explain to a computer how to see. How to catch. How to understand the words of a language. It turned out that computers and simple robots found it very hard to learn the skills infant humans quickly acquire.

Advanced robots will have to learn just like humans: by experience. They'll have to use trial and error, try speaking the language, try bumping into tables, try singing a song. They'll have to get it wrong again and again if they're to learn something. We won't be able to just slip them the rules, because nobody can learn a language from its grammar; not even robots.

It's a myth that man learns by rules. Thus, neither can robots. They have to try out the world for themselves. The most important role of the nursery teacher is not feeding rules and tables to the kids, but supporting and comforting them. Just as parents do: baby tries out the world and ouch! he bumps himself and needs to be comforted. Love is the secret behind man's fabulous ability to learn: the knowledge that you're from a loving environment that can give you comfort and relief from pain means you have the courage to get out there and try things out.

It sounds pretty romantic, but in the future it will be a no-holds-barred export policy: robots will need training and nobody will do a better job than nursery school teachers. They've put up with generations of snot-nosed kids, so they'll have no trouble coping with a couple of generations of robots that aren't picky, happily nap after lunch, and never pee in the sandbox. No other country has nursery schools as good as Denmark's and so they won't be able to compete with the quality of Denmark's robots. In the future the rich of southeast Asia will want their breakfast orange juice served by a cute robot. So they'll look for the brand known as *From Scandinavia with Love.*

The robots will be able to reproduce themselves; the technical stuff with its circuits and gizmos will be child's play for them. But that doesn't mean they'll automatically acquire the ability to incorporate experiences of love and curiosity into their systems. This can't be done on the basis of *rules*; it takes *experiences* of great affection and even greater patience.

So the robots will have to be sent to nursery school.

IF THIS IDEA has anything to it, there are reasons to believe that we'll be able to create a society and environment in which the human wisdom that lies beyond *Homo economicus* will continue to prevail. But it will be a pretty decisive cultural battle, and it's not too soon to join it. Because otherwise we'll soon end up playing the Ultimatum game with a counterpart who corresponds more to our myth about ourselves than our reality.

We must create a *Robot reciprocans,* or perhaps even the slightly louche *Robot generosus.*

THE OTHER REASON for concern at where technological progress is taking us is biotechnology, particularly the part of it involved in controlling human reproduction—

i.e., the way new humans are made. "Sex is fun, but not necessarily the best way of making new people," one researcher into human reproduction said back in the eighties.[3]

Sexual selection, which has created so many fantastic traits in man, is characterized by the fact that it's completely distributed throughout society, among all its members. Everybody is attracted sexually by others. Most have the urge to reproduce. They choose partners and mate. Evolution continues.

In many contests it's the women who make the greatest impact on this selection, because they're the ones who do the propagation grunt work. But irrespective of whether women or men have the greater impact on sexual selection, it's hard to see human sexual selection as a sensible, rational activity. Love is, as we know, inscrutable. Selection is intuitive more than anything else.

In other words, sexual selection is a distributed, intuitive administration of man's evolution as a species.

The decisions on how man's evolution is to proceed are made from the phenomenon of desire/lack of desire in people's homes, in bars, and in discos.

Nobody can tell how man would've turned out if the decisions had been made another way: centralized and rationally. But isn't that the way biotechnology is taking us? Instead of a sequence of choices independent of one another that determine who makes whom weak in the knees, reproduction is becoming a centrally controlled, rational event resulting in shrewd medical considerations and techniques and objectively reasoned decisions as to which eggs are to be rejected and which children to be born.

It's not only a matter of doctors performing non-stop amniotic fluid tests and turning many pregnant moms into patients. It's also a matter of potential parents no longer being allowed to listen to their own intuitive desire to mate with another human, but beginning to get rational ideas about preferring a girl baby, preferably a brunette, preferably one who can jump, preferably a genius, but also musical, and a non-smoker.

The designer baby, created through rational choice and deliberate priorities, by using centrally developed technology and according to a set of ethics drawn up by a state committee, is a very different child from a love child resulting from the coming together of two humans.

Cloning enables the creation of humans who are not the fruit of two people's embrace but of the intense desire of one human to see himself created once more.

Biotechnology therefore involves the possibility, at least, of a radical, drastic transformation of evolution from distributed, intuitive control to centralized, rational control. But what if the beauty of man is due to a hitherto unrecognized wisdom in distributed, intuitive selection? Where will we be then?

But is it that certain that distributed, intuitive selection is the right method of managing our future? Might there not be plenty of shrewdness in rationality: a great deal of suffering we could save ourselves and lots of beauty we can create?

In my view, the most important human experience that can shed light on this question is the *demographic transition,* in many respects one of the most important events in the history of mankind.

ANIMALS DIFFER. SOME reproduce at a tremendous pace, but in return their mortality rate is high. Others reproduce slowly and peacefully, but live much longer.

Rabbits, rats, and insects are examples of the former way of managing the population; biologists call it an *r-strategy*. Myriad animals are born, but mortality is enormous, so the population remains constant over a longer period of time, though with large fluctuations. The individual animals are small, short-lived, and are born in large litters of which the majority perishes. The interval between births is brief, and the generations rapidly succeed one another.

The other way of managing the population is known as a *k-strategy*. It's familiar from elephants, humans, and other large animals that live in something resembling balance with the environment. Pregnancy and life are both long, offspring are born individually and at considerable intervals, enabling some serious parental care. The birth rate is low but so is the mortality rate, at any rate compared to that of rats.

Both strategies can lead to stable populations, because the birth and death rates are equal, although at very different levels.[4]

If we regard humanity as one large population, we are currently engaged in a transition from an r-strategy to a k-strategy. Mankind's original ecological niche—adaptation to a life as hunters and gatherers, originally took us into a k-strategy situation with a low birth rate; but agriculture and then industrialization created enormous population growth making everything more like an r-strategy (even though in the broader, biological perspective we've always belonged to the k-strategists).

The transition from high birth rates and high death rates in our part of the world took place from the end of the eighteenth century to the middle of the twentieth century.

The mortality rate fell first, because sanitation improved. Clean water, good nutrition, better housing, and broken chains of infection enabled man to better resist parasites, which had besieged man with great infectious diseases for many of the early centuries in modern times. We learned to cheat the parasites by making a sharp distinction between the body's *input* and *output* (water, food, and feces).

Once the mortality rate had begun to fall, the birth rate also diminished, although with some delay (about a century). Then the two quantities stabilized (accession and demise) until they were roughly the same size. The population was stable again.

During this process there was a period of lower mortality rates but in it the birth rate remained high: the population therefore grew to several times its original size. But then it stabilized.

The industrial nations of the world have all passed through this shift from r-like population dynamics to k-like ones. Since, the population has been stable or even declined.

It's this shift that is known as the demographic transition. It's brought about considerable changes to society and is nowadays taking place at a global level, because the developing countries are beginning to catch up. The UN population statistics suggest that the world population, currently at six billion, will stabilize at the end of this century at around ten billion.[5]

What is remarkable is that this transition has taken place in almost every part of the world for hundreds of years without being the result of a conscious, central decision. Everywhere in the world where sanitary improvements have reduced the mortality rate, after a delay of a couple of generations, the birth rate has begun to fall as well.

The fall in the mortality rate may be the result of efforts society has decided to make. Better drains, a ban on dangerous foods, urban planning, and health services play a part. For society, welfare pays, because sickness costs.

But the birth rate is not something anyone decided on. There were no authorities with the power to decide how many children a Danish woman was to have in 1927. It was up to her, along with her husband and the technical options available to her. Today, when all kinds of contraceptives are freely available, the decisions have become a bit easier to implement, but it was not contraception that caused the birth rate to fall: it was the fall in the mortality rate.

Everywhere in the world a fall in the mortality rate has been followed by a falling birth rate. Totally distributed throughout society, highly intuitively and emotionally, the couples of this world decide whether to have more children; they each make the decision based on their life expectancy. Yet we see one society after another obeying the law of demographic transition.

Why? Because man is an animal who makes highly

practical biological decisions on reproduction; once we see that two or three children are enough to ensure that there are sufficient surviving offspring to help us at the rest home, we stop having lots of children. Not as the result of a centrally directed, rational policy, but as the result of powerful emotional decisions in the family home.

This shows that man is able to make extremely practical decisions on matters of life and death (literally), even if the authority to make them is distributed throughout society and is administered intuitively. A most remarkable state of affairs. Can we say anything even vaguely similar about the centrally determined birth-control programs being attempted in various places around the world?

Decentralized, intuitive administration is not only possible; it has proved astonishingly effective. Because, biologically speaking, the transformation of the birth rate taking place in the world today is the main event, while stock prices, athletics results, and the whims of fashion houses are mere ripples.

*K*EEP SEXUAL SELECTION! This will be one of the most important political and cultural demands in the future: man's genetic future must be managed de-centrally and intuitively, not centrally and rationally. But sexual selection is under threat from biotechnology.

You may think that it's irrational and bad management to allow decisions as important as the future of mankind to be made in society's double beds by flattered women propagating with drunken suitors. But it is this irrationality to which we owe the origin of man's most wonderful facets: generosity, empathy, kindliness, tolerance, morality, altruism, willingness to cooperate, and creativity.

Passion is the root of all good. *Stay horny!*

When the technologists, scientists, and the rest of them argue that opponents of biotechnology and cloning are just romantic opponents of scientific progress and of the continued dynamism of human civilization, we may suitably retort: *What do you think will happen to art, science, culture, athletics, society, civilization, and the conquering of outer space if you deprive us of sexuality?*

We want to make babies with our dicks! If not we'll do a *reverse Lysistrata:* no art, no science, and no voluntary service until we get sex back. Real sex of the kind that results in babies.

Without sexual selection, no effort.

SOME OF WHAT gives life meaning is that we constantly have to make sure we're competent to win a mate to mate with. Sexual selection takes place constantly in the sense that sex and stroking are not things you only want when you're about to make a baby. Sexuality today has been liberated from the purely reproductive act. This is why the need to show off our talents, so we can be desired by our partner, is a lifelong project. And hence an effort.

But if they deprive us of reproduction and turn sexuality into nothing but a private stimulant with no biological significance, we'll lose the meaning of life and become, in many ways, *unproductive.*

IT'S NOT ABOUT group selection, or our strange, abstract, good sides, or our ideals, or the better angels of our nature. It's about generosity, effort, Zahavi's handicap, and sexual selection. We are social; we support other people because it's in our interests to do so. That's what is so special about us humans:

Effort gives you sex
Gifts give relationships
Generosity gives pleasure

This, I assert, is what defines man; this is man's secret, which sets him apart from all other animals; this is our own very special discovery.

Man is the creature that decided sexual selection should be according to effort, that we should choose a mate according to how much effort has been made. Man is therefore the creature that has most of all evolved himself, his mind, and his surroundings, into a fantastic world.

However beautiful the blue whale, the elephant, and the gorilla may seem to us, their world is nothing compared with the matchless world man has created in his quest for a mate. Oh, yes, they are splendid, these lovely animals, but quite honestly, and no matter how rich their singing and grunting maybe, they are no match for us.

GENEROSITY AND CREATIVITY are a consequence of our sexuality and its special selection. It is not for nothing that the word generosity comes from the Latin word *genus,* which means sex, kin, family.

When generosity is rooted in kinship and sexuality, this also means that it's constantly being refueled: we want strokes, kindliness, affection, friendship, and physical contact. Every day. Twelve hugs a day. It's a *drive* in everyday life: we want love, so we're creative and generous.

Every time we have sex it reassures us that our genotype is okay. Another human selects our phenotype as attractive because our phenotype signals a good genotype. Sex is good for your quality of life partly because it's the ultimate form of acceptance.

Sexual selection has led to us, because it chose the people who displayed generosity, public spirit, and a sense of commitment. The people who were prepared to share won the jackpot. We are their descendants. We must nurture this inheritance.

We have got to realize that while perhaps "gentlemen prefer blondes," as they say,[6] it is far more important and correct to say that "blondes prefer gentlemen." And to remember that gentlemen are men who behave decently.

The division of the species into two genders, whose members each select an example of the opposite sex, creates a motor, a power, a dynamism that keeps all the wheels turning. It really is all about love.

"Love is all there is, it makes the world go round," as Bob Dylan sings.[7]

S EXUAL SELECTION IS a greater change in the perspective of biological evolution than you might think at first. In my case, it shook the very foundations of my view of the world: the notion that the universe is full of living creatures with cultures and civilizations as rich as those of man.

For decades I've been following research into the possibility of life beyond Earth, and seen it move in twin directions: on the one hand, the purely scientific preconditions for believing that there are other living creatures in the universe have improved markedly—there are countless planets out there; the foundations for the chemistry of life are formed spontaneously in almost-empty space; self-organization is an important property of so-called dead nature.

But on the other hand, there are pretty powerful arguments for stating that there cannot be very many civilizations in our Milky Way: if there had been, they'd have been so prominent in the galactic landscape that we would have spotted them ages ago; if they were out there they would already be here, the argument goes, and it is annoyingly compelling.[8] The point is that the universe is already old enough that if there were many civilizations out there at least some of them would've already conquered the entire galaxy, including Earth. So if they're out there, they're already down here. But they're not down here, so they can't be out there.[9]

Annoying, because I so much want to believe there is life out there with which we can make contact. There are still good reasons for believing there might be. But that it evolves brains like ours, cultures like ours, or science like ours is less credible, because human evolution is the result of man's sexual preferences. And why should they be distributed throughout the cosmos?

If we look at the fauna of our own little planet, it's characteristic that many of its most remarkable products are similar inventions made many times independently of one another. The dolphin and the shark are extremely different if we look at their evolutionary history and inner structure, but they both agree entirely on the best possible hydrodynamics for a sea creature.

But the human propensity to build technological equipment, colossal libraries, or to gaze at the stars is unique. Neither the whale nor the elephant, both of which have larger brains than man, has dedicated itself to creativity, art, or moon landings. She-elephants and she-whales apparently look for more significant things in a potential mate.

In other words, the history of mankind is quite special: it's the result of a completely open, non-directional sexual selection; selection according to individuals with the ability and the desire to make an effort, to reach out for the world and to transform it.

We may therefore be completely alone in the universe when it comes to lifeforms with a powerful urge for space travel. There may be loads of whales, elephants, and microbes out there, but the little woman won't give them any lovin' in return for exploring the universe. The women of the cosmos may not have a predilection for world conquerors. Perhaps we're entirely alone in painting pictures in order to get our rocks off. Sexual selection out there in the galaxy may be based on principles entirely different from ours; these extraterrestrial creatures may never have discovered that effort leads to making out and hence to matchless results.

Are we alone in the cosmos with this discovery?

THE NEXT STEP in the history of the world will be to learn for real to take the hard way out. We don't just have to get to the moon and the stars: we have to get to one another here on Earth. Will you agree to help to save the world? Will you agree to be generous everywhere you go—in the bedroom, in the polling booth, at the sailing club? Will you agree to be magnanimous, open-handed, tolerant, creative, community-minded, world saving, visionary, forward-thinking, courageous, giving, sharing, and thorough? No, I can't get my head around it either.

Nor do I say you *have to.* You'll survive anyway, and I'm sure everything will work out all right. All I'm saying is that if you don't, you won't get enough you-know-what.

I won't pretend I'm an expert on love or generosity, certainly not in practice. But now that I've started, I might as well try to summarize the whole business. How about something as insane as a set of simple rules for living:

1. Pursue self-interest: be generous.
2. Be selfish: share everything.
3. Show your individuality: create community.
4. Be greedy: make an effort.
5. Make an effort with your mate.
6. Make space: every man unto his own effort.
7. Fight cloning: make babies with pleasure.
8. Demand love from your robot.
9. Save the world: have sex.

Epilogue

"I'll give you something you can't get on the Internet!" said the artist Jens Jørgen Thorsen. He raised a bucket of yellow paint above his head and poured it all over himself. Drenched in yellow paint from his long hair down to his leopard-skin pants, he went back to work on his six large canvasses, gesticulating and talking away. A *performance* continued.

The Sønderborg Sales and Advertising Association had organized a major event. Hundreds of business people from the Danish province on the German border had consumed their plates of pork with trimmings and were now seated in long rows in what just happened to be called the Dyers Hall of the Erhvervs Uddannelses Center Syd (that is, the Business Training Centre South). It was Thursday, November 2, 2000.

At one end of the hall Thorsen scurried about, working away at the gigantic painting as the process was captured on video and broadcast on the Web, where you could bid for the painting; after the auction the money would go to the Red Cross. "I paint to get laid," Jens Jørgen Thorsen shouted enthusiastically as he doused himself and his canvas with paint.

At the other end of the hall I was giving a talk on the Internet and the impact digital technology would have on the future. My starting point was the dissolution of the headquarters-thinking that the Internet is based on. The distributed network made up of immeasurable connected nodes is superior to the centralized network with its vulnerable headquarters. This technological model is inspired by living nature, where the central nervous systems of living creatures are organized according to the same principle that we've since used for the Internet: a massive number of connections comprising a network that can regulate itself, and that is highly robust, ensuring that there will almost always be connections left even if major damage is inflicted on it.

The challenge to central control and surveillance is the secret behind the success of mammals, I explained. You . can't tell in advance which knowledge and skills a creature as advanced as a human is going to need in his lifetime. So you can't equip him with predetermined rules that instruct about life. He has to learn by trial and error and to take the knocks that come his way. That's why love is the very recipe for a mammal: its offspring are born weak and unable to cope unaided, but they're able to learn about the world by doing so under their parents' tender care. We can't understand the world by studying the rules for it; we have to run into the wall time and time again. The only way of ensuring that we can survive the inevitable head trauma that follows is tender loving care and parental willingness to invest time and effort in the wee ones. Let's hear it for the mammals.

The crowd in the Dyers Hall had to crane their necks and turn their heads to keep up with this bizarre show in which Thorsen babbled about pussy at one end of the hall while I preached mammalian glands at the other. To each his own.

JENS JØRGEN THORSEN died unexpectedly but quietly during a siesta a couple of weeks later. A gentle demise. No more films, *situationist* actions, performances, paintings, television appearances, and crazy ideas. In his lifetime he painted quite a few pictures and got even more pussy. This small, happy, generous man with his blinking eyes and huge talent for intimacy and provocation didn't need to be in a room for many seconds before he'd picked out a woman with whom he could flirt unashamedly. There was nothing to be ashamed of. Thorsen was into pussy. And art. There's no contradiction there: just life and creation.

THE FORMULA WAS simple but it contained a tiny disparity that explains so much of human life it's almost beyond comprehension: *Thorsen got pussy. The rest of us got paintings.*

The disparity in the formula regards the fact that for Thorsen the ultimate driving force was aimed at obtaining something pleasurable from the object of his desire (that is, pussy). But in the process he produced something that gave pleasure to lots of other people, too; and continues to do so.

Sexual selection is about the fact that we want something from *one* other, but to attain it we create something that pleases *many* others. Our instinct is to couple—a meeting between two people—but in order to get it we've developed generosity, creativity, altruism, and fellowship for the benefit of the many.

To win her, we give something to everyone else—creative works or just common decency. To win her, we create togetherness: to-get-her-ness . . .

WHAT DO YOU think? Thorsen didn't stick to one *other*, but sowed his seed all over the place, did he not? I suppose so; but the disparity still holds good. Even with Picasso, maybe he was as fond of the ladies as we've been told, but however hard he tried he couldn't have gotten through to nearly as many ladies with his dick as he did with his paintings. A great deal of us developed our visual sense through acquaintanceship with Picasso's works; far more people than Picasso ever actually met. I'm sure John Lennon and the other Beatles also had all the girls they wanted, but there are still far more who delight in their music.

THE DISPARITY IS simple but the consequences are huge: in courtship one party reaches for another and satisfaction is consummated in the meeting between the two; but the game results in the spin-offs of self-expression, beauty, and creativity, often to the benefit of many. To win her, he gives something to all of us. Two people meet, and the violins play.

This is not just the story of painting resulting in pussy and effort resulting in making out. It's also the story of pussy resulting in paintings and making out resulting in effort. But okay, it's the same story, of course.

We have our desire and our sexual drive to thank for compelling us to create so much beautiful art and to make such an effort in general: to the delight of ourselves, because it finds us a mate, and to the delight of others, because it inspires our creative drive and our willingness to cooperate.

Love lifts us up where we belong.[1]

Through all the world
there goes one long cry
from the heart of the artist:
"Give me leave to do my utmost!"[2]

Notes

CHAPTER 1

1 For an overview, see Werner Güth and Reinhard Tietz: "Ultimatum Bargaining Behavior: A Survey and Comparison of Experimental Results," *Journal of Economic Psychology 11*, 417–449, 1990; Herbert Gintis: *Game Theory Evolving*, Princeton: Princeton University Press, 2000, 252–254.

2 The expression *Homo economicus* is so common that no original source is ever credited. I have been unable to ascertain where it comes from, but its current usage may be seen in D. Rutherford: *Dictionary of Economics*, London: Routledge, 1992, 208; and in J. Eatwell, M. Milgate, and P. Newman: *The New Palgrave Dictionary of Economics*, London: Macmillan, 1987, Vol. 1, 587. The variant "economic man" is also current; see A. Barnard and J. Spencer (eds.): *Encyclopedia of Social and Cultural Anthropology*, London: Routledge, 2002 [orig. 1996], 603.

3 Joseph Henrich, Robert Boyd, Samuel Bowles, Colin Camerer, Ernst Fehr, Herbert Gintis, and Richard McElreath: "In Search of *Homo economicus:* Behavioral Experiments in 15 Small-Scale Societies," *American Economic Review 91(2)*, 73–78, 2001.

4 For an overview, see: Robert H. Frank, T. Gilovich, and D. T. Reagan: "Does Studying Economics Inhibit Cooperation?," *Journal of Economic Perspectives 7(2)*, 159–171, 1993.

5 John Carter and Michael Irons: "Are Economists Different, and If So, Why?," *Journal of Economic Perspectives 5(2)*, 171–177, 1991.

6 Ibid., 173.

7 The analysis of the data in terms of individual players was undertaken by the Swedish economist Jan Tullberg in his working paper "The Ultimatum Game Revisited," Stockholm School of Economics WP 1999, available at http://swoba.hhs.se/hastba/papers/hastba1999_002.pdf.

8 For an authoritative and extremely comprehensive overview see John H. Kagel and Alvin E. Roth: *The Handbook of Experimental Economics*, Princeton: Princeton University Press, 1995.

9 Ernst Fehr and Simon Gächter: "Altruistic Punishment in Humans," *Nature 415*, 137–140, 2002.

10 *Encyclopedia Britannica*, Chicago, 1993, vol. 1, 302.

11 Karl Sigmund, Ernst Fehr, and Martin A. Nowak: "The Economics of Fair Play," *Scientific American*, 83–87, January 2002.

12 Robert Frank: *Passions within Reason*, New York: W.W. Norton, 1988, x.

13 Ibid., 11.

14 Gregory Berns quoted in Natalie Angier: "Why We're So Nice: We're Wired to Cooperate," *New York Times*, July 23, 2002.

15 James K. Rilling et al.: "A Neural Basis for Social Cooperation," *Neuron 35*, 395–405, 2002.

CHAPTER 2

1 An excellent historical overview is to be found in: "A Chronology of Game Theory," http://www.econ.canterbury.ac.nz/hist.htm.

2 J. Bronowski: *The Ascent of Man*, London: BBC, 1973, 432.

3 Herbert Gintis: *Game Theory Evolving*, Princeton: Princeton University Press, 2000, xxiii. See also Herbert Gintis: "The Contribution of Game Theory to Experimental Design in the Behavioral Sciences," *Behavioral and Brain Sciences 24*, 411–412, 2001; and

the rest of the discussion on the target article by R. Hertwig and Andreas Ortmann: "Experimental Practices in Economics: A Methodological Challenge for Psychologists?," *Behavioral and Brain Sciences 24,* 383–453, 2001.

4 *Stanford Encyclopedia of Philosophy:* "Game Theory," 33, http://plato. stanford.edu/entries/game-theory.

5 Brian Skyrms: *The Stag Hunt,* Presidential Address, Pacific Division of the American Philosophical Association, March 2001, available at http://hypatia.ss.uci.edu/lps/home/fac-staff/faculty/skyrms/Hunt.PDF.

6 Quoted from William Poundstone: *Prisoner's Dilemma,* New York: Anchor Books, 1992, 220. From *Discours sur l'origine de l'inegalité,* 1755.

7 Robert H. Frank: *Luxury Fever: Money and Happiness in an Era of Excess,* Princeton: Princeton University Press, 1999, 152 et seq.

8 Sylvia Nasar: *A Beautiful Mind,* London: Faber & Faber, 2001 [orig. New York, 1998], paperback, 118. See also Poundstone (1992), 101 et seq; and for a variation Gintis (2000), 19–20, in which the car thieves are replaced by lawyers who cheat with the bill.

9 Gintis (2000), xxiv.

10 See R. Hertwig and Andreas Ortmann, 383–453.

11 Tor Nørretranders: "Civilisationens sårbare centre," *Børsens Nyheds-magasin,* September 17, 2001. Tor Nørretranders: "The Vulnerability of Headquarters," www.edge.org, September 21, 2001.

12 A critique of altruism as an ethical precept is to be found in Jan and Birgitta Tullberg: *Naturlig Etik: En Uppgörelse Med Altruismen,* Stockholm: Lykeion förlag, 1994. But apart from the critique of altruism as a program there are not many similarities between the Tullberg ethic of reciprocity and the ethic of dissimilarity developed in the present book.

13 See for example Matt Ridley: *The Origins of Virtue,* New York: Penguin, 1998 [orig. 1996], 6.

CHAPTER 3

1 Charles Darwin: *On the Origin of Species,* Hertfordshire: Wordsworth Classics of World Literature, 1998. Another frequently utilized photographic reproduction of the first edition of Darwin's work uses an abbreviated title on its title page: *On the Origin of Species by Charles Darwin. A Facsimile of the First Edition,* Cambridge, MA: Harvard University Press, 1964. Darwin originally wanted the title *An Abstract of an Essay on the Origin of Species and Varieties through Natural Selection,* but his publisher, John Murray, had the initial padding removed, according to Thomas Hylland Eriksen's *Charles Darwin,* Copenhagen: Tiderne Skifter, 2000 [orig. 1997], 74.

2 Charles Darwin: *On the Origin of Species.*

3 Daniel C. Dennett: *Darwin's Dangerous Idea,* Harmondsworth: Penguin, 1996 [orig. 1995], 21: "Let me lay my cards on the table: If I were to give an award for the single best idea anyone ever had, I'd give it to Darwin, ahead of Newton and Einstein and everyone else. In a single stroke, the idea of evolution by natural selection unifies the realm of life. . . ."

4 Thomas Hylland Eriksen, 7.

CHAPTER 4

1 For a detailed study of Haldane and other British researchers/ Marxists between the wars such as Haldane, J. D. Bernal, Joseph Needham, and others, see Gary Werskey: *The Visible College,* London: Allen Lane, 1978. Haldane's background see p. 52 et seq. For a discussion of his style and what became of him see Tor Nørretranders: "Fysik, Mystik, Politik," *Hug 35,* Copenhagen, 1982, 4–13, printed in Tor Nørretranders: *Person på en planet,* Copenhagen: Aschehough, 1995, 230–246.

2 The story is reproduced in numerous locations in the literature,

though not always with the same figures. The numbers three and nine are to be found in John Casti: *Paradigms Lost,* New York: Avon, 1990, 166 (where the coaster is mentioned), and John Troyer: "Human and other natures," in: L. D. Katz (ed.): *Evolutionary Origins of Morality,* Thorverton: Imprint Academic, 2000, 62–65, here p. 65. Other accounts give two siblings, eight cousins, e.g., Lee Dugatkin: *Cheating Monkeys and Citizen Bees,* New York: The Free Press, 1999, 40 (where the episode is dated in the thirties) and in Steven Rose: "Escaping Evolutionary Psychology," in: H. and P. Rose (eds.): *Alas, Poor Darwin,* London: Vintage, 2001, 247–265, here p. 249. We will return to the numbers later.

3 J. B. S. Haldane: "Population Genetics," *New Biology 18,* 1955, 34–51, here p. 44. See also Richard Dawkins: *The Selfish Gene,* Oxford: Oxford University Press, 1989 [orig. 1976], 96; A. and A. Zahavi: *The Handicap principle,* Oxford: Oxford University Press, 1997, 163.

4 William Hamilton: *Narrow Roads of Gene Land, The Collected papers of W. D. Hamilton,* W. H. Freeman, Oxford: 1996, 26.

5 W. D. Hamilton: "The Genetical Evolution of Social Behavior," *Journal of Theoretical Biology 7,* 1964, 1–52.

6 Ibid., 1.

7 Hamilton's rule puts it simply: $rb > c$ where r is the degree of kinship, b is the payoff for the kin, and c is the cost to you.

8 Dugatkin (1999), 44, for a table of degrees of kinship.

9 This is the explanation for why Haldane's coaster calculations ought to result in the numbers three and nine: two brothers only contain exactly the same quantity of your own genes as you do, so two brothers equal no gain from the genetic point of view (and what's more, you get wet). But three brothers have more of your genes than you have. Similarly, eight cousins only have the same amount of your genes as you do, while nine cousins have more.

10 Richard Dawkins: *The Selfish Gene,* Oxford: Oxford University Press, 1989 [orig. 1976].

11 Trivers grew up in Copenhagen as the son of an employee of the United States embassy. Anders Pape Møller, personal information.

12 Robert L. Trivers: "The Evolution of Reciprocal Altruism," *The Quarterly Review of Biology 46*, 1971, 35–57.

13 Ibid., 36.

14 Yogi Berra as quoted in Robert D. Putnam: *Bowling Alone. The Collapse and Revival of American Community*, New York: Simon & Schuster, 2000, 20.

15 For a superb introduction to this pioneering experiment, see e.g.: Douglas Hofstadter: "The Prisoner's Dilemma Computer Tournaments and the Evolution of Cooperation," in: D. Hofstadter: *Metamagical Themes*, New York: Basic Books, 1985, 715–734; John Casti (1990), 198–202; William Pundstone: *Prisoner's Dilemma*, New York: Anchor Books, 1992, 236–255.

16 Robert Axelrod: *The Evolution of Co-operation*, London: Penguin, 1990, 3.

17 Ibid., 12.

18 Ibid., 69.

19 See Lewis Wolpert and Alison Richards: *A Passion for Science*, Oxford: Oxford University Press, 1988, interview with JMS 122–137, here 124.

20 Gintis (2000).

21 R. Axelrod and W. D. Hamilton: "The Evolution of Cooperation," *Science 211*, 1981, 1390–1396. The article is reprinted, slightly revised, as Chapter 5 in Axelrod (1990), 88–105.

22 Ullica Segerstråle: *Defenders of the truth*, Oxford: Oxford University Press, 2000, 23.

23 In Denmark too, where the periodical *Naturkampen—Socialistisk tidsskrift for naturvidenskab, teknik og medicin*, of which I was a co-editor, published a series of articles criticizing sociobiology and neo-Darwinism, of which a number were later published in

book form as Jesper Hoffmeyer: *Evolution, Økologi, Historie. Neo-darwinismens krise,* Copenhagen: politisk revys forlag, 1980.

24 Funny, if you supported Wilson's critics. His supporters didn't find it at all funny then and they still don't. They didn't find the criticism reasonable or the critics fair, see e.g. John Alcock: *The Triumph of Sociobiology,* Oxford: Oxford University Press, 2000, 3 and 20.

25 A comparison of the global agenda from the sixties with one from the millennium reveals that many of the apparently insurmountable problems of the sixties have actually progressed considerably; cf. Tor Nørretranders: *Frem i tiden,* Copenhagen: Tiderne Skifter, 1999.

26 Trivers (1971), 52.

27 Ibid., 53.

28 R. D. Alexander: *The Biology of Moral Systems,* New York: Aldine de Gruyter, 1987.

29 Richard Alexander quoted in Martin A. Nowak and Karl Sigmund: "The Dynamics of Indirect Reciprocity," *Journal of theoretical Biology 194,* 561–574, 1998, here p. 562.

30 Claus Weedekind and Manfred Milinski: "Cooperation Through Image Scoring in Humans," *Science 288,* 2000, 850–852.

31 Martin A. Nowak and Karl Sigmund: "The Dynamics of Indirect Reciprocity," *Journal of Theoretical Biology 194,* 1998, 561–574.

32 Martin A. Nowak and Karl Sigmund: "Evolution of Indirect Reciprocity by Image Scoring," *Nature 393,* 1998, 573–577, here. p. 576; Regis Ferriere: "Help and You Shall Be Helped," *Nature 393,* 1998, 517–519.

33 Olof Leimar and Peter Hammerstein: "Evolution of Cooperation through Indirect Reciprocity," *Proceedings of the Royal Society of London Series B, 268,* 2001, 745–753, here p. 753.

34 Rebecca Bliege Bird et al.: "Risk and Reciprocity in Meriam Food Sharing," *Evolution and Human Behavior 23,* 2002, 297–321, here.

p. 317f. See also Gilbert Roberts: "Competitive Altruism: From Reciprocity to the Handicap Principle," *Proceedings of the Royal Society of London Series B 265,* 1997, 427–431.

35 G. S. Wilkinson: "Reciprocal Food Sharing in the Vampire Bat," *Nature 308,* 1984, 181–184.

36 Bernd Heinrich and John Marzluff: "Why Ravens Share," *American Scientist 83,* 1995, 342–349.

37 Samuel Bowles and Herbert Gintis: *"Homo reciprocans,"* Nature *415,* 2002, 125–126.

38 Ibid., 251–252.

39 On group selection among primates and humans as the origin of our social traits, see Christopher Boehm: *Hierarchy in the Forest: The Evolution of Egalitarian Behavior,* Cambridge, MA: Harvard University Press, 1999.

40 Charles Darwin: *The Descent of Man,* Amherst: Prometheus Books, 1998 [orig. 1871], 134–135.

41 Ibid., 137.

42 Lee Dugatkin: *Cheating Monkeys and Citizen Bees,* New York: The Free Press, 1999, 140.

43 George C. Williams: *Adaptation and Natural Selection: A Critique of Some Current Evolutionary Thought,* Princeton: Princeton University Press, 1966, see esp. chapter 4, 92–124.

44 Elliott Sober and David Sloan Wilson: *Unto Others. The Evolution and Psychology of Unselfish Behavior,* Cambridge, MA: Harvard University Press. 2000 [orig. 1998], 23f. See also John Maynard Smith: *Evolutionary genetics,* 2nd ed., Oxford: Oxford University Press, 2001, 173f.

45 Sober and Wilson: *Unto Others,* 33.

46 Ibid., 9.

47 Herbert Gintis: "Solving The Puzzle of Procociality," 2001, *Rationality and Society,* available at http://www-unix.oit.umass.edu/~gintis/.

48 A major portion of the modern criticism of Darwinism is due to

precisely this factor. We will be returning to critics like Steven Jay Gould.

49 Charles Darwin: *On the Origin of Species,* 143.

50 A brilliant overview of the evolution of the eye as a problem of evolutionary theory is to be found in Richard Dawkins: *Climbing Mount Improbable,* London: Viking, 1996, 126–179. Dawkins also discusses the passage just quoted from *Origin.*

51 "The sight of a feather in a peacock's tail, whenever I gaze at it, makes me sick!" Darwin in a letter to Asa Gray, printed in *The Correspondence of Charles Darwin, Volume 8: 1860,* Frederick Burkhardt et al. (eds.), Cambridge: Cambridge University Press, 1993, 140.

CHAPTER 5

1 Mike Robson: "Darwinismens modtagelse i Norden," N. Bonde, J. Hoffmeyer, and H. Stangerup (ed.): *Naturens Historiefortællere I,* Gad Copenhagen, 1985, 365–382, here p. 375.

2 "Et brev om Darwinismen" reprinted in J. P. Jacobsen and Vilhelm Møller: *Darwin. Hans Liv og Lære,* Copenhagen: Gyldendalske Boghandels Forlag, 1893, 237–241. This quotation is from p. 241.

3 Charles Darwin: *The Descent of Man and Selection in Relation to Sex,* Volume I & II, London: John Murray, 1871.

4 Charles Darwin: *On the Origin of Species,* 5th ed., London: John Murray, 1869, 6.

5 Stephen Jay Gould: *The Panda's Thumb,* New York: W. W. Norton, 1982, 49–50.

6 Charles Darwin: *On the Origin of Species,* Hertfordshire: Wordsworth Classics of World Literature, 1998, 69.

7 See e.g. Anders Pape Møller: *Sexual Selection and the Barn Swallow,* Oxford: Oxford University Press, 1994.

8 See: Bent Jørgensen and Pernille Kløvedal Helweg: *Sex hvad er meningen, Kønslivets naturhistorie,* Copenhagen: Høst & Søn, 2001.

9 *The Complete Works of Lewis Carroll,* New York: Modern Library, 166. This celebrated passage is in *Through the Looking-Glass,* published in 1871 and strictly speaking not part of *Alice's Adventures in Wonderland.*

10 Matt Ridley: *The Red Queen: Sex and the Evolution of Human Nature,* London: Penguin, 1994 [orig. 1993].

11 Malte Andersson: *Sexual Selection,* Princeton: Princeton University Press, 1994, 3.

12 Alfred Russel Wallace: *Darwinism: An Exposition of the Theory of Natural Selection with Some of Its Applications,* London: Macmillan and co., 1889, 294–296.

13 Quoted from Gould (1982), 55

14 Wallace (1889), 472.

15 Ibid., 473.

16 Ibid., 478.

17 Biosemiotics, which is widespread in Danish academia in an anti-neo-Darwinist variety (see e.g. Jesper Hoffmeyer: *En snegl på vejen, Betydningens naturhistorie,* Copenhagen: Omverden/Rosinante, 1993), is based on a valid idea because signals and signs play an enormous part in biology. But the way it distances itself from modern Darwinism and thus the center of gravity of modern biology is quite unnecessary. A consistent explication of Darwinism such as that attempted by the present book also leads to a focus on signals and signs, but without uncoupling the rest of biological theory and research. On semiotics see also: John Maynard Smith: "Why Fruitflies Dance. The Variety and Reliability of Animal Signals," *The Times Literary Supplement,* No. 5131, August 3, 2001, 11–12.

18 Quoted from Gould (1982), 56.

19 John Maynard Smith: "Foreword," in: Helene Cronin: *The Ant and the Peacock,* Cambridge: Cambridge University Press, 1991, ix–x, here ix.

20 Geoffrey Miller: *The Mating Mind,* London: Vintage, 2000, 63.

21 Ibid., 61.

22 Ibid., 59.

23 Ibid., 51.

24 J. P. Jacobsen, "Mogens," *Samlede Værker,* Copenhagen: Gyldendal, 1888, 271–327.

25 Denson K. McLain, Michael P. Moulton, and Todd P. Redfearn: "Sexual Selection and the Risk of Extinction of Introduced Birds on Oceanic Islands," *OIKOS 74,* 1995, 27–34. Denson K. McLain and Stephen P. Vives: "Sexual Selection and Community Structure: An Island Biogeographic Analysis with Beetles," *OIKOS 82,* 1998, 271–281.

26 John J. Wiens: "Widespread Loss of Sexually Selected Traits: How the Peacock Lost Its Spots," *Trends in Ecology & Evolution 16,* 2001, 517–523.

CHAPTER 6

1 *Encyclopedia Britannica,* Chicago, 1993, Vol. 12, 286, mentions Veblen's Norwegian background, for example.

2 Thorstein Veblen: *The Theory of the Leisure Class,* New York: Prometheus, 1998 [orig. 1899], 75.

3 Ibid., 96, 98.

4 John Updike: "Poor Little Rich Boy," *The Guardian,* June 21, 2003.

5 Geoffrey F. Miller: "Waste: A Sexual Critique of Consumerism," *Prospect,* Feb 1999, 18–23.

6 Tor Nørretranders: "Pengenes armod," *Børsens Nyhedsmagasin 18,* June 2001.

7 On the reception given to Veblen's ideas by economists and sociologists see: Wilfred Dolfsma: "Life and Times of the Veblen Effect," *History of Economic Ideas VIII/3,* 2000, 61–82.

8 Michael Spence: "Job Market Signaling," *Quarterly Journal of Economics, 87(3),* 1973, 355–374.

9 Paul A. Johnsgard: *The Pheasants of the World, Biology and Natural*

History, 2nd. ed., Washington, D. C.: Smithsonian Institution Press, 1999, 356–7.

10 Søren Ryge Petersen: *Livet er en fugl,* Copenhagen: Høst & Søn, 2000, 119.

11 Robert L. Trivers: "Parental Investment and Sexual Selection," in: Bernard Campbell: *Sexual Selection and the Descent of Man 1871–1971,* Chicago: Aldine Publishing Company, 1972, 136–179, here p. 173.

12 Quoted at http://www.quotes.dk.

13 Richard Dawkins: *The Selfish Gene,* London: Oxford University Press, 1999 [orig. 1976], 160.

14 Ibid., 309.

15 Marion Petrie and Amanda Williams: "Peahens Lay More Eggs for Peacocks with Larger Trains," *Proceedings of the Royal Society of London B,* 251, 1993, 127–131. See also Malte Andersson: *Sexual Selection,* Princeton: Princeton University Press, 1994, 335.

16 Amotz Zahavi: "Mate Selection: A Selection for Handicap", *Journal of Theoretical Biology 53,* 1975, 205–214, here p. 210.

17 Helena Cronin: *The Ant and the Peacock,* Cambridge: Cambridge University Press, 1991, 113.

18 Anders Pape Møller: *Sexual Selection and the Barn Swallow,* Oxford: Oxford University Press, 1994. A rich overview of swallow research may be found at http://hirundorustica.com/.

19 Karl Grammer, Berhard Fink, Anders P. Møller, and Randy Thornhill: "Darwinian Aesthetics: Sexual Selection and the Biology of Beauty," *Biological Review.*

20 Zahavi (1995), 2–3.

21 Anders Pape Møller (1994), 7.

22 See Dawkins (1999/1976), 170–171.

23 Four examples are listed in Marc D. Hauser: *The Evolution of Communication,* Cambridge, MA: MIT Press, 1997 [orig. 1996], 27. In an extensive overview article, Rufus A. Johnstone: "Sexual Selection, Honest Advertising and the Handicap Principle: Reviewing the Evidence," *Biological Reviews 70,* 1995, 1–65, a very large number

of possible examples are listed. The conclusion is that there are clear examples but not many in which it is demonstrated that the handicap leads to better reproduction (p. 51). Johnstone writes on p. 52 that there are several more examples of females going for direct advantages in mate choice, e.g., food offered by the male. Zahavi and Zahavi (1998) provide a number of examples, but not all are recognized by colleagues.

24 William Hamilton "Sindet, Skønheden og Fremtiden," DR2, 1996, produced by the Mindship Fonden for Danmarks Radio. Interview: Tor Nørretranders. Hamilton took part in a seminar under the Mindship art and science seminar when Copenhagen was European Capital of Culture in 1996. The seminar was on the biology of beauty, among other things, and participants included Hamilton, Anders Pape Møller, Randy Thornhill, Karl Grammmer, Steve Gangestad, and other modern pioneers of sexual selection.

25 W. D. Hamilton and S. P. Brown: "Autumn Tree Colours as a Handicap Signal," *Proceedings of the Royal Society B, 268,* 2001, 1489–1493.

26 John Whitfield: "Trees Tell Pests to Leaf Off," *Nature Science Update,* July 10, 2001.

27 Amotz and Avishag Zahavi: *The Handicap Principle,* Oxford: Oxford University Press, 1997, 40.

28 Jared Diamond: *Den tredje chimpanse,* Copenhagen: Akademisk Forlag/Nepenthes Forlag, 1997, 207.

29 Ibid., 213.

30 *Dagbladet Politiken,* August 15, 2002, 1st (news) section, 7.

31 Susan Kelley and R.I.M. Dunbar: "Who Dares, Wins: Heroism Versus Altruism in Women's Mate Choice," *Human Nature 12,* 2001, 89–105. The study is referred to in Elisa Batista: "Science Says Women Dig Fast Cars," *Wired.*

32 Randolph M. Nesse: "How Selfish Genes Shape Moral Passions," in Leonard D. Katz: *Evolutionary Origins of Morality: Cross-Disciplinary Perspectives,* Bowling Green, OH: Imprint Academic, 2000, 227–231, here p. 227.

CHAPTER 7

1 Irwin Tessman: "Human Altruism as a Courtship Display," *OIKOS* *74*, 157–158, 1995, here p. 157.

2 Ibid., 158.

3 James L. Boone: "The Evolution of Magnaminity," *Human Nature 9*, 1998, 1–21.

4 Richard Sosis: "Costly Signaling and Torch Fishing on Ifaluk Atoll," *Evolution and Human Behavior 21*, 2000, 223–244.

5 Eric Alden Smith and Rebecca L. Bliege Bird: "Turtle Gunting and Tombstone Opening: Public Generosity as Costly Signaling," *Evolution and Human Behavior 21*, 2000, 245–261.

6 Michael Gurven: "'It's a Wonderful Life': Signaling Generosity Among the Aché of Paraguay," *Evolution and Human Behavior 21*, 2000, 263–282.

7 Zahavi (1975), 212–213.

8 Amotz Zahavi: "Altruism as a Handicap: The Limitations of Kin Selection and Reciprocity," *Journal of Avian Biology 26*, 1995, 1–3.

9 Zahavi and Zahavi (1997), 125.

10 Zahavi (1995), 2.

11 Zahavi and Zahavi (1997), 134.

12 Richard Conniff: "Why We Take Risks," *Discover*, Vol. 22 No. 12, December 2001.

13 Ibid.

14 Jonathan Wright: "Helping-at-the-Nest in Arabian Babblers: Signaling Social Status or Sensible Investment in Chicks?," *Animal Behavior 54*, 1997, 1439–1448, here p. 1447.

15 Jonathan Wright: "Altruism as a Signal: Zahavi's Alternative to Kin Selection and Reciprocity," *Journal of Avian Biology 30*, 1999, 10–115.

16 Amotz Zahavi: "Babbler Altruism and Kin Selection: A Reply to Jon," *Journal of Avian Biology 30*, 1999, 115.

17 Lynn Hunt: "A Rewarding Tale," *New Scientist 161:2176,* March 6, 1999, 8.
18 Miller (2000), 339.

CHAPTER 8

1 Miller (2000), 318, 339.
2 G. F. Miller: "Mental Traits as Fitness Indicators: Expanding Evolutionary Psychology's Adaptationism," *Annals of the New York Academy of Sciences 709,* 2000, 62–74.
3 Edgar Rubin: "Et grafologisk eksperiment" in: *Mennesker og Høns,* Berlingske Forlag, Copenhagen 1937, 80–87, here p. 81.
4 Ibid., 82–83.
5 Steven Rose (ed.): *Alas, Poor Darwin,* London: Vintage, 2001. See especially Rose's summary pp. 247–265.
6 "Status symbol" and "Form of exchange" are discussed in the chapters on goods and gifts onwards.
7 Mark Hertsgaard: *The Beatles,* Copenhagen: Munksgaard Rosinante, 1996 [orig. 1995], 357–358.

CHAPTER 9

1 Brian Eno in John Brockman: "A Big Theory of Culture: A Talk with Brian Eno," *Edge # 11.5,* April 1997. I also quoted this passage in my book *Frem i tiden,* Copenhagen: Tiderne Skifter, 1999, 138–139.
2 Geoffrey F. Miller: *The Mating Mind,* London: Vintage, 2000, 134.
3 The count was carried out in Denmark, led by a woman doctor: Bente Pakkenberg and H. J. G. Gundersen (1997) "Neocortical Neuron Number in Humans: Effect of Sex and Age," *Journal of Comparative Neurology 384,* 1997, 312–320.

4 Miller (2000), 168.

5 Miller (2000), 168.

6 Dire Straits: "Money for Nothing," *Brothers in Arms,* Vertigo, 1985.

7 Hertsgaard (1996), 62.

8 J. B. Sidgwick: *Amateur Astronomer's Handbook,* London: Faber and Faber, 1955, 425.

9 Tor Nørretranders: "Understanding Understanding," Sture Allén (ed.): *Nobelsymposia 92: Of Thoughts and Words,* Singapore: Imperial College Press, 1995, 193–206.

10 Thomas Kuhn: *Videnskabens revolutioner,* Copenhagen: Fremad, 1973 [orig. 1962], 179–180.

11 Robert M. Pirsig: *Lila: En undersøgelse af moral,* Copenhagen: Schønberg, 1995 [orig. *Lila: An Inquiry into Morals*, New York: Bantam Books, 1991], 110.

12 The classic example is Francis Cricks and James Watson's discovery of the structure of the DNA molecule; the classic description of this is James Watson: *The Double Helix,* New York: Signet Books, 1969.

13 Emil Weichert, 1896, quoted in Freeman Dyson: *Infinite in All Directions,* New York: Harper & Row, 1988, 36. I quoted the same passage in *Verden vokser,* 1994, 181.

14 Ole Fogh Kirkeby: *Secunda Philosophia,* Frederiksberg: Samfundslitteratur, 1999, 8. See also his *Loyalitet,* Frederiksberg: Samfundslitteratur, 2002.

15 *Ordbog over det danske Sprog,* Bind.

16 Sober and Wilson (2000), 199f; Robert Frank (1988), 51.

17 I'm grateful to Pia Maria Marquard for this brief course in elementary management.

18 Satoshi Kanazawa: "Scientific Discoveries as Cultural Displays: A Further Test of Miller's Courtship Model," *Evolution and Human Behavior 21,* 317–321, 2000, here p. 321.

19 *Encyclopedia Britannica* 8: Chicago, 1993, 440.

20 See Tor Nørretranders: *Hengivelse—en debatbog om mænds orgasmer,* Copenhagen: Informations Forlag, 1991.

21 Tor Nørretranders: *The User Illusion* (1991), Chapter 5. The word has entered the English language: see www.quinion.com/words/turnsofphrase/tp-exf1.htm.

22 Nørretranders(1991), Chapter 4.

23 Signals that are not costly can be controlled by social control: M. Lachmann, S. Szamado, and C. T. Bergstrom: "Cost and Conflict in Animal Signals and Human Language," *Proceedings of the National Academy of Sciences USA, 98,* 2001, 13189–13194.

24 Quoted in James L. Gould and Carol Grant Gould: *Sexual Selection,* New York: Scientific American Library/HPHLP, 1989, 258.

25 David M. Buss: "Sex Differences in Human Mate Choice Preferences: Evolutionary Hypotheses Tested in 37 Cultures," *Behavioral and Brain Sciences 12(1),* 1989, 1–49, here p. 13, column 1. Buss's article with his presentation of the study is on pp. 1–14, whereafter a number of other researchers comment on his results; this is typical of the *Behavioral and Brain Science* journal.

26 The same applies to David Buss's textbook *Evolutionary Psychology: The New Science of the Mind,* Boston: Allyn and Bacon, 1999, in which human mate choice is discussed for ninety pages without its being made particularly apparent that gender differences rather than the most highly prioritized criterion are being considered; see for example 108–109.

27 Miller (2000), 201–203. The model mentioned is about fitness matching.

28 Karl Grammer, Berhard Fink, Anders P. Møller, and Randy Thornhill: "Darwinian Aesthetics: Sexual Selection and the Biology of Beauty," *Biological Review.*

29 Martie G. Haselton and Geoffrey Miller: "Ovulatory Shifts in Attraction to Artistic and Entrepreneurial Excellence," paper at HBES 2002, Rutgers, June 22, 2002. G. Miller, personal comment.

30 Dinah Caruthers: "Ovulatory Cycle Effects on Perceived Mate

Attractiveness as a Function of Male Sense of Humor," typescript, University of New Mexico. G. Miller, personal comment.

31 The existentialists include philosophers such as Kierkegaard, Sartre, Jaspers, etc.

CHAPTER 10

1 Marcel Mauss: *The Gift,* New York: W.W. Norton, 2000 [translation; orig. 1990].

2 Mauss (2000/1924), 6.

3 Ibid., 19.

4 Ibid., 20.

5 Marshall Sahlins: *Stone Age Economics,* New York: Gruyter, 1972, 150. Sahlins contributes a detailed textual analysis of the one (!) Maori passage in which the meaning of the term is documented in Mauss.

6 Thomas Hylland Eriksen and D. O. Hessen: *Egoisme,* Copenhagen: Høst & Søn, 2000 [orig. Oslo 1999].

7 Claude Levi-Strauss: *Introduction to the Work of Marcel Mauss,* London: Routledge, 1987 [orig. 1950], 48.

8 Jacques Derrida: "The Time of the King," in: Alan D. Schrift: *The Logic of the Gift,* New York: Routledge, 1997, 121–147, here p. 124.

9 Pierre Bourdieu: *Af praktiske grunde. Omkring teorien om menneskelig handlen,* Copenhagen: Hans Reitzels Forlag, 2001 [orig. 1994], 175–176. Bourdieu uses the Latin term *habitus* to describe society-building relations.

10 Karl Polanyi: *The Great Transformation: The Political and Economic Origins of Our Time,* Boston: Beacon Press, 2001 [orig. 1944], 44.

11 The market-field analogy is borrowed from Herbert Gintis: *Game Theory Evolving,* (2000), 46. Strictly speaking, theories of equilibrium are the only ones that take this formal form.

12 Fred Block: "Introduction," in Polanyi (2001/1944), pp. xviii-xxxviii, here note 10, xxiv.

13 The description of gifts as redundant was developed especially in David Cheal: *The Gift Economy*, London: Routledge, 1988, 12 et seq.

14 John Davis: *Exchange*, Minneapolis: University of Minnesota Press, 1992, 49.

15 Mary Douglas: "Foreword," in: Marcel Mauss: *The Gift*, New York: W.W. Norton, 2000 [translation; orig. 1990], vii–xviii, here p. xv.

16 UNDP: *Human Development Report 1995: Gender and Human Development*. I am grateful to Wilfred Dolfsma for referring me to the report.

17 Ibid., 87.

18 Ibid., 93.

19 Ibid., 94.

20 Ibid., 97.

21 Gintis (2000), 244.

22 Kari Martinsen: *Fra Marx til Løgstrup. Om etik og sanselighed i sygeplejen*, Copenhagen: Munksgaard Danmark, 2002 [orig. 1993], 186.

23 Løgstrup quoted in Martinsen (2002/1993), 82.

24 Ibid., 82.

25 See e.g. this brilliant work on stewardesses among others: Arlie Hochchild: *The Managed Heart: The Commercialization of Human Feeling*, Berkeley: University of California Press, 1983. See also Arlie Russell Hochschild: "The Economy of Gratitude," in: *Contemporary Studies in Sociology 9*, 1989, 95–113.

CHAPTER 11

1 Lewis Hyde: *The Gift: Imagination and the Erotic Life of Property*, New York: Vintage, 1999 [orig. 1979], here p. xi. I am grateful to Howard Rheingold for referring me to Hyde's analysis.

2 Paul McCartney quoted in Hertsgaard (1996), 146.

3 Hyde (1999/1979), xii.

4 Ibid., xiii.

5 Nørretranders (1998).

6 See his biography at http://www.edge.org/3rd_culture/bios /csik.html.

7 Mihaly Csikszentmihalyi in: *Flow: The Psychology of Optimal Experience,* New York: Harper and Row, 1990.

8 A splendid guide to the difficulty of having the courage to say yes and thereby expose oneself is: Keith Johnstone: *Impro: Improvisation og teater,* Copenhagen: Hans Reitzels Forlag, 1987, see p. 118 in particular.

9 In his wonderful book *Ind i musikken,* Gyldendal, 1987, the musician Peter Bastian describes the phenomenon that aversion to music is often aversion to part of yourself.

10 Tor Nørretranders: *Verden vokser,* Aschehoug, 1994, 172.

11 Jacob Jensen: *Anderledes men ikke mærkeligt. En designers erindringer,* Copenhagen: Gyldendal, 1997, 186.

12 Warren Hagstrom: *The Scientific Community,* New York: Basic Books, 1964. On the link between the science of sociology and anthropological gift economy theory, see also Leslie Sklair: *Organized Knowledge,* London: Paladin, 1976, 63 et seq.

13 Thorstein Veblen: *The Place of Science in Modern Civilisation and Other Essays,* New York: B. W. Huebsch, 1919. The essay that lent its title to the book dates from 1906. The term *idle curiosity* is introduced on p. 6.

14 Helga Nowotny, Peter Scott, and Michael Gibbons: *Re-Thinking Science: Knowledge and the Public in an Age of Uncertainty,* Oxford: Polity, 2001, and Michael Gibbons et al.: *The New Production of Knowledge: The Dynamics of Science and Research in Contemporary Societies,* London: Sage, 1994.

15 I have not been able to pinpoint the origin of this proverb but it may be found in many places on the Internet. I heard it via *labcom,*

Kolding, whose head, Carsten Borch, chose it as the motto for this center for knowledge-sharing among businessmen, scientists, artists, and others.

16 A splendid description of the Danish term *Fælled* can be read in the first issue of the culture magazine *Fælleden,* 1975. The English term *commons* and the problem of creating social cooperation is discussed in depth in Elinor Ostrom: *Governing the Commons: The Evolution of Institutions for Collective Action,* Cambridge: Cambridge University Press, 1990.

CHAPTER 12

1 The fax example was inspired by Kevin Kelly: *New Rules for the New Economy,* London: Fourth Estate, 1999 [orig. 1998], 40.

2 Carl Shapiro and Hal R. Varian: *Information Rules: A Strategic Guide to the Network Economy,* Cambridge, MA: Harvard Business School Press, 1999, 184.

3 For an outline history of the computer see M. Campbell-Kelly and William Aspray: *Computer: A History of the Information Machine,* New York: Basic Books, 1996.

4 Lawrence Lessig: *The Future of Ideas,* New York: Random House, 2001, 51–52.

5 Eric P. Raymond (ed.): *The New Hacker's Dictionary,* 3rd ed., Cambridge, MA: The MIT Press, 1996, 233.

6 Pekka Himanen: *The Hacker Ethic and the Spirit of the Information Age,* London: Secker & Warburg, 2001, vii and ix.

7 Max Weber: *The Protestant Ethic and the Spirit of Capitalism,* London: Routledge, 2001 [orig. 1930].

8 Bob Young quoted in Lessig (2001), 279.

9 Josh Lerner and Jean Tirole: "The Simple Economics of Open Source," National Bureau of Economic Research *Working Paper 7600.* The same point is elaborated in David Lancashire: "Code,

Culture and Cash: The Fading Altruism of Open Source Development," *First Monday 6:12*, 2001.

10 Richard Stallman: "The GNU Operating System and the Free Software Movement," in: C. DiBona et al. (eds.): *OpenSources*, Sebastopol, CA: O'Reilly, 1999, 53–70, here p. 64. Richard Barbrook: "The Hi-tech Gift Economy," *First Monday 3:12,* 1998. The webzine *First Monday* has published many articles on the topic; see www.firstmonday.org.

11 Steven Weber: "The Political Economy of Open Source Software," *BRIE Working paper 140,* accessible at http://brie.berkeley. edu/~briewww/pubs/wp/wp140.pdf of Weber's book *The Success of Open Source,* Cambridge, MA: Harvard University Press, 2002.

12 Eric P. Raymond: *The Cathedral & The Bazaar: Musings on Linux and Open Source by an Accidental Revolutionary,* Sebastopol, CA: O'Reilly, 1999, here p. 67.

13 For a little Ode to Bill Gates about his short-sightedness and the joy openness could bring him see Peter Schwartz, Peter Leyden, and Joel Hyatt: *The Long Boom: A Future History of the World 1980–2020,* London: Orion Business Books, 2000, 30–36.

14 One good example is Ole Grünbaum: *Teknofetichismen—og drømmen om det gnidningsløse samfund,* Copenhagen: Tiderne Skifter, 2001. An almost manic self-showdown from one of the most talented prophets of the Information-Technology Age. The author of the current book did not escape, either. My vision of an 11 Mbps infrastructure for Denmark was criticized, though on very thin grounds: the money would be better spent inviting foreign chefs to Denmark than on developing networks with taste and smell (p. 36); pornography is the only thing broadband connections are used for today (47–8); it is no good claiming that information technology can improve democracy, because it doesn't work to start with (84–87).

15 My book on the Internet, *Stedet som ikke er* (1997), praises the web without mentioning (apart from with a sneer) the commer-

cial aspect, which wasn't really a player in 1997. I may therefore conclude with peace of mind that it was not dot-com that inspired my own enthusiasm, but the actual potential of the technology. Which still exists.

16 Ibid., 203.

17 Nørretranders (1998), chapter 6.

18 In Denmark, the Åben Æter [Open Airwaves] association has been founded for the purpose of disseminating 802.11b. Its Web site is at www.aaae.dk.

CHAPTER 13

1 Samuel Bowles and Herbert Gintis: "Reciprocity, Self-Interest, and the Welfare State," *Nordic Journal of Political Economy 26,* 2000, 33–53, here p. 33.

2 On the "supposedness" of the quotation, see T. Vogel-Jørgensen, *Bevingede Ord,* 5. ed., Copenhagen: Gad, 1979, column 582.

3 Matt Ridley: *The Origins of Virtue,* New York: Penguin, 1998 [orig. 1996].

4 See Fred Block: "Introduction," in Polanyi (2001/1944), xviii–xxxviii, for an outline of the debate.

5 Manuel Castells: *The Information Age: Economy, Society and Culture,* Vol. I–III, London: Blackwell, 1997, 2000, and 2000.

6 Manuel Castells: *The Internet Galaxy,* Oxford: Oxford University Press, 2001, 2.

7 Paul Baran: *On Distributed Communications,* accessible at http://www.rand.org/publications/RM/baran.list.html.

8 See Tor Nørretranders: *Stedet som ikke er,* Copenhagen: Aschehoug, 1997, 27 et seq in particular.

9 Albert-László Barabásin: *Linked: The New Science of Networks,* Cambridge, MA: Perseus, 2002, is a superb introduction to network theory that emphasizes the irregularity. Bernardo Huberman: *The Laws of the Web: Patterns in the Ecology of Information,* Cambridge,

MA: MIT Press, 2001, is elegant in its succinctness but more difficult to read.

10 Robert D. Putnam: *Bowling Alone. The Collapse and Revival of American Community*, New York: Simon & Schuster, 2000, 113.

11 Ibid., 239.

12 The idea that the good news and the bad news about the Internet are one and the same is borrowed from the writer Howard Rheingold, who has been saying for years that the good news and the bad news about the Internet is that anyone can say anything he wants.

13 Samuel Bowles and Herbert Gintis: "Is Equality Passé? *Homo Reciprocans* and the Future of Egalitarian Politics," *Boston Review,* Fall 1998. Accessible at http://bostonreview.mit.edu/BR23.6/ bowles.html.

14 Samuel Bowles and Herbert Gintis: "Reciprocity, Self-Interest, and the Welfare State," *Nordic Journal of Political Economy 26,* 2000, 33–53, here p. 34.

15 Ibid., 252 and 278.

16 The calculation behind the figure of 16¢ per day is presented in my book *Frem i tiden,* Copenhagen: Tiderne Skifter, 1999, 113–120. You can make your contribution at www.netaid.org.

17 Parts of this argument were presented in the article "Velfærd på verdensplan," *Moment,* February 2002, 8.

18 The expression "The Scandinavian Dream" comes from Thomas Ryan Jensen.

19 The idea with the pies is hundreds of years old and appears in the French Utopian socialist Charles Fourier: *Stammefællesskabet,* Copenhagen: Rhodos, 1972, 101–108. The fragment "The battle of the pies" is from 1817.

20 The idea of a sex strike is thousands of years old. In Aristophanes's play *Lysistrata* (411 BC) the women go on a "sex strike" until war is ended.

21 See Geoffrey Miller: "Moral Vision," 2000, accessible at http://www. unm.edu/~psych/faculty/moral_vision.htm.

22 Ibid., 325.

23 Mary Douglas: "No Free Gifts," Foreword to Marcel Mauss: *The Gift,* New York: W. W. Norton, 2000 [foreword orig. 1990], vii.

24 "The Coming Flood: Philanthropy in this Decade, a GBN Report," *Global Business Network,* May 2002, accessible at www.gbn.com.

25 Thomas B. Murphy quoted in: Stephanie Strom: "The Newly Rich are Fueling a New Era in Philanthropy," *New York Times,* April 27, 2002.

26 John J. Havens and Paul G. Schervish: *Millionaires and the Millennium: New Estimates for the Forthcoming Wealth Transfer and the Prospects for a Golden Age of Philanthropy,* accessible at www. bc.edu/swri/.

27 On anonymity, see: Paul G. Schervish: "The Sound of One Hand Clapping: The Case For and Against Anonymous Giving," *Voluntas 5:1,* 1994, 1–26, accessible at www.bc.edu/swri/.

28 Thomas Nagel: *The Possibility of Altruism,* Princeton: Princeton University Press, 1978 [orig. 1970], 1.

CHAPTER 14

1 John F. Kennedy: "Address at Rice University in the Space Effort," September 12, 1962, accessible on the web at http://www.rice.edu/fondren/woodson/speech.html.

2 Hans Moravec: *Robot,* New York: Oxford University Press, 1999. Ray Kurzweil: *The Age of Spiritual Machines,* London: Orion Business Books, 1999. See also *Stedet som ikke er* og *Frem i tiden om dette.*

3 Quoted in Ove Nyholms film *Fremtidens børn,* 1984.

4 Massimo Livi-Baccin: *A Concise History of World Population,* 2nd. ed., Oxford: Blackwell, 1997.

5. Wolfgang Lutz et al.: "Doubling of World Population Unlikely," *Nature 387,* 1997, 803–805.

6 The expression comes from Anita Loos's novel (1926): *Gentlemen Prefer Blondes.* In 1928 Loos followed up with *But Gentlemen Marry Brunettes;* cf. T. Vogel-Jørgensen: *Bevingede Ord,* 5th ed., 3rd imprint. G. E. C., Copenhagen: Gads forlag, 1979, 317.

7 Bob Dylan: "I Threw It All Away," *Nashville Skyline,* Columbia, 1969.

8 Michael H. Hart: "An Explanation for the Absence of Extraterrestrials on Earth," *Quarterly Journal of the Royal Astronomical Society 16,* 1975, 128–135. See also Ben Zuckerman and Michael H. Hart: *Extraterrestrials: Where are they?,* 2nd. ed., Cambridge: Cambridge University Press, 1995.

9 I discuss related issues in my books *Om kapitalistisk naturvidenskab,* 1976, *Den blå himmel,* 1987, and *Frem i tiden 1999.*

EPILOGUE

1 The chorus "Love lifts us up where we belong" comes from the lovely song "Up Where We Belong" by Will Jennings, Jack Nitzsche, and Buffy Sainte-Marie. It may be most familiar from Joe Cocker and Jennifer Warnes's recording from 1982 for the movie *An Officer and a Gentleman.* It is also available in Buffy Sanite-Marie's recording on the anthology album *Up Where We Belong,* Angel Classics, 1996.

2 Isaak Dinesen [Karen Blixen]: here*: Babette's Feast, Anecdotes of Destiny,* Harmondsworth: Penguin Books Ltd, 1986, 68.

Index

A

abstract altruism, 285
adaptation, 79–80, 116, 132, 157–58
Alexander, Richard, 59, 60, 61
altruism
    and egoism, xiii
    and emotions, 12
    and evolution, 65–67
    explanation of, 11–12
    and generosity, 121–30
    and group selection, 67–68
    and handicap, 121–30
    and happiness, 14
    and helping others, 36, 45, 64
    and morality, 284
    and natural selection, 43
    types of, 37–70, 127, 129, 196,
        274–75, 285
Andersen, Vilhelm, 86
anonymity, 198–99, 206
Ant and the Peacock, The, 108
apes, 71–72, 84–85, 151
Arabian Babblers, 89, 99, 125–27
arms race, 20, 56
art, 219–32. *See also* creativity
artificial intelligence, 294–95
AT&T, 244–45

attraction, 110–11, 148–50
Axelrod, Robert, 47–48, 50, 54

B

bacteria, 77, 79
Baran, Paul, 266
Beatles, 146, 153, 220, 312
Beautiful Mind, A, 21
beauty, xi, 110–11, 152, 168, 182–87,
    225–26, 297, 312
behavior, causes of, 167–71
Berra, Yogi, 46
Bible, 29
biology, 53, 58, 62, 68–69
biotechnology, 57, 98, 232, 240, 253,
    295–97, 301–2
Black Panthers, 57
Boas, Franz, 192
Boone, James, 122
Bourdieu, Pierre, 197
Bowles, Samuel, 259, 271
Bowling Alone, 267
brain capacity, 148–49, 151, 306
Bronowski, Jacob, 16
Buss, David, 182–83, 185–86

C

calculation, 52–53
camouflage, 80–81
Campbell, Bernard, 100
capitalism, 56, 58, 231–32, 249, 269
Castells, Manuel, 264, 269
cells, 77–78
charity, xiii, 128–29, 225, 275, 277, 281–83
cloning, 297, 302, 307
cocooning, 268, 270
Coming Flood, The, 282
commodities, 198–218, 231–32
communication, 179–81, 233–37, 276
communism, 267
community, xiii, 24, 307. *See also* societies
computer games, 14, 47–48, 54
computer programs, 242–47
computers, 13–14, 47–49, 291
Comte, Auguste, 11–12
concrete altruism, 285
Conniff, Richard, 126
conservatism, 267
conspicuous consumption, 91–95, 107, 122, 235–37, 284
contract work, 216–17
contraction, 155–57
cooperation
    benefits of, 14, 19–21, 27, 54–55
    conundrum of, 40
    and evolution, 65–67, 69
    and experimental economics, 62
    and game theory, 53–54
    and group selection, 67–68
    and natural selection, 43
    and prisoner's dilemma, 48–49
    and selfishness, xiii, 46–47
costly signals
    and generosity, 121, 123–24, 127, 130, 252
    and information, 180–83, 250
    and moon landing, 289–90
    and sexual selection, 97–98, 107, 110–17, 138, 148, 154, 162, 166
creationism, 29, 32
creativity
    and altruism, 99
    and generosity, 286
    and gifts, 219–32
    and sexual selection, xi–xiii, 149, 169, 184, 188–89, 302–3, 306, 310–12
Cronin, Helena, 108
Csikszentmihalyi, Mihaly, 222
cultivation, 32, 74–75
cultural activities, 147–90

D

Darwin, Charles, xii, 29–37, 54, 58, 64, 69–89, 100, 113, 131–46
Darwinism, 35, 64, 72, 75–76, 142–43, 159
Das Kapital, 203
Davis, John, 210
Dawkins, Richard, 44, 63–64, 105
democracy, 274
demographic transition, 297–300
Dennett, Daniel C., 30, 31
Derrida, Jacques, 196
Descent of Man, The, 71–73, 77, 100
desire. *See* sexual desire
Diamond, Jared, 117–19, 153

dinosaurs, 158

Dire Straits, 153

Discover, 126

Dogme 95, 165

Dolfsma, Wilfred, 211, 213

dot-com collapse, 235, 254

Double Darwin, 131–46

Douglas, Mary, 210, 211

Dunbar, Robin, 120

Dylan, Bob, 56, 304

E

e-commerce, 198–99

economics, 4–7, 58, 133. *See also* experimental economics

economy. *See* gift economy; market economy

efficiency, 133, 145

effort, xii, 160–67, 303, 307, 312

egoism, xiii, 44, 47, 54–56, 65–67, 69

Einstein's theories, 239

emotions, 12–13

End of History, 269

"End, The," 146

Eno, Brian, 147, 163

equilibrium, 18–19, 21, 25–26

Eriksen, Thomas Hylland, 195

Essai sur le don (The Gift), 192–93, 210

eugenics, 57

evolution

    of cognition, 159

    and game theory, 53–55

    and group selection, 68

    mechanisms behind, 108–9

    and natural selection, xii, 29–33, 41–43, 54, 58, 68, 73–74, 76, 81–83

    and selfishness, 65–67

    and sexual selection, xii, 151, 296, 304–7

    theory of, xii, 37, 39, 58

Evolution and Human Behavior, 123

Evolution of Cooperation, The, 54

Evolution of Reciprocal Altruism, The, 45

evolutionary biologists, 67, 73, 76

evolutionary levels, 170

evolutionary psychology, 139–40

evolutionary stable strategy, 50–54

exformation, 180

expansion, 155–57

experimental economics

    and cooperation, 62

    and game theory, 24, 58

    and generosity, 134

    and human behavior, xii, 8, 13, 26, 59, 206, 214–15, 274, 291–92

    and strong reciprocity, 271

    and welfare state, 259–60

extinction, 27, 88, 103

F

Fehr, Ernst, 10, 12

fellowship, 27, 279, 311

female choices, 81, 84–89, 106–7, 171–72

Fink, Bernhard, 111

Fisher, Ronald A., 39, 87–88, 106, 151

Fitzgerald, Scott, 94

flow, state of, 222–23

Frank, Robert, 12–13, 206, 292

Free Software Foundation, 245–46, 250

Freud, Sigmund, 163

Fukuyama, Francis, 269
Future of Ideas, The, 249
future of world, 287–307

G

Gächter, Simon, 10
game theory
    and analytical tools, 23
    and assumptions, 23–24
    and economics, 24, 58
    equilibrium of, 18–19
    and evolution, 53–55
    and political measures, 17
    and predictions, 23, 271
    purpose of, 16–17
    and selfishness, 1–3, 9, 13, 58
    strategies of, xii, 13–27
    and war, 17
    see also specific games
Gates, Bill, 243, 251
generalized altruism, 59
generosity
    and altruism, 121–30
    conundrum of, 40
    and evolution, 133–35
    and gift-giving, 196
    global generosity, 277–83
    and group selection, 67
    and kinship, 303–4
    pleasure of, 60–61, 303
    and reciprocity, 145–46, 196–97
    and science, 241–42
    and sexuality, xiii, 303–4, 307
    with strangers, 271

genes
    good genes, 103, 106, 110–11, 121–23,
        167, 179, 188–89
    and human nature, 56–57
    study of, 39–40
genetic filtering, 57
genetic mapping, 57
Genetical Evolution of Social Behavior,
    The, 41
genotypes, 39–41, 44–45, 55, 64
gift economy
    and commodities, 191–92, 200, 208,
        213, 215, 226–27, 269
    and creativity, 226–32
    and sharing, 244, 247–48, 250, 265,
        293
Gift, The, 192–93, 210
gifts
    giving, 191–218, 271, 285–86
    as reciprocity, 191–218
    and relationships, 194–95, 197, 199,
        209–10, 303
    see also hau
Gintis, Herbert, 17, 22–23, 63, 68, 215,
    259, 271
Global Business Network (GBN), 282,
    283
global economic competition, 293
global generosity, xiii, 277–83
global welfare, 257, 275–82, 285–86
globalization, 259–86
GNU, 245–46, 249
Goth, Werner, 2
Gould, Steven Jay, 76, 142, 159
Grafen, Alan, 106
Grammer, Karl, 111

Gray, Asa, 70
Great Transformation, The, 200
greed, 4–7, 10, 13, 278, 290–91
group altruism, 68
group selection, 63, 65–68
group solidarity, 27

H

hackers, 248–50
Haldane, J. B. S., 37–40, 50, 106
Hamilton, William, 40–46, 54, 60, 115, 127
Hammerstein, Peter, 62
handicap, 91–130
Handicap Principle, 99–106, 113, 115–17, 222
Handicap Principle, The, 114
Haselton, Martie, 188
hau, 194–96, 200, 217, 225, 265, 267, 271–74, 293. *See also* gifts
Hayek, Frederick, 264
headquarters, 261, 263, 270–71, 310
helping others, 35–70, 215–17, 271, 277–78, 280–81
heredity, 31–34, 39, 57–58, 73, 132
Hertsgaard, Mark, 154
hierarchies, 265–71
Himanen, Pekka, 248
Homo economicus, xiii, 1–14, 58, 134–35, 143–44, 206, 214, 242, 274, 291–93, 295
Homo generosus, xiii, 134–35, 143–44, 242
Homo parochius, 274

Homo reciprocans, 62–63
Hyde, Lewis, 219–20

I

IBM, 247
immediate cause, 167–69, 171
indirect reciprocity, 60–62
industrial society, 34, 213, 236–37, 249, 288
Information Age, The, 264
information technology, 232, 264–66
Inquiry into Values, An, 161
Internet, 233–35, 254–55, 261, 270, 309–10
intoxicants, 117–19
intuitive selection, 297, 301
isolation, 268, 270

J

Jacobsen, J. P., xii, 72, 86
Jensen, Jacob, 225
Johannsen, Wilhelm, 39

K

k-strategy, 298–99
Kamikaze pilots, 25
Kanazawa, Satoshi, 173–74
Kelly, Susan, 120
Kennedy, John F., 287–89
Kingdom, The, 25

kinship selection, 127, 135
kinship theory, 40–43, 58–60
Klein, Jesper, 105
knowledge
    owning, 238–40
    sharing, 229–31, 240–41, 252–57
    and technology, xii, 287–90
    by trial-and-error, 310
Krüger, Mr., 140–41
Kuhn, Thomas, 159

L

Lamarck, Jean-Baptiste, 30
language, 237–38
laws of nature, 238–39
Leimar, Olof, 62
Lennon, John, 154, 312
Lessig, Lawrence, 249
Lévi-Strauss, Clause, 196, 197
liberalism, 267
life
    civil life, 267–69
    and creativity, 311
    philosophy of, xiv
    risking, 37–38
    rules for, 307
    value of, 25–26
Lila—an inquiry into morals, 161
Linux, 246, 247, 249
Løgstrup, K. E., 215–16
Louis XIV, King, 261, 271
love, 143–46, 187, 304, 307, 312

M

males, choosing, 74–75, 81, 84–89,
    106–7, 171–72
market economy, 198–219, 228–34,
    253, 292
market mask, 135, 199, 206, 263, 265,
    292
market mechanisms, 198–218
Martinsen, Kari, 215–16
Marx, Karl, 203–5
Marxism, 37–38
mates, selecting, 182–86. See also males,
    choosing
Mating Mind, The, 148
Mauss, Marcel, 192–94, 196, 197, 210
McCartney, Paul, 145, 220
Mendel, Gregor, 39
Metcalfe, Bob, 236
Metcalfe's law, 236–37, 256
Microsoft, 243, 246, 247
Miller, Geoffrey, 85, 139, 148–50,
    173–74, 188
"Mogens," 86
Möller, Anders Pape, 108, 111, 113
monogamous species, 102, 109, 113, 186
Monrad, D. G., 72
moon landing, 287–90
morality, 64, 161–62, 216, 275, 284, 302
Morgenstern, Oskar, 15–16
mortality rates, 298–300
Murphy, Thomas B., 283
muses, 174
mutations, 34, 78

N

Nagel, Thomas, 284
Nash equilibrium, 21–22, 25, 52–53
Nash, John, 21
natural selection
    and evolution, xii, 29–33, 41–43, 54,
        58, 68, 73–74, 76, 81–83
    and humans, 133–34
    and nature, 69–70
    and sexual selection, 104–7, 132
Nature, 10
nature, 69–70, 238–39
Nesse, Randolph, 120
network externalities, 236–37
network society, 209, 237, 264–66, 310
New Scientist, 127
New York Times, 283
Newton, Huey, 57
Newton's laws, 238–39
Nielsen, Richard Møller, 46
Nobel Prize for Economics, 95, 97, 98
Nowak, Martin, 61
nuclear arms race, 20
nursery schools, 293–95

O

On the Origin of Species, 29–30, 34, 70,
    72, 73, 76, 138
Open Source software, 245–47, 250, 251
openness, 233–57
origins of man, xii. *See also* evolution

P

parasites, 79–80
partners, selecting, 182–86. *See also*
    males, choosing
peacock, 99–120
pharmaceuticals companies, 251–52
phenotypes, 39–41, 44–45, 55, 64
philanthropy, xi, 280–83
Picasso, Pablo, 312
Pigou, Arthur Cecil, 212
Pirsig, Robert M., 161–62
Polanyi, Karl, 200, 207, 264
polygamous males, 101–2, 113
population management, 298–300
potlatch, 191–92
poverty, 275–76, 278
predators, 42–43
prisoner's dilemma game, 14, 19–21,
    46–50, 61, 291
psychological levels, 170
psychology, 139–40
puberty, 109–10
public good games, 8–12
public spirit, 259–86
punishment, 10–11, 13, 271
Putnam, Robert D., 46, 267–69

R

r-strategy, 298–99
racism, 56, 57
RAND Corporation, 19–20, 47

Rapoport, Anatol, 47, 48
rationality, xii, 3, 9, 13, 23–26, 52–54
reciprocity
    and altruism, 37–70, 127, 129, 196,
        274–75
    and generosity, 145–46, 196–97
    indirect reciprocity, 60–62
    and love, 145–46
    and redistribution, 200–203
    strong reciprocity, 271
Red Queen hypothesis, 78–79
redistribution, 200–203, 259
reiteration, 54, 143, 269
relationships
    and gifts, 194–95, 197, 199, 209–10,
        303
    length of, 187–89
    logic of, 166
    and society, 270–71, 303
reproduction, 74, 77–78, 80, 296–302,
    307
Robot economicus, 292–93
Robot generosus, 295
Robot reciprocans, 295
robots, 292–95, 307
Rose, Steven, 142
Rousseau, Jean-Jacques, 18
Rubin, Edgar, 141

S

scarcity society, 284
Schleimann, Mr., 96–97
scientific knowledge, 227–31, 240–42,
    252–57

selection. *See* group selection; natural
    selection; sexual selection
self-interests, 13, 206, 215, 250, 272, 307
self-selection, 190
selfish altruism, 68
selfish gene, 63–64
Selfish Gene, The, 44, 105
selfishness
    assumptions of, xii, 23–27
    and cooperation, xiii, 46–47
    and evolution, 65–68
    and game theory, 1–3, 9, 13, 58
    and group solidarity, 27
    and sharing, 307
    view of, 43–44
semi-suppressed levels, 170
September 11, 2001, 24–25, 285
sexual desire, xi, 168–71, 176–77, 296,
    304, 307, 310–12
sexual differences, 182–86
sexual fantasies, 167, 177–79
sexual selection
    and attraction, 149–50
    benefits of, 137–40
    and biotechnology, 301–2
    and costly signals, 97–98, 107,
        110–17, 138, 148, 154, 162, 166
    and creativity, xi–xiii, 149, 169, 184,
        188–89, 302–3, 306, 310–12
    and culture, 154–55, 168–71, 181
    and evolution, xii, 151, 296, 304–7
    explanation of, 72–74, 76, 80–81
    and female choices, 84–89
    and humans, 110, 133–34, 136–40
    and love, 144–45, 187
    and male choices, 101–2

and natural selection, 104–7, 132
preoccupation with, 178–79
result of, 157–58
as self-selection, 190
and sexual differences, 182–86
Sexual Selection and the Descent of Man 1871–1971, 100
sexuality, xiii, 77–80, 303–4, 307
shared knowledge, 227–31, 240–41, 252–57
sharing, 233–57, 265, 271, 293, 307
Sigmund, Karl, 61
Simpson paradox, 66–67
Smith, Adam, 215
Smith, John Maynard, 50–51, 53, 65, 85, 113
Sober, Elliot, 67
social behavior, 55, 57, 62
social capital, 268–69
social status, 176
socialism, 267
sociality, 13, 23, 67, 133, 136–40, 190, 303
societies
decline of, 267–68
and globalization, 260–61
and Internet, 261
and markets, 207–11
and relationships, 270–71, 303
types of, 209, 237, 264–66, 284, 310
value of, 268
Sociobiology, 55
software, 242–47
Sørensen, Villy, 222
Spence, Michael, 95–96
spiritualism, 83–84

stable strategy, 50–54
stag hunt, 17–19, 253
Stallman, Richard, 245–46
Stanford Encyclopedia of Philosophy, 17
status symbols, 234–37
strong reciprocity, 271
subconscious levels, 170
sublimation, 163
suicide bombers, 25–26
superfluity society, 284
surveillance, 267, 310
survival
of fittest, 27, 34, 35, 74
and natural selection, 131–32, 138
struggle for, 152, 166
systems of national accounts (SNA), 211–13

T

tautology, 31
technology
future of, 265, 291–307, 309–10
and generosity, 241–42
and knowledge, xii, 287–90
sharing, 254–57, 276
terrorism, 24–26
Tessman, Irwin, 122
Theory of Games and Economic Behavior, The, 15–16
Theory of the Leisure Class, The, 92
thermodynamic depth, 180
Third Chimpanzee, The, 117
Thomson's gazelle, 114–15
Thornhill, Randy, 111

Thorsen, Jen Jørgen, 168–69, 309, 310, 311

Tit-for-Tat, 48–50, 193

tournament experiment, 47–49

Trivers, Robert, 45–47, 49, 57, 59, 60, 101, 127

trust, 14, 19, 21, 26, 113, 187, 253, 270

Tucker, Al, 20

U

ultimatum game, 1–6, 167–69, 285–86, 290–91

umage, 160–61

United Nations Development Programme (UNDP), 211–13

UNIX, 244–45

User Illusion, The, 180, 221, 223, 238

V

variation, 31–34, 132

Veblen, Thorstein, 92–95, 107, 122, 192

virtues, 157, 165, 263

voluntary service, 267–68, 280–81, 302

von Linné, Carl, 80

von Neumann, John, 15–16

von Trier, Lars, 25

W

Wallace, Alfred, 34, 81–84, 143

warning cries, 42–43, 47

wastefulness, 93–94

wealth, xiii, 91–95, 277–78, 285–86

Weber, Max, 249

Weekendavisen, 96

welfare society, xii, xiii, 259–86

Wiechert, Emil, 164

Williams, George C., 65

Wilson, David Sloan, 67

Wilson, Edward O., 55, 56

wisdom, xi, xiii, 54, 165, 295–97. *See also* knowledge

women's movement, 174–76

world future, 287–307

World Trade Center, 24

Wright, Jonathan, 127

X

xenophobia, 56, 68

Xerox, 247

Z

Zahavi, Amotz, 99, 105–7, 112–17, 124–26, 153, 157, 181

Zahavi, Avishag, 114

Zen and the Art of Motorcycle Maintenance, 161